IN T
LINE O.

THE GREAT OPENING
BATSMEN OF TEST CRICKET

by

Richard Sydenham

COUNTRY BOOKS

CONTENTS

AUTHOR'S NOTE

The duel between quick bowler and opening batsman is as captivating as Test cricket gets. The excitement, the tension, the unpredictability - all are elements that make this battle so compulsive at the start of an innings, particularly on the first morning. The partnerships of Gordon Greenidge and Desmond Haynes for the West Indies was the factor responsible in my taking an added interest into the role of the opening batsman. Their unorthodox, typically Caribbean way of attacking from the outset was too great a spectacle for a young lad to ignore. Seeing them play, whether as television viewer or as a spectator, was a truly rewarding experience. Right from their entrance into the arena as they walked down the pavilion steps, when the sighting of their deep red crash helmets amongst the members would stir the forever-atmospheric West Indian crowd into carnival, to the moment of their dismissal, was cricket at its best for me. When I played league cricket I soon became an opening batsman myself; a decision influenced heavily by the exhibitions of Greenidge and Haynes. Years later, as a journalist, I suppose it was inevitable that I would write this book. I'm sure we'll continue to see many more opening batsmen in the calibre of Greenidge and Haynes further into the future. The likes of Michael Slater, Mark Taylor, Sanath Jayasuriya, Michael Atherton and Saeed Anwar are current role models for today's kids and they are terrific examples to youngsters aspiring to become opening batsmen. If their exhibitions can influence tomorrow's cricketers like Greenidge and Haynes influenced me and so many others, then I'm sure there will be an abundance of talented openers years on. The openers that I have interviewed have all been extremely open with their opinions and particularly, I found it interesting to discover how they thought (or think) when facing a Wes Hall, a Dennis Lillee or a Wasim Akram. Coaches throughout the world preach the cover drive, backward defence and so on, but it's not often you get the chance to learn how to prepare yourself mentally when up against pace, spin, different conditions, or yourself when riddled with self-doubt. As New Zealand's John Wright said, 'Eighty-five percent of the game is played up here (in the mind).' I realise that some people may consider other players not featured in the book worthy of a chapter, but I have had to devise strict qualifications in order to set some kind of a precedent. It is easy to recall so many opening batsmen who have excelled in Tests at some point or other, but I wanted to narrow the field down to reveal the very best that opened consistently in Test cricket. There are obviously harsh factors that eliminate some very fine openers: Like Barry Richards - a victim of politics, and Australia's Bill Woodfull and Bill Ponsford, who did not play the amount of Test cricket in the twenties and thirties that we see today, which has meant their run tallies are not all that high. However, the qualifications are: Batting average must be over

37.00; Test runs must be more than 2,500; and 60% of their Test match innings' must be as an opening batsman.

Obviously, without the kind contributions from the cricketers that gave their time to recall team-mates, adversaries or their own experiences, this book would not have seen the light of day. So I want to thank the following who were interviewed for the book: Dennis Amiss, Bishan Bedi, Sir Alec Bedser, Richie Benaud, David Brown, Greg Chappell, Mike Denness, John Edrich, Farokh Engineer, Graeme Fowler, Sunil Gavaskar, Graham Gooch, Tom Graveney, Tony Greig, Desmond Haynes, Ron Headley, Mike Hendrick, Michael Holding, Conrad Hunte, Alan Jones, Tony Lewis, Dennis Lillee, Colin McDonald, Geoff Marsh, Arthur Morris, Martyn Moxon, Mudassar Nazar, Mushtaq Mohammed, Phil Neale, Mark Nicholas, Brian Rose, Saeed Anwar, Navjot Sidhu, Bobby Simpson, Michael Slater, John Snow, Keith Stackpole, Bob Taylor, Mark Taylor, John Wright.

Particularly, I am very grateful to Jeff Thomson who gave his opinions on old rivals for the foreword. I'm sure you'll agree that he has not held anything back.

References:
The Barry Richards Story, Faber & Faber (London), 1978
Big Bird Flying High, Arthur Barker (London), 1988 by Joel Garner
Botham - My Autobiography, Collins Willow (London), 1994
Boycott -The Autobiography, Corgi Books (London), 1987
Clive Lloyd - The Authorised Biography, Grafton Books (London), 1986 by Trevor McDonald
The Collins Who's Who of English First-Class Cricket, Collins Willow (London), 1985 by Robert Brooke
Desmond Haynes - Lion of Barbados, H.F. & G. Witherby (London), 1993 by Rob Steen
It's Knott Cricket, MacMillan (London), 1985 by Alan Knott
John Arlott's Book of Cricketers, Sphere Books (London), 1982
Len Hutton - Fifty Years in Cricket, Star (London), 1986
Marshall Arts, MacDonald-Queen Anne Press (London), 1987 by Malcolm Marshall & Patrick Symes
Playfair Cricket Annual (several), Headline (London) Edited by Bill Frindall
Richard Hadlee - At The Double, Stanley Paul (London), 1985 by Tony Francis
South Africa - The Years of Isolation, Lennard-Queen Anne Press (London), 1994 by Mike Procter
The Wisden Book of Test Cricket 1877-1984, Guild Publishing (London), 1985 by Bill Frindall
Also Wisden Cricket Monthly, The Cricketer & Sky Sports.

FOREWORD

by JEFF THOMSON (Australia 1972/73 - 1985)

'I've had many great battles with some of the players featured in this book and I treasure each one. I used to love the competition with the opening batsmen. The good thing about this book is the amount of interviews with the players themselves, particularly in this case, the opening batsmen. It's interesting to know how they thought, about their own game and also about the various bowlers they faced. From my point of view, I used to love the excitement at the start of an innings, when I opened the bowling against some of these guys. It was a great buzz. There are stories in the book about how the batsmen coped with sheer pace: People ask me whether I enjoyed hitting batsmen and the simple answer is it certainly never bothered me. I just felt that it was part of my repertoire. There are some great players featured, though there are also players that aren't in who I rated very highly. Having said that, statistics speak for themselves. I have different memories of all the players. To recount some:

Gordon Greenidge: I can only talk from my experience and fortunately, Gordon didn't really get going for a bloke that scored so many runs around the world. He had unbelievable power, whether driving, cutting, pulling - he really gave it the full whammy. He didn't have that good a time against Dennis (Lillee) and myself; we seemed to knock him out of the way fairly quickly. Still, he was a great bloke and a dangerous opener.

Desmond Haynes: Desmond, who got us a few times, was a different sort of batsman and was a bit unpredictable. You'd give him a real good ball and then give it to him again next ball, as you tend to do, and he'd smash it for four. He was disconcerting for a bowler, quite unorthodox in a fashion but a very effective opener. I bowled at him in Antigua on his debut in the one-dayers. Simmo said, 'This bloke can't bat.' He got 148!

Roy Fredericks: Freddo was one of the blokes who I really rated highly. He was a very good cutter and puller - not a big front foot player - but he was probably one of the best back foot players around. I can remember hitting him absolutely flat out, that would have knocked any other bloke out that I ever hit on the head - he never even rubbed it! He just took it like a hammer hitting a concrete wall; it was a waste of my time. When Freddo scored that 169 in Perth, it was against our top bowling side as well. It didn't matter what we bowled that day, he was just hooking, pulling and driving everything; top innings that.

John Edrich: I caught him towards the end of his career and beat him for pace a lot. I always liked bowling to left-handers, though. He was a gutsy, stodgy player who squirted them around. I never gave him much to squirt around.

5

Graham Gooch: After the seventies, he got me back at the end of my career in '85, but I wasn't bowling well that series. Goochie was a little unorthodox, but effective. He worked really hard at his game and got the rewards from that.

Geoffrey Boycott: I didn't get to bowl too much to him because he went off the scene when Dennis and myself were at our peak. He came back in '77 when I was carrying an injury and bowling at half pace, and Dennis wasn't there. Boycs was a very effective opening bat, though very boring, very selfish and he didn't make a lot of friends out there.

Sunil Gavaskar: I rated him highly. Sunny played me pretty well and used to duck and weave and only play when he wanted to. I found the guys that knew where their off stump was, usually made good opening batsmen, and this was the case with Sunny.

Dennis Amiss: He was a lot better bat than his stats show against Australia; he had a rough time out there. I remember one innings in Melbourne when he got 90, and I said to Dennis, 'Why doesn't he play like this all the bloody time?' Fortunately, Dennis knocked him over early a few times, but there's not much you can do if you get a good ball early on.

John Wright: Wrighty was ugly as a batsman but effective. He was steady and had guts. The guts men always hang around and give you a hard time; they don't do anything stupid. Wrighty wasn't a blazer, he was a grafter.

Keith Stackpole: He was just before my time, but he was a dangerous guy who went for his shots. He was a good back foot player. Stacky was a guy that people liked to watch; they like to see openers hit the ball, like Slater and Sidhu do nowadays'.

Jeff Thomson, March 1998.

AAMIR SOHAIL - PERSONAL FILE

FULL NAME: Aamir Sohail

DATE OF BIRTH: 14th September, 1966

BIRTHPLACE: Lahore

PLAYING ROLE: Left Hand Bat, Slow Left Arm

TEAMS: Pakistan; Lahore City Whites, Lahore

TEST DEBUT: 1992 v England, Birmingham

TESTS: 44

MOST PRODUCTIVE GROUND H: Karachi, 480 runs (68.57) in 4 Tests
                       A: Manchester, 206 runs (103.00) in 1 Test

FIRST-CLASS DEBUT: 1983-84

HIGHEST SCORE: 205 Pakistan v England, Manchester, 1992

BEST BOWLING: 7-53

NICKNAME: Amma

PERCENTAGE OF TEST INNINGS AS OPENER: 94.80%

FOR THE RECORD: Played in the 1992 World Cup in Australia & New
Zealand. Scored 114 v Zimbabwe; Played in the 1996 World Cup in India,
Pakistan & Sri Lanka. Scored 111 v South Africa; In only his third Test match,
Sohail scored 205 at Old Trafford from just 284 balls. All runs were scored on the
first day; At Lord's in July 1998, Aamir played in an MCC XI against a
World XI in a game that was played to raise funds for the Princess Diana
Memorial Fund; Captained Pakistan in the series defeat at home against
Australia in 1998-99. Was also captain in South Africa in 1997-98 in the
absence of the injured Rashid Latif.

AAMIR SOHAIL (Pakistan)

For such a talented stroke-maker, this elegant left-handed batsman has not achieved as much in his career as he once threatened to, after arriving in the Test arena in emphatic style when making his highest Test score of 205 in only his third Test match against England in 1992. That initial glimpse of him clearly illustrated that he was a batsman with a great deal of potential, though his performances thereafter have not been consistent enough to continue this belief with any real conviction. It is fair to say Aamir Sohail has not done himself justice, when you analyse the bare statistical truths of his fluctuating international career: Five centuries in 44 Tests (two in the same series) is way below his capabilities, and his average has dropped alarmingly as his career has progressed. Averages of 45.11 against Australia and 58.28 against the West Indies prove his true worth as a Test-class opening batsman. These are the two strongest countries in the world, yet with the exception of England (49.00), he averages higher against those two countries than the others. Averages of 30.77 against New Zealand, 31.62 against Sri Lanka and 27.64 against Zimbabwe paint a confusing picture of his Test career; of a man who has proved his talent when up against the best bowlers in the world like Warne, McGrath, Ambrose and Walsh, yet has problems with application against the less-powerful nations.

Former Pakistan captain, Mushtaq Mohammed, who was coach of the Pakistan team in the mid-nineties while Sohail was a leading member of the squad, said. "He has tremendous ability and a real good cricket brain. He thinks about the game very well, but unfortunately, Aamir Sohail is his own worst enemy. He is paranoid and thinks everyone is against him. He doesn't allow himself to concentrate enough on his batting out in the middle because he develops these ideas and this anger comes through in his batting, which can only have destructive results. This is a great shame given Sohail's cricket ability. In particular, I feel he is a very good captain and would be even better if he could control his emotions. When he was captain on the South Africa tour when Rashid Latif was injured, I thought he did a fine job." To emphasise this opinion, it has been said of him previously that he once felt so betrayed by his team that instead of travelling back to the team hotel with his colleagues, he chose to travel on a different bus with the kit! This is an element of Aamir Sohail that has prevented his skill, undoubted that is, to really come to the forth in world cricket. Along with his Pakistan opening partner, Saeed Anwar, the two have previously been touted to have enough talent to challenge the feats of Greenidge and Haynes, though this would now seem highly unlikely in light of patchy form by both players and unproven corruption claims aimed at Sohail that continue to smear the sport in Pakistan; another sorrowful episode to the bumpy career of Aamir Sohail.

Following that 1992 tour of England, where he averaged 51 after experiencing his first taste of Test cricket in the five-Test series, he went on to Hamilton in New Zealand and registered a pair; stealing from him any premature ideas he may still have had of conquering the big time. Months later, he visited the Caribbean, which further proved to him how tough Test cricket can be, given his scores of 55 (at Trinidad), 15, 10 and 4. His scores throughout his Test career have been consistent if not prolific. The fact he has only five Test centuries does not really paint a true reflection of his batting, as he has scored seven fifties over the 70 mark. His 99 at Brisbane in 1995-96 against a strong Australian side with a bowling attack consisting of McDermott, McGrath, Warne and Reiffel, emphasised his talent yet displayed his shortcomings at the same time. The best batsmen can fall just short of their century when getting a good ball at the wrong time, but this cannot explain Sohail's unfortunate missed opportunities on all such occasions. However, it is his fluent stroke-play that has brought him all of his runs and this shouldn't be used as a weapon to hang him. It is a mere statement that such batting skill could be taken even further.

His finest period in Test match cricket was during the home series against the West Indies in 1997-98. It was an emphatic triumph for Pakistan in winning the series 3-0, with two innings victories and another by ten wickets, though the personal success that Sohail enjoyed was equal to the team's effort to say the least. Although he began the series poorly scoring just four at Peshawar, in the following Test matches at Rawalpindi and then Karachi, he registered 160 on both occasions. In the second Test at Rawalpindi, Aamir put on a match-winning third-wicket partnership of 323 with Inzaman-ul-Haq. Then at Karachi he shared an opening stand of 298 with Ijaz Ahmed. Such achievements are regularly undermined whenever the West Indian pace bowlers are met with slow wickets, but when you talk of Courtney Walsh, Curtly Ambrose and Ian Bishop, these are experienced and highly skilled Test match bowlers that still have much to offer irrespective of any pace deficiency. Much of Pakistan's success in that rubber was based on the tremendous foundations that Sohail created for his side; though supported by wonderful bowling from Akram, Mushtaq, Saqlain and Azhar Mahmood. After these performances against the West Indies, it is then exasperating to see Aamir register just 75 runs in six innings on tour in South Africa. It is this kind of inconsistency that has plagued his career; proved further by his recent failings at home to Australia though with an excellent 133 at Karachi.

AAMIR SOHAIL - TEST MATCH STATISTICS   ( ) = As Opener

TESTS: 44   INN: 77 (73)   RUNS: 2760 (2591)
AVERAGE: 37.29 (37.01)   HS: 205 (205)   50: 13 (13) 100: 5 (4)

OVERALL RECORD   + = Opened in every innings against that country

V AUSTRALIA
TESTS: 9   INN: 17 (16)   RUNS: 767 (662)
AVERAGE: 45.11 (41.37)   HS: 133 (133)   50: 4 (4) 100: 2 (1)

V ENGLAND
TESTS: 7   INN: 12+   RUNS: 490
AVERAGE: 49.00   HS: 205   50: 1 100: 1

V NEW ZEALAND
TESTS: 5   INN: 9+   RUNS: 277
AVERAGE: 30.77   HS: 88   50: 3 100: 0

V SOUTH AFRICA
TESTS: 5   INN: 9 (7)   RUNS: 150 (105)
AVERAGE: 16.66 (15.00)   HS: 38 (36)   50: 0 100: 0

V SRI LANKA
TESTS: 5   INN: 8+   RUNS: 253
AVERAGE: 31.62   HS: 74   50: 2 100: 0

V WEST INDIES
TESTS: 5   INN: 7+   RUNS: 408
AVERAGE: 58.28   HS: 160   50: 1 100: 2

V ZIMBABWE
TESTS: 8   INN: 15 (14)   RUNS: 387 (368)
AVERAGE: 27.64 (28.30)   HS: 63 (63)   50: 2 (2) 100: 0

DENNIS AMISS - PERSONAL FILE

FULL NAME: Dennis Leslie Amiss

DATE OF BIRTH: 7th April, 1943

BIRTHPLACE: Harborne, Birmingham

EDUCATION: Oldknow School, Birmingham

PLAYING ROLE: Right Hand Bat, Occasional Slow Left Arm

TEAMS: England; Warwickshire 1960 - 1987

TEST DEBUT: 1966 v West Indies, The Oval

TESTS: 50

MOST PRODUCTIVE GROUND - H: The Oval, 492 runs (70.28) in 5 Tests
                                        A: Kingston, 289 runs (289.00) in 1 Test

FIRST-CLASS DEBUT: 1960

FIRST-CLASS RUNS: 43,423

FIRST-CLASS WICKETS: 18

HIGHEST SCORE: 262* England v West Indies, Kingston, 1973-74

BEST BOWLING: 3-21 Warwickshire v Middlesex, Lord's, 1970

NICKNAME: Sacker

PERCENTAGE OF TEST INNINGS AS OPENER: 78.40%

FOR THE RECORD: Wisden 1974; Benefit 1975 (£34,947); Played in Kerry Packer's World Series Cricket in Australia in 1977-78. While in Australia, his idea fashioned the trend for the wearing of batting helmets; Toured South Africa in 1981-82 as a member of the England 'rebel' squad and was banned from Test cricket for three years; Testimonial 1985 - donated part of the proceeds to schools cricket in Warwickshire; After his career, he worked as a Sales Executive and Company Director; In 1994, he became Chief Executive at Warwickshire C.C.C.

DENNIS AMISS (England)

Former Warwickshire coach Ernest 'Tiger' Smith said to a young Dennis Amiss, "When you get a hundred, go on and make it into a big hundred, because those runs will make up for the times you miss out." Smith played in the same England team in the early 1900s with Jack Hobbs and Wilfred Rhodes, and had been an opener himself for Warwickshire, so he knew the trade as well as most. Amiss followed his mentor's advice religiously and, in time, developed a determination that allowed him to compile big totals. He scored eleven Test centuries and eight of them were above 150. He admits: "I was always very determined, but I just loved batting and always wanted to be at the crease." Originally, Dennis was a middle-order batsman, where he played for England in his first nine Tests, but it was the switch to the top of the order that sparked his Test career into life. He relates: "At Edgbaston in '72, I was struggling for form a bit and competing with Kanhai, Kallicharran and MJK for a spot in the middle-order. John Jameson and John Whitehouse opened the innings and weren't having a lot of success, so I asked to open because it was the only way back for me. The skipper agreed and I then got Bob Willis and David Brown to bowl at me in the nets with a new ball to get used to those conditions."

The change was a successful one and earned him a recall to the England squad and a place on the 1972-73 tour of India. Sadly the runs still never came, as he struggled to come to terms with the prodigious Indian spinners Chandrasekhar and Bedi, who captured 60 wickets between them in the five-match series. Dennis managed just 90 runs in six innings' before he was dropped. "I used to get a bit tense and tight when they had fielders around the bat and the ball was turning," Amiss admitted. In his Test career, those two tormentors each accounted for his wicket on seven occasions. The contest though, wasn't always a one-way thing and in England in 1974 Dennis got his revenge. He recalls: "Chandrasekhar had bowled so well in India with his leg-breaks and googlies, making it bounce like a tennis ball; but he wasn't quite on song this time and you can sense as a batsman when a bowler's not got it right, so I knew it was time to get my own back. For all the trouble they'd given me in the past, I wanted to pay them back." He did so in style, amassing 370 runs in four innings', including 188 at Lord's - a dismissal he was annoyed at; he felt he should have registered 300 which was a milestone that always eluded him much to his disappointment. This is a typically modest reflection from a tenacious player who was always in search of more runs, however big his score may have been. On avenging the Indian spin bowlers he said: "What did the trick was a net I had when I was left out (of the fourth Test) on the Indian tour previously. I couldn't find any of our bowlers but Bishan Bedi said, 'I'll bowl to you' and then Prasanna said, "I'll bowl to you," but Chandra never came out. They made me play as if there were fielders all around the bat and I never got out - that was the turning point. They got into trouble for it and Bedi won't let me forget it." To rub salt further into the wounds of the now-beaten spinners, Amiss made 179 at Delhi in 1976-77, which was his final Test match century. "I threw it away with a tired shot when I should have gone on to get a big 200," he said.

Dennis wasn't normally the type to offer his wicket cheaply. In fact he sold it at a price most bowlers could not afford. On the 1973-74 West Indies tour, Amiss was the difference between the sides. He made three centuries in the five-match rubber, becoming the first Englishman to do so against the West Indians. The series ended 1-1 but things could have been much different. After losing the first Test in Trinidad, despite a fighting 174 from Dennis that nearly salvaged a draw, England again found themselves in a similar position at Jamaica in the second Test. This time however, Amiss produced a magic 262 not out that thwarted the Windies' victory push, in batting out two days; an innings he rates as his best ever. "The wicket was good, there were a lot of Warwickshire supporters out there which helped and I thought if I could see off the new ball, I could hang around for a while. I saw off about three or four new balls in the end. I had to concentrate hard, but I found that if you really enjoy it, you don't notice the hardship and tiredness - it was like having a long net." Tony Greig, a member of that England side, has the greatest of respect for that achievement. "He was a perfuse sweater and I remember we gave him some brandy during the intervals! Dennis was a real big hundred merchant. When he got going, he loved it so much that he wanted to make it count when he was seeing it big. He had that sort of mentality which is rare, but he saw it as an opportunity to make up for the times he missed out." He followed that up with 118 in Guyana, before England drew level in Trinidad in the fifth Test.

Although he faced a difficult attack in the Caribbean of Boyce, Julien, Holder, Sobers and Gibbs, the advent of the West Indian pace quartet was soon paraded and Dennis had his viewing in 1976. A young and fiery Michael Holding put a dent in his skull in a tour game at Lord's when Amiss was playing for the MCC and this led to his absence for much of the summer. He had lost all confidence against fast bowling now, also thanks to a previous hammering from Lillee and Thomson. Such desperate times called for desperate measures and from his sabbatical, he returned with a new 'back and across' stance. After rebuilding his game, Dennis was given the fifth Test at The Oval to prove himself once more, while England had already lost the series. Although this match went the same way as the previous two defeats, Amiss made 203 on a good batting track and announced his return with real character. "It was quite a flat wicket; Viv Richards scored 291 on it. Once I played myself in I was hoping to get 300, but

Michael Holding was bowling superb," he recalls, about the bowler who accounted for his wicket twice in the match. "Michael's rhythm that day was the best I've ever seen from a fast bowler. He didn't seem to break the batting line once in 30 overs. Along with Jeff Thomson he was the quickest bowler I faced."

Despite a Test career average against the West Indies of 70.62, things were much less prolific in the early days. On his debut at The Oval, the occasion got the better of him. "When suddenly you're playing for England it is a very daunting situation. I got to the team hotel and was told that I was rooming with Ken Higgs. In the room there was my sweater, tie and England cap and I didn't want to lose sight of them. I always tell the story of how I went to bed in my cap and sweater! I never in fact did, but I thought about it. I was totally overawed by the situation. When I went out to bat I passed Wes Hall who said, "Good luck young man," which was encouraging; but when I was on 17, I went back to one that I should have gone forward to and was lbw to Wes. I was so nervous I could hardly play a bloody shot!"

It was nearly seven years after his debut before Dennis enjoyed any real success in the Test arena. From his first 12 Test matches he was averaging just 18.31, but in 1972-73 on tour in Pakistan he began to adapt successfully as an opening bat having only played there in three Tests previously. He took full advantage of the innocuous, flat wickets in a three-match series that saw every game drawn. On his first major success he commented: "It was nice to break through. For people like Keith Fletcher and myself, when you looked at your predecessors like Cowdrey, Barrington, Dexter and May, you think, 'My gosh, how can I be as good as those blokes?' But suddenly when they retire and go out of the picture, you realise it's down to you and that you must produce the goods to keep your place." His new mature attitude brought him 112 at Lahore in the first Test and he followed that with 158 at Hyderabad in scorching-hot conditions, as he remembers. "They were good batting wickets and didn't turn as much (as they do today). I had two days off after that innings in Hyderabad - I was absolutely dehydrated. The boys had been in the field for two days while I was resting at the hotel and I thought I'll do them some tea and toast for when they got back. I'll always remember Norman Gifford telling me where to stuff the toast and tea; he had burnt lips, his skin was peeling off and he was as red as a beetroot; he said he nearly died out there! Nowadays you have nutritionists to tell you what to eat to help you in those conditions, but we never had any of those things. I used to sweat a lot and those conditions really took a lot out of me." In the third Test at Karachi, Dennis made 99 and narrowly failed to register his third hundred in three consecutive Tests - in somewhat harsh circumstances when given out caught at bat-pad. "That was disappointing because I don't think I hit it," he says. "There were fielders all around the bat

14

and they all appealed and the umpire gave me out. Mushtaq Mohammed said to me later that he didn't think I hit it, but they had to get rid of me because they didn't want me scoring 300!"

The saddest aspect of his career is his lack of success against the Australians. He became one of many to suffer at the hands of Dennis Lillee and Jeff Thomson - the opening pair who terrorised batsmen with immense hostility. In Australia in 1974-75, Amiss scored 175 runs in nine innings including 90 at Melbourne. Reliving the pain, Dennis said: "It felt like the whole world had fallen in because I couldn't get a run. Every time I felt I was playing okay I got out. Other times you might have a bit of luck, but here, whenever I nicked it they caught it. They caught some great catches. We'd have a beer after play in one of the dressing rooms and I remember Ian and Greg Chappell both saying about Lillee and Thommo, 'Thank god we've got'em on our side.' Viv Richards said the same in 1976 about Roberts and Holding. When fast bowlers get you out a lot it knocks your confidence. Lillee was very fit and strong and had an ability to keep going, bowling an off-stump line consistently and with bounce, getting the odd one to nip back. Thommo was just *so* fast who got bounce from nowhere. They both had a lot of aggression and kept coming at you." His last three knocks in that series failed to register a single run as he fell to Lillee on each occasion. "In the last Test match I couldn't have got a run whatever I did because I was mentally gone. Everything I'd tried hadn't come off and you feel in total despair. I would loved to have scored a hundred against the Australians - the arch enemy, it was a big disappointment." His modest record against them is surprising, for a batsman who was a good player of fast bowling, as he proved time and again when facing the West Indies. He reasoned: "Pace and bounce is difficult to play from high-class fast bowlers, but if you've got consistent bounce from the pitch then it helps an awful lot. It was a regular thing in Australia for Lillee and Thomson to bowl bouncers that comfortably cleared Rodney Marsh's head never mind the batsman's. There is no easy solution against good, hostile bowling, it's just a case of applying yourself and trying to wear them down. You have got to be strong-willed and strong-minded." Amiss had an obvious affinity to opening, clearly visible when compared with his scores down the order. He was a fighter who relished the danger of the new-ball attack. He feels batting at the top of the order requires a great deal of mental toughness. "If you get up one day out of the wrong side of the bed and feel weak mentally, when you get out in the middle and the ball flies past your ear you tend to think, 'Bloody hell this is going to be a contest - I don't know if I fancy it.' Another day you wake up very strong and you're thinking, 'Right I'll take you today and if I play well enough I'm going to be smacking you by the end of the day. I really loved smacking them!"

15

DENNIS AMISS - TEST MATCH STATISTICS   ( ) = As Opener

TESTS: 50   INN: 88 (69)   RUNS: 3612 (3276)
AVERAGE: 46.30 (53.70)   HS: 262* (262*)   50: 11 (9) 100: 11 (11)

OVERALL RECORD   + = Opened in every innings against that country

V AUSTRALIA
TESTS: 11   INN: 21 (15)   RUNS: 305 (227)
AVERAGE: 15.25 (16.21)   HS: 90 (90)   50: 2 (1) 100: 0

V INDIA
TESTS: 14   INN: 24 (19)   RUNS: 965 (877)
AVERAGE: 41.95 (48.72)   HS: 188 (188)   50: 4 (4) 100: 2 (2)

V NEW ZEALAND
TESTS: 5   INN: 7+   RUNS: 433
AVERAGE: 86.60   HS: 164*   50: 1 100: 2

V PAKISTAN
TESTS: 10   INN: 18 (11)   RUNS: 779 (626)
AVERAGE: 55.64 (69.55)   HS: 183 (183)   50: 2 (1) 100: 3 (3)

V WEST INDIES
TESTS: 10   INN: 18 (17)   RUNS: 1130 (1113)
AVERAGE: 70.62 (74.20)   HS: 262* (262*)   50: 2 (2) 100: 4 (4)

MICHAEL ATHERTON - PERSONAL FILE

FULL NAME: Michael Andrew Atherton

DATE OF BIRTH: 23rd March, 1968

BIRTHPLACE: Failsworth, Manchester

EDUCATION: Manchester Grammar School; Downing College, Cambridge

PLAYING ROLE: Right Hand Bat, Leg Break Bowler, Slip and Gully Fielder

TEAMS: England; Cambridge University 1987 - 1989; Lancashire 1987 - .

TEST DEBUT: 1989 v Australia, Nottingham

TESTS: 84

MOST PRODUCTIVE GROUND -H: Nottingham, 865 runs (61.78) in 9 Tests
                          A: Sydney, 263 runs (87.66) in 2 Tests

FIRST-CLASS DEBUT: 1987

FIRST-CLASS RUNS: 17,599

FIRST-CLASS WICKETS: 108

HIGHEST SCORE: 199 Lancashire v Durham, Gateshead, 1992

BEST BOWLING: 6-78 Lancashire v Nottinghamshire, Nottingham, 1990

NICKNAME: Athers

PERCENTAGE OF TEST INNINGS AS OPENER: 90.96%

FOR THE RECORD: Captained England U19 at the age of 16; Became the youngest Lancastrian to score a Test century in 1990, when he made 151 against New Zealand at Trent Bridge; Wisden 1990; Young Cricketer of the Year 1990; Along with N.H. Fairbrother, Atherton set a new county record for the 3rd wicket when they put on 364 against Surrey at The Oval in 1990; Benefit 1997; OBE 1997; Holds record for captaining England in the most Tests (52), surpassing Peter May's former record; Currently, he is England's 8th highest run scorer in Test history.

MICHAEL ATHERTON (England)

Fewer England batsmen have been possessed with the same amount of fight than Michael Atherton, who is at his best during a crisis; whether scrapping for survival or maintaining an advantage. He displays certain aspects of his personality through his batting, most notably his stubbornness. His gritty refusal to be beaten by the bowler has played as great a part in his success in Test cricket as his batting skills alone. This is a strength he has carried with him from his youth, though it probably multiplied when he became captain of England. Graeme Fowler, who opened the batting for England in the early eighties, can remember the way in which Michael made his entrance into a relatively tough Lancashire dressing room, when he had completed his education at Cambridge University. "There were two things that I noticed about Michael initially when he had just left Cambridge: One, was that he was a very good player and two, how mentally inflexible he was. He had these very strong opinions and no matter what, if you tried to discuss them with him, he would disagree with it. That aspect of his game has improved over the years. He still has very strong ideas but he's now willing to listen. It does say a lot about his character, though, as he walked into quite a fierce dressing room from Cambridge. Most of us had been playing for 12 years, some of us in Test cricket, so he wasn't going to get an easy ride. Mike knew what he wanted to do and he basically knew how he wanted to do it. He was like a 'mini complete player', who would never ask you outright for advice as he was too proud to do that; he would listen to discussions and pick things up indirectly."

That precocious, tough youngster went on to break the record for Test match appearances as England captain, beating Peter May's record (of 41). Although he led an England team that often struggled, his tenacity contributed significantly toward the plus points of the team. For too long he was relied upon as the man who would bail England out of trouble. From the summer of 1993 against Australia, when Michael eventually inherited the captaincy from Graham Gooch, to mid-way through the summer of 1996, Atherton was the rock that England depended on to build the foundations of an acceptable total. He compensated regularly for the shortcomings of players who never fulfilled their potential. Between the mentioned period above, Atherton averaged 48.29 in 36 Tests. Further evidence that begs admiration is the fact that most of those Tests were played against the more powerful cricket nations: Australia (11), South Africa (8) and West Indies (9). This just goes to prove that Michael Atherton has been a much better opening batsman for England than his current figures show, and also proves that he possesses the sufficient talent to cope against the very best. In the 20 Tests up to the end of the 1997-98 West Indies tour,

Atherton averaged 28.73. Pundits suggested that he continued longer than he deserved, but someone with Atherton's ability and mental toughness cannot simply lose his class. His lone fight for his country for three years deserved such faith. On his loss of form, Fowler commented: "He was the longest running England captain ever, and if you've got that weight of responsibility it takes its toll. You have to bare in mind that for the majority of that time he's played in what has been a side that has let him down and he's had to carry it. If you carry that weight of responsibility for so long, there are times when you've only so much left in the barrel. I don't think form matters to him to be honest. He is just so strong mentally that it doesn't make any difference. He has this incredible mental capacity to deal with everything that has gone on; all the attention that has been given to him and all the criticism from the press he's received has all added to that pressure, yet he's come through it and come through it. He obviously grew up a lot being the England captain all that time. I still rate him as one of the best openers in the world."

Atherton has great strength of mind to graft out a long innings, though such a compliment could mislead anybody who has not seen him play. He is a player more likely to save a Test match than win one, but he can be a very enterprising batsman with a handsome array of attacking strokes. He plays the hook and pull shot well, is equally comfortable driving, particularly through the cover region, and there are few players as punishing to deliveries that stray on to leg stump. There are numerous examples that exemplify his application to compile long and vital totals. His 105 in Sydney in 1990-91; his 88 in Sydney in 1994-95, after England had slumped to 17 for the loss of three wickets on the first day and his Test best 185 not out in Johannesburg in 1995-96, that, along with Jack Russell, helped to save a Test match that appeared to be heading for sure defeat. In New Zealand at Christchurch in 1996-97, Atherton carried his bat for the first time in Test cricket, for 94. This was enough to keep England in the match, but were still 118 runs adrift of the Kiwis first innings total. After a good England bowling display in New Zealand's second innings, Mike then struck 118, ensuring a fine England win, and also narrowly avoided an amazing milestone. He spent 26 hours and 28 minutes on the field of play - all but 156 minutes of the whole of the Test. If he could have remained not out in his second innings he would have become only the fifth Englishman to have been on the field of play throughout a completed Test match. Graeme Fowler attributes much of these successes to his mental approach. "When he walked through the door at Lancashire with those very strong opinions and wouldn't change his mind, that was the seed that grew into him having the best temperament in world cricket, along with Steve Waugh, for batting long periods at the crease."

When Atherton made his Test debut against Australia in 1989, he batted at number three, the same position where he batted for Lancashire. In fact it was only when he became an opening batsman in Test cricket that Lancashire realised his talent for the role. In only his third Test match he made 151 for England against New Zealand at Nottingham in 1990; this was his first Test as an opening batsman. Still he batted at number three for Lancashire, while the established opening pair of Graeme Fowler and Gehan Mendis were there. "He was quite happy to bat at three and didn't see any difference between opening the batting and going in at three," Fowler said. "He batted there at Cambridge and for most of his life. It was only when he started opening the batting for England that people felt he should open for Lancashire. When Mendo and myself left, he moved up, but he didn't mind either way. At number three you have to have the ability to come in under any situation, but most importantly, to come in and face the new ball. He was obviously technically and mentally equipped to do that so there wasn't a big change for him to make between three and one at all."

From that match in Nottingham, where incidentally he has scored four centuries, Atherton soon went on to establish himself in the England side. In 1990, against New Zealand and then India, Michael registered 735 runs in the six Test matches at 66.81. Although he was praised accordingly, his performances were overshadowed somewhat by the even greater feats of his opening partner Graham Gooch, who scored 1058 runs at 96.18, including his infamous 333 at Lord's. However, those performances were more than enough to show the nation that he would be a very fine opening batsman for England for many years to come. The following year, when the West Indies were touring, the story was very different. He scored just 79 runs in five Tests at a derisory average of 8.77. It was to be the beginning of a fateful encounter with Curtly Ambrose, whose superior bowling has plagued him throughout his career like a terminal disease. Atherton has still shown enough courage and ability to earn the respect of the West Indies pace attack, as they realise just how important his wicket is to their destiny. Despite Michael's undoubtedly impressive batting displays against them, two of his three hundreds against the West Indies were made on flat, lifeless wickets: At Antigua (when Brian Lara scored 375) and Nottingham, when Ambrose was absent through injury. His disappointing tour there in 1997-98 when he averaged just 18.09, spelled the end as far as his captaincy went, but he is not the only one to have been exposed to mediocrity against the West Indies; there have been many more before him, and many of those cannot boast three centuries against them irrespective of pitch conditions. "If you consider the firepower that the West Indies have had through the years, to still average in the early thirties against a West Indies attack is no mean feat," says Fowler.

One of the lowest points of Atherton's career was his form in Zimbabwe on England's first ever tour there in 1996-97. The Zimbabwe team was raw, though not without a fair sprinkling of talent. England drew the series 0-0 and maybe underestimated the opposition somewhat. This low for Atherton, following on from a barren series against Pakistan, created a feeding frenzy for the media that portrayed the proverbial circling of vultures ready to move in for the kill. It is in these circumstances when Atherton is most dangerous, like the typical wounded animal. He went on to New Zealand and scored 325 runs at 108.33 in the three Tests; two of which were won and the other was saved by a record New Zealand tenth-wicket partnership. The series after though, against Australia, proved to be another slide for Atherton and again the media questioned his future both as captain and as player. His personality has often been described as dour by the media and his communicative skills, which is a vital duty nowadays for a Test captain, as less than complimentary. In support of his former county colleague, Graeme Fowler counters: "Mike doesn't suffer falls gladly, he never has done. He has his own way of talking to the press. He is very guarded because they have stuffed him out of sight on a number of occasions. I've been in press conferences with him when he's had everybody in the room laughing, but I've also been in the room when somebody's asked him a completely ridiculous question and he has cut them dead - quite rightly so."

During that 1997 Ashes battle, Atherton struggled to come to terms with the bowling of Glenn McGrath and Shane Warne. Along with Ambrose these two have dismissed him more than any other bowler. Nevertheless, there are plenty more bowlers in world cricket who can say they have been the victim of Michael Atherton; of his craft as a batsman, of his unwavering temperament, but more likely, of his steely, resilience that is so difficult to break. If every England player was possessed of the same tenacity, there would be a lot less matches lost to a lack of fight. In the 1998 series against South Africa, when still under the media microscope, he scored 103 at Edgbaston to defy his many critics. Without the burden of captaincy Atherton continued throughout that series in prolific and typically uncompromising form making 493 runs at 54.77. Along the way, he encountered his trademark confrontation with a fast bowler with a problem, who, in this case, was Allan Donald. On the Sunday evening at Trent Bridge, the two shared one of the most electrifying ding-dongs that more befitted a contest between Leonard and Duran. Michael would appear to have the same affect on fast bowlers like that of a red rag to a bull. With his wide, Lancashire grin, quick bowlers seem to develop an instant desire to remove the teeth that Atherton models so regularly; though the opener thrives on such adrenaline and would be, I'm sure, terribly upset if pace bowlers began to smile and exchange pleasantries with him, as opposed to the normal grunt, expletive and customary bouncer.

MICHAEL ATHERTON - TEST MATCH STATISTICS ( ) = As Opener

TESTS: 84	INN: 155 (141)	RUNS: 5935 (5717)
AVERAGE: 39.83 (40.83)	HS: 185* (185*)	50: 37 (36) 100: 12 (12)

OVERALL RECORD + = Opened in every innings against that country

V AUSTRALIA
TESTS: 24	INN: 48 (43)	RUNS: 1569 (1493)
AVERAGE: 34.10 (35.54)	HS: 105 (105)	50: 13 (13) 100: 1 (1)

V INDIA
TESTS: 7	INN: 13 (11)	RUNS: 689 (641)
AVERAGE: 57.41 (64.10)	HS: 160 (160)	50: 4 (4) 100: 2 (2)

V NEW ZEALAND
TESTS: 9	INN: 13+	RUNS: 955
AVERAGE: 79.58	HS: 151	50: 5 100: 4

V PAKISTAN
TESTS: 6	INN: 10 (7)	RUNS: 307 (243)
AVERAGE: 30.70 (34.71)	HS: 76 (76)	50: 3 (2) 100: 0

V SOUTH AFRICA
TESTS: 13	INN: 24+	RUNS: 1090
AVERAGE: 49.54	HS: 185*	50: 7 100: 2

V SRI LANKA
TESTS: 1	INN: 2+	RUNS: 15
AVERAGE: 7.50	HS: 7.50	50: 0 100: 0

V WEST INDIES
TESTS: 22	INN: 41 (37)	RUNS: 1276 (1246)
AVERAGE: 31.12 (33.67)	HS: 144 (144)	50: 5 (5) 100: 3 (3)

V ZIMBABWE
TESTS: 2	INN: 4+	RUNS: 34
AVERAGE: 8.50	HS: 16	50: 0 100: 0

EDDIE BARLOW - PERSONAL FILE

FULL NAME: Edgar John Barlow

DATE OF BIRTH: 12th August, 1940

BIRTHPLACE: Pretoria

EDUCATION: Pretoria High School; Witwatersrand University

PLAYING ROLE: Right Hand Bat, Right Arm Medium Pace, Slip Fielder

TEAMS: South Africa; Transvaal 1959/60 - 1963/64 & 1967/68; Eastern
      Province 1964/65 - 1966/67; Western Province; Boland; Derbyshire
      1976 - 1978 (capt)

TEST DEBUT: 1961-62 v New Zealand, Durban

TESTS: 30

MOST PRODUCTIVE GROUND H: Johannesburg 566 runs (47.16) in 7 Tests
                        A: Adelaide 248 runs (248.00) in 1 Test
FIRST-CLASS DEBUT: 1959-60

FIRST-CLASS RUNS: 18,212

FIRST-CLASS WICKETS: 571

HIGHEST SCORE: 217 Derbyshire v Surrey, Ilkeston, 1976

BEST BOWLING: 7-24 Western Province v Natal, Durban, 1972-73

NICKNAME: Bunter

PERCENTAGE OF TEST INNINGS AS OPENER: 91.22%

FOR THE RECORD: Took a hat-trick and four wickets in five balls while
playing for the Rest of the World against England in 1970 at Leeds; Played in
Kerry Packer's World Series Cricket; Promoted South African sport while
based in London, ran a vineyard, coached at Gloucestershire C.C.C., cricket
manager with Orange Free State, Transvaal and Griqualand West, and has
worked with Ali Bacher on developing cricket in the townships.

EDDIE BARLOW (South Africa)

This pugnacious cricketer proved how it is possible to succeed in the tough environment of Test cricket with a never-say-die temperament - a strength which exceeded his skills as a batsman alone. Eddie Barlow was one of the fiercest competitors of his era, and it was that fighting streak that inspired his performances out in the middle, whether as opening bat, middle-order bat or as bowler; he was always battling for his team. These characteristics were foremost in his career, though such a description should not undermine his ability with the bat. He may not have been in the same league as fellow countrymen Barry Richards and Graeme Pollock, in terms of value-for-money or graceful exhibitionism, but his uncompromising technique was certainly effective. Eddie's unrelenting spirit at the top of South Africa's batting order was often responsible for laying the foundations of a testing total, or alternatively, useful in denying an opposition in their push for victory. "He might not have been the best to watch," says former England wicketkeeper Bob Taylor, who was a colleague at Derbyshire, "but he used to fight it out. He was a fine, gutsy competitor, like a typical South African, and he was a particularly good player of fast bowling. He always gave 110 percent."

Eddie made his bow in Test cricket against New Zealand at Durban in 1961-62, registering ordinary scores of 15 and 10. Although, his performances improved that series with two forties in the next Test at Johannesburg, and fifties in the following three Tests at Cape Town, Johannesburg again and Port Elizabeth. It was in his next Test series in 1963-64 in Australia that he really launched his name on the cricketing world. The first match at Brisbane saw him make his first Test century of 114. He scored nought in the second innings of that Test, but it paled into insignificance when the series was finally complete, after he had scored 603 runs in the five-match rubber. At Melbourne in the second Test he made his second consecutive century (109). It was within the picturesque setting of the Adelaide Oval, though, where Eddie impressed most that series. In Australia's festival state, he held his own celebration in striking 201 and 47 not out in the second innings, to set up a ten-wicket win and square the series at 1-1 (which became the eventual series aggregate). In making his 201, he shared a third-wicket partnership of 341 with Graeme Pollock (175). To polish off a tremendous match-winning performance Eddie also chipped in with 3-6, from five overs of his briskish medium pace, in Australia's second innings.

After that Adelaide clash, his first nine Test matches had realised 896 runs at an impressive average of 56, showing him to be a quick learner in the highest arena possible. Barlow's old South Africa team-mate, Mike Procter, sums up his game with a cutting honesty, but with huge admiration for his attitude at the same time. "His batting technique was a little shaky," Procter admits, "he would play across the line and sometimes lose his timing. That's when he showed his character, because he would graft away, refusing to buckle to the bowlers, playing his way out of his bad form."* Bob Taylor added, about his former Derbyshire colleague: "He was like Geoff Boycott in the way he frustrated bowlers. He tried to occupy the crease and certainly wouldn't give his wicket away. When he got out he was always very annoyed - like most top players."

The season following the 1963-64 tour of New Zealand, Barlow was a key member of the South Africa side that entertained Mike Smith's English tourists. He began that series with two and nought at Durban, which contributed to his poor overall average at that venue of seven from four Tests. From there, he went on to scale much better heights, scoring 71 in Johannesburg in the second Test, 138 and 78 at Cape Town, 96 and 42 at Jo'Berg once more, followed by 69 and 47 in the fifth Test at Port Elizabeth. England won the first Test at Durban and that result settled the series, 1-0 in England's favour. The Springboks had their revenge though, months later, when touring England for a three-Test rubber. Barlow failed to emulate his achievements from the previous series but still managed to register fifties at Lord's (52) and at Nottingham (76) where they clinched the series 1-0. Barlow's feats in Test cricket, particularly against England, formed part of the reason why he later joined Derbyshire in the mid-seventies. Not only were the county looking to benefit from his batting and bowling skills, they felt his refreshing approach to the game would do a great deal for the club. Bob Taylor can remember a specific instance from the Derbyshire dressing room when the South African's upbeat temperament shone brighter than ever. "When he took over as captain, his first words to us were: 'One of the problems with you English players is that you worry too much about weather. We know it's inclement, but I want you all to get in the right frame of mind and focus positively. I don't want you thinking that you're not going to be playing because of rain, I want you all in a positive mood and expecting to start on time.' His attitude and fighting spirit rubbed off on the players, and from his time at the club we kicked on and managed to win a trophy shortly after." Derbyshire team-mate, Mike Hendrick, added: "The one thing that struck me about Eddie was how much he seemed to enjoy his cricket. He liked to lead from the front."

Despite a disappointing home series against Australia, personally, in 1966-67 when he made only 186 runs from five Tests, Barlow duly compensated in his

* Mike Procter, South Africa - The Years of Isolation, Leonard - Queen Anne Press (London), 1994

next Test series that came three years later - also against the Aussies. He began the rubber with 127 batting in the middle-order, which helped towards South Africa's first victory of an emphatic 4-0 series win. After a fine 110 in Johannesburg in the third Test, he was then restored to the opener's berth along side Barry Richards for the final Test match of his career at Port Elizabeth. It became the last Test that South Africa would play for 22 years due to politics, but Eddie bowed out in style with 73 and 27 to help complete the rout of Australia. "His mental toughness was a vital ingredient in our success against Australia before isolation," says Mike Procter. "At the time he was 30, a very experienced Test player and due to be Ali Bacher's vice-captain on the 1970 tour. His confidence just seeped through to the rest of us, so that we always believed we could turn a game round." South Africa proved to the world they were, probably, the strongest team around. Sadly, politics prevented such an opinion from being further put to the test, and also prematurely curtailed many a promising Test career - not least that of Eddie Barlow, who had posted an impressive average of 45 from his 30 matches.

EDDIE BARLOW - TEST MATCH STATISTICS   ( ) = As Opener

TESTS: 30	INN: 57 (52)	RUNS: 2516 (2290)
AVERAGE: 45.74 (45.80)	HS: 201 (201)	50: 15 (14) 100: 6 (5)

OVERALL RECORD   + = Opened in every innings against that country

V AUSTRALIA
TESTS: 14	INN: 26 (23)	RUNS: 1149 (999)
AVERAGE: 47.87 (47.57)	HS: 201 (201)	50: 3 (3) 100: 5 (4)

V ENGLAND
TESTS: 8	INN: 16 (15)	RUNS: 742 (666)
AVERAGE: 46.37 (44.40)	HS: 138 (138)	50: 6 (5) 100: 1 (1)

V NEW ZEALAND
TESTS: 8	INN: 15+	RUNS: 625
AVERAGE: 41.66	HS: 92	50: 6 100: 0

GEOFF BOYCOTT - PERSONAL FILE

FULL NAME: Geoffrey Boycott

DATE OF BIRTH: 21st October, 1940

BIRTHPLACE: Fitzwilliam, Yorkshire

EDUCATION: Hemsworth Grammar School

PLAYING ROLE: Right Hand Bat, Occasional Right Arm Medium Pace

TEAMS: England; Yorkshire 1962 - 1986

TEST DEBUT: 1964 v Australia, Nottingham

TESTS: 108

MOST PRODUCTIVE GROUND H: Lord's, 1189 runs (45.73) in 16 Tests
A: Port-of-Spain, 478 runs (59.75) in 5 Tests
FIRST-CLASS DEBUT: 1962

FIRST-CLASS RUNS: 48,426

FIRST-CLASS WICKETS: 45

HIGHEST SCORE: 261* MCC v WICB President's XI, Bridgetown, 1973-74

BEST BOWLING: 4-14 Yorkshire v Lancashire, Leeds, 1979

NICKNAME: Fiery or Boycs

PERCENTAGE OF TEST INNINGS AS OPENER: 98.96%

FOR THE RECORD: Cricket Writers Club Young Player of the Year 1964; Wisden 1964; Benefit 1974 (£20,639); Became the first Englishman to average over a hundred in a season in 1971 (100.12). He repeated this feat in 1979 (102.53); Was the first player to score his hundredth century in a Test match in 1977 at Leeds; Toured South Africa with a 'rebel' England squad in 1981-82 and was banned from Test cricket for three years; Testimonial 1984; He has the best career average of all batsmen who have scored over 35,000 first-class runs (56.83); Now a TV commentator and newspaper columnist.

GEOFF BOYCOTT (England)

This tenacious, stubborn, cricket-loving Yorkshireman was one of the most talented batsmen of his generation, and his Test match statistics reflect such a tribute. He was a player that broke bowlers hearts, with his uncompromising approach, watertight defence and a fine all-round technique. Boycott's greatest strength though, was concentration. He could shut out all distractions and focus solely on the job in hand, which to him was occupying the crease, rarely playing the kind of loose shots that batsmen often perish to. Geoff was always hungry to compile large totals for himself, and he was subsequently labelled a selfish player, but his opinion was the more runs he amassed - the more his team would benefit. That may be, though the criticism still came. In his time as a journalist after his cricket career, Sir Len Hutton, another fine Yorkshire and England opener, saw much of Boycott and rated him highly, but considered his over-cautious approach to batting somewhat of a waste of talent. In his autobiography, *Fifty Years in Cricket*, Len wrote: "Geoffrey would have been a far better player had he played in the thirties. He is a fine player, but he bats with the one thought in mind of not getting out. While Bradman, Hammond, Compton and myself, to name but a few, looked for a scoring opportunity as the bowler ran in, Geoffrey is absorbed with the defence of his wicket. Defence is his first thought; attack is his second. I cannot think of a batsman in his class who has allowed more bad balls to go unpunished."

Boycott's opening partner at Yorkshire in the early to mid-eighties was Martyn Moxon. Batting with Geoffrey Boycott was an experience he is proud to recall, though in the early days, it was a slightly unnerving experience for him. "I watched him as a kid, so when I first went out to bat with him I was a bit overawed and was in awe of him so much that I was frightened to talk to him. He wasn't the sort of bloke who would offer young players advice. It was only in later years when I found out that his theory was players should go to him if they wanted help. The more I got to know him and the more we played together the more I got to talk to him on a casual basis." Despite the flack that Geoffrey has received for particular aspects of his game, the fact remains that he was a class performer and Moxon certainly knew this when he was looking on from 22 yards. He admits: "Just by being at the other end to him, I learned a lot about the techniques of batting. He was totally dedicated to his profession, never left anything to chance, he prepared as well as anybody ever could, and he was mentally strong as well. He said very little in between overs; he was so wrapped up in what he was doing and concentrating that much."

It is a great shame that Boycott is so famously remembered for his slow scoring and stout defence, as he was such a good player that if he could have allowed himself to play a few more shots, which he did possess, things may have been different. However, the technique he did employ was still effective and often paramount to an England batting line-up that sometimes looked a little thin. People knew that with Boycott at the top of the order to provide the anchor role, there was always going to be a certain amount of solidity to the batting. It's not uncommon nowadays for television commentators to say, "England could do with a Boycott in this situation," when the side is up against it. There was nobody more gritty and determined than Geoff, as Pakistan's Mushtaq Mohammed relates: "He had such a tremendous temperament. The way he batted used to frustrate sides and I can remember when we gave him a lot of stick, just because we couldn't get him out. We'd say, 'Come on you boring bastard, it's not a ten-day match. But he used to absorb all the stick and just get on with his batting. His concentration was magnificent." Tom Graveney, a former England colleague, was another who admired Boycott's skill but, again, was not agreeable to his approach to batting. Having said that, Tom did play with one of the greatest openers ever in Len Hutton, so it's not easy for any batsman to live up to such high standards. "With all due respect, I think the first thing that Geoffrey thought of was what was going on underneath number one and the side didn't matter quite so much; where as Len Hutton always played for the side. However, Geoffrey was technically a very good player, there's no doubt about that. I loved batting with him. People say he was a manufactured player but that's ridiculous. He was very good indeed, though he was a grafter who was more likely to win you a game on a bad wicket." The subject of Geoff's self-interest has been discussed time and again, in Yorkshire and England dressing rooms, commentary boxes, pubs and offices. Folk have different opinions on this; but one thing is certain according to Martyn Moxon, and that is that Boycott's ability as an attacking player was far greater than many gave him credit for. He said: "I've seen it where we needed to get maximum batting points from a certain amount of overs and we've failed, and in that time he scored particularly slowly, so there have been occasions where you could argue that he had been selfish and not played for the team - I know this has been said about him. But he also had the ability to take attacks apart as and when he felt it necessary - and he has done that. It's difficult to say whether he batted the way he did on purpose. I just think that he had worked his game plan out to such fine detail that he eliminated any risks of getting out, because he wanted to go on and score hundred plus."

The chief reason for Boycott's technique of occupying the crease was simply due to the fact he just loved batting so much. Staying out there in the middle was a sure way to extend his passion. New Zealand's Richard Hadlee, one of the greatest fast bowlers in the history of the game, had a lot of respect for Boycott's fighting style and said as much in his book '*At The Double* '. He wrote: "If you get him out (and I haven't too often) you know you've really earned his wicket. I've found him probably the hardest guy I've ever bowled to. He's a player that every bowler must respect because he's so professional. His application, concentration and dedication are second to none and he never gives anything away. All he wants to do is occupy the crease and score runs and he's prepared to wear the bowler down to get what he wants. Boycott's so run-hungry that he won't take any chances. If you do beat his bat and get through his defences, it's a major triumph." Geoff was technically as good as anybody - his carefully mapped-out technique was sublime. He could handle the quicks, but he was equally as good against the spinners. Some of his best innings' were against top-class spin bowlers on turning wickets. He knew his game plan inside out and he probably knew also, how each particular bowler would be trying to get him out.

Having contributed so much detailed preparation into his game, the times he did miss out were very hard moments for him to take, whether in Test cricket or even in county cricket. In 1973 against New Zealand at Trent Bridge, Geoff was the victim of a poor call by his opening partner Dennis Amiss, and was run out for one. It was hard enough for him to accept a dismissal by a good ball, but to get run out at that stage of the innings was not something he accepted easily. Amiss, who went on to register an unbeaten 138, recalls apologetically: "I called him for a two then I suddenly realised that Dick Pollard was on to it and I said 'no', but he kept coming. I went back into my crease, which he didn't appreciate, and after calling me a few names he was heard in the pavilion saying, 'Look at the bastard scoring all my runs!' We never spoke for a while after that and captain Ray Illingworth had to have a word with us about how England's cause is greater than any personal feud. It took a while for us to resume our opening partnerships successfully. We had a few hiccups and stop-starts because we had lost trust in one another." On another forgettable occasion for Geoff, Martyn Moxon remembers how distraught his partner was after getting out just prior to the close of play. This was after he and Moxon had shared a stand of 351 for the first wicket against Worcestershire in 1985. It was the highest opening partnership by a Yorkshire pair since Holmes and Sutcliffe's stand of 555 in 1932. "I was out first for 168 and then he got out caught at long leg hooking for 184, off the last ball of the day," Moxon recalls. "He came in and basically sat in a corner with a towel over his head for 45 minutes and never said a word to anybody. He was absolutely distraught that he'd got out playing the hook shot at that time of day, so I think that sums up his mentality on batting - he wanted to be there the next day to go on and get 200, 300 whatever."

Geoff's Test career began in 1964 against Australia at Nottingham. Inevitably, it was a very edgy occasion for him, but he still managed to record a useful 48. He recalls: "I remember being nervous at first, so nervous that I picked up my bat to play the opening delivery from Graham McKenzie and it was in Grout's gloves before I had time to play a shot!" His scores in that series were solid and showed him to be a man with a fine temperament - a strength that was prominent in his make-up. Although he averaged a more than respectable 48.50 in that series, he still realised his deficiencies: He was struggling to come to terms with Graeme Corling's out-swinger's and promptly sought the help of Bill Bowes, the former Yorkshire and England bowler who was then writing on an evening Yorkshire newspaper. Together they came up with some ideas to help improve his technique against the moving ball. It seemed to work given his next score of 58 at Manchester. Although it was his 113 at The Oval in the next Test that proved he was properly over his weakness. That hundred also earned him a place on his first MCC tour, to South Africa. On that tour Boycott struggled to adjust to the conditions initially where the pitches were harder and faster than he had previously encountered, but still finished the series with two seventies and a hundred in the final Test at Port Elizabeth.

The career of Geoffrey Boycott is scattered with triumphs and controversies, and nothing was ever more intriguing than his omission from the England team in 1967 - after he had scored 246 not out! It was against India on a flat wicket at his home ground in Leeds, and the selectors ruled that he had batted too slowly and was promptly served a one-Test suspension as a disciplinary measure. Harsh it may seem and Geoff was inevitably upset at the treatment. "The decision stunned me at the time," he said, "though looking back I now see that it had become inevitable. I was mortified with embarrassment and filled with an angry, burning sense of injustice, which I can remember clearly and painfully to this day. Even after 20 years and with plenty of opportunity to ponder all the aspects of the affair, I still feel the selectors were wrong. They inflicted upon me a stigma which I cannot believe I deserved but one which I will take with me to my grave. Being dropped by England then was an indelible stain on my record; more, it was a stain on my character which has been used as an official endorsement of the accusation that I played the game selfishly and with total disregard for others. When the circumstances have long been forgotten, the fact that I was dropped for slow scoring will remain. I still believe I was the victim of a miscarriage of justice." *
Geoff scored slowly on the first day of the Test to finish 106 not out, but he accelerated on the second day adequately. However, his scoring rate from day

* Geoffrey Boycott, Boycott - The Autobiography, Corgi (London), 1988

one had already triggered a witch-hunt from the press and much pressure was put on the selectors to leave Boycott out for the next match - which they did of course. Geoff had gone into that game in pretty bad form and his former Yorkshire and England team-mate, Brian Close, understood the situation more than most. He said: "One needs to understand Boycott's frame of mind as an out-of-form batsman trying to prove himself good enough for England; and to study the innings in this context to reach a charitable understanding of why he played as he did. Such tenacity, in different conditions, would have been hailed as a masterly exhibition of the bulldog spirit; but on this first day of a Test it was being viewed in a different light." After serving his one-match suspension, Geoff returned for the third Test in Birmingham, but by this time the scars were already inflicted and were never likely to heal.

One of Geoff's most prestigious moments of his career came in 1977, when he scored his 100th century on his home ground at Leeds against Australia in a Test match. He scored 191 and reached the milestone against a good Aussie pace attack of Thomson, Pascoe and Walker. It is just another statistical highlight of a career littered with them. When you scan through Boycott's Test career, there are so many consistent contributions that one feels, despite the criticism he received, there would always be a place in an England side for a player like Geoffrey Boycott. Yes he batted patiently, yes he was never one to enthral Test match crowds, but at the same time he frustrated bowlers to the point of submission, where he could eventually score freely off them with an ease only associated with the classiest and most workmanlike of batsman. It is sad to think that three years of his career were bypassed from 1974 to 1977, due to his differences with Mike Denness's captaincy. He lost a further three years of his Test career after he toured South Africa with a 'rebel' England side. Considering he lost six years in Test cricket for these reasons, one can't help wondering how many runs he could have ended up with had he have played throughout these periods. Such, though, was the strength and opinionated nature of Boycott's principled attitude. We see him today as a prominent figure of the cricketing media, and nobody would ever want him to change his forthright manner that personifies the outspoken Yorkshireman and reflects the way he played the game - honestly and tenaciously. As Dennis Amiss concludes, "By statistics Geoff will go down as one of England's greatest players. He had tremendous concentration and was always very determined."

GEOFF BOYCOTT - TEST MATCH STATISTICS   ( ) = As Opener

TESTS: 108   INN: 193 (191)   RUNS: 8114 (8091)
AVERAGE: 47.72 (48.16)   HS: 246* (246*)   50: 42 (42) 100: 22 (22)

OVERALL RECORD   + = Opened in every innings   against that country

V AUSTRALIA
TESTS: 38   INN: 71+   RUNS: 2945
AVERAGE: 47.50   HS: 191   50: 14 100: 7

V INDIA
TESTS: 13   INN: 22+   RUNS: 1084
AVERAGE: 57.05   HS: 246*   50: 2 100: 4

V NEW ZEALAND
TESTS: 15   INN: 25+   RUNS: 916
AVERAGE: 38.16   HS: 131   50: 6 100: 2

V PAKISTAN
TESTS: 6   INN: 10+   RUNS: 591
AVERAGE: 84.42   HS: 121*   50: 3 100: 3

V SOUTH AFRICA
TESTS: 7   INN: 12+   RUNS: 373
AVERAGE: 33.90   HS: 117   50: 2 100: 1

V WEST INDIES
TESTS: 28   INN: 53 (51)   RUNS: 2205 (2182)
AVERAGE: 45.93 (47.43)   HS: 128 (128)   50: 15 (15) 100: 5 (5)

JOHN EDRICH - PERSONAL FILE

FULL NAME: John Hugh Edrich

DATE OF BIRTH: 21st June, 1937

BIRTHPLACE: Blofield, Norfolk

EDUCATION: Brackendale School, Norwich

PLAYING ROLE: Left Hand Bat

TEAMS: England; Surrey 1958 - 1978

TEST DEBUT: 1963 v West Indies, Manchester

TESTS: 77

MOST PRODUCTIVE GROUND - H: Leeds, 849 runs (53.06) in 9 Tests
                                                      A: Sydney, 340 runs (56.66) in 4 Tests
FIRST-CLASS DEBUT: 1958

FIRST-CLASS RUNS: 39,790

HIGHEST SCORE: 310* England v New Zealand, Leeds, 1965

PERCENTAGE OF TEST INNINGS AS OPENER: 64.56%

FOR THE RECORD: Played for Norfolk 1954 & 1979-80; Scored against every first-class county except his own; During his 310* in 1965 for England v New Zealand, he scored the most boundaries in a Test innings; Became the 17th batsman in first-class cricket to score a hundred centuries (101* Surrey v Derbyshire, The Oval, 1977); MBE 1977; Cousins include B.R. Edrich (Kent & Glamorgan), E.H. Edrich (Lancashire), G.A. Edrich (Lancashire) and W.J. Edrich (Middlesex & England); Served as an England selector in 1981 and as England batting coach under R. Illingworth's regime in the mid-nineties; He is now a successful businessman.

JOHN EDRICH (England)

The dream of representing your country is the thought that clouds most young cricketers minds, but in the case of John Edrich, things were different. "I didn't think about it much when I was a youngster, but with being born into the Edrich family I soon realised that I could play cricket and was then obviously encouraged. We lived in a farmhouse in Norfolk and my father laid about fifteen yards of concrete behind the house where he'd spend hours and hours bowling at me," John recalls. He was playing minor counties cricket for Norfolk in his mid-teenage years, but still, lofty ambitions never once hindered his career priorities. When he joined Surrey as a seventeen-year-old, it was as if he had joined an England team already, with names such as Barrington, Bedser, May, Loader, Laker and Lock; getting into the Surrey side alone was a more than useful step to Test cricket. "In those days it was an achievement in itself just to get into the Surrey side, but once I achieved that, I then started to think about playing for England. We were encouraged straight away to try and become the best, but if you lost sight of your priorities you were soon knocked down to size." His mentor at Surrey could not have been better equipped to mould Edrich into a Test match opening batsman, as Andrew Sandham was himself a great opener who partnered Jack Hobbs for so long with Surrey and England. Sandham's England career would have spanned much longer than 14 Tests had it not been for the presence of Herbert Sutcliffe. Under the guidance of Sandham, he soon impressed at The Oval, and a beckoning Test career inevitably followed.

After establishing himself as an opener with Surrey, John adopted a liking for the position. "I preferred opening, I think it suited my game and I never did like hanging around waiting to go in." He batted at two on his Test debut against the West Indies, in a top three also containing his Surrey colleagues Mickey Stewart and Ken Barrington. John feels his debut could not have been harder. "It was a quick learning process and was a bit of a shock as I'd never faced anybody as quick as Wes Hall and Charlie Griffith before. That would be the best side that I played against throughout my career; there was also Sobers, Gibbs, Kanhai, Worrell, Hunte and Butcher - one couldn't have got a harder baptism. I realised very early on that for me to be successful in Test cricket I had to play at my best and tighten up my game." This was something he did to perfection. Edrich was a player that made the bowler earn his wicket and he eliminated the kind of shots that are often punished by dismissal in that arena. He said: "Colin Cowdrey told me early on that Test cricket was all about nudging and pushing ones and twos and the odd four, because it's a big innings game. It can be difficult going in first and your main job should be to see the first session off and not look to play too many risk shots. Shot selection is vital for an opener - fortunately I never had a problem with concentration so I was able to leave a lot of balls that I never had to play." His introduction to Test cricket from Griffith and Hall proved to be a helpful exercise for later life, as John became quite adept at handling the quick stuff.

He scored 120 against Australia at Lord's in 1964 - his first Test century. It was the first of three hundreds Edrich made on the ground, but it wasn't until the following summer against New Zealand that he really launched his career. At Headingley, John opened the innings in the absence of Geoff Boycott and scored a massive 310 not out. He batted for 532 minutes and hit five sixes and 52 fours - a record for boundaries hit. It was the first triple century by an Englishman in a Test since Len Hutton's 364 in 1938. He shared a partnership of 339 with his Surrey colleague Ken Barrington for the 2nd wicket. "It's strange how things work out because I was only brought in because Geoffrey Boycott had hurt his back. I felt as though I could have batted for another day, everything just seemed to come off the middle of the bat. I wasn't concerned at going for Gary Sobers' world record (365) at the time, but after, I thought it would have been nice to have another hour before MJK Smith declared." Still this innings wasn't enough to cement his name at the top of the order. When Boycott returned in the next Test against South Africa that summer, Bob Barber kept his opening spot while John had to drop down to three. Edrich says: "They used to do things like that in those days. After getting 300 I thought, 'That's it, I'll be opening next match', but it wasn't to be. Having got used to opening, I then had to adjust again to waiting around and batting at three." Without complaint, John continued at first wicket down and responded in the appropriate manner by scoring two centuries on the Australian tour in 1965-66. Despite his heavy run scoring, it wasn't until 1967-68 on tour in the West Indies that he finally became a regular fixture in the England team and an opener at that. In Barbados, he scored 146 which was the only hundred he made against the West Indies, despite his 96 in Jamaica the previous Test. "In Barbados it was a lovely wicket to bat on as you get a nice even bounce. I should never have got out, but I nicked one to the keeper after Charlie (Griffith) had bowled me one down the leg side."

John's form was consistently good against Australia and in 1968, this was the case once more, averaging 61.55 including a superb 164 on his home ground. The Aussie attack wasn't awesome in any way but it did consist of Graham McKenzie who John felt "bowled a few loose balls but also the odd unplayable one." His most rewarding time against the Australians was on tour in 1970-71. He registered 648 runs in the series at 72. In the 6th Test at Adelaide, which has always been a batsman's paradise, he had his first glimpse of Dennis Lillee who was making his Test debut. Although the fiery young Aussie finished the 1st innings with figures of 5-84, including John's wicket, Edrich had already plundered a fine 130. He recalled: "This young man was charging in, all arms and legs and banging it down as fast as he could, but this was before he learnt too much about the game. Even then we knew he was going to be a good bowler." Despite a lean home series in 1972, John returned to his best in 1975, scoring 175 at Lord's in the 2nd Innings. This time he had to combat a much more polished and mature Lillee, added to his even quicker strike partner Jeff Thomson. On the battle he says: "I tried to wear them down. The trick was not to play too many shots. When you hit at the ball at that pace, more often than not you're going to be guiding it towards the slips, so I was happy to be patient and pick up the ones and twos and knew if I did that for a day, I was going to have a hundred. I always liked playing against Australia because they were very competitive as I was. To do well against them was the supreme achievement for me." Dennis Lillee has a lot of respect for Edrich, and remembers just how difficult a task it was to remove him. "I always found with Edrich that to get him out it was going to be hard work and that you had to bowl well at him, as he always valued his wicket so much - he was a grafter. John was never prepared to take you on; he preferred to grind you into the ground," Dennis said.

Typical of an opening batsman, John was never keen on the lesser paced bowlers from India and Pakistan, reflected honestly in his figures. "I couldn't get used to the twiddly bowlers," he admits with a smile, but does acknowledge the problems people like Bhagwat Chandrasekhar gave him. John Edrich is best remembered when at war with the quick bowlers, blunting the sharpest of opening attacks ever to surface on a cricket field such as Hall and Griffith, Lillee and Thomson, Roberts and Holding and Peter Pollock - the South African that felled him in 1965. He concludes: "When Pollock hit me on the head I learnt an important lesson and I never took my eye off the ball again after that. Dennis Lillee broke two ribs when I thought it was going to bounce a bit more, but generally, I was always happier playing the quicks."

There is nothing more satisfying to a professional sportsman than hearing a former adversary praising your skill. John's combative, uncompromising spirit on the cricket field was such that he commanded a healthy respect from those who admired his talent as a batsman and his fight as a competitor. Edrich feels there has never been a finer opening batsman than South Africa's Barry Richards, who was sadly deprived a prolonged Test arena due to politics. However, the respect is mutual, as Barry regards John as one of *the* great players. He praised: "Those who regard him as a dour grafter would do well to remember that in the early sixties his style was to set about the county attacks;

he had a spell when he hit more sixes than any other player in the country. But when he was entrusted with the job of stabilising the England batting line-up, often in sides that were under the collar against the Australian and West Indian pace attacks, he set about the task with maximum efficiency and responsibility. Don't forget either that although he limited his strokes to get the innings off to a sound start he would still hit the ball very hard later in his innings when the pressure was off. By nature Australians are from generous with their praise but their top players all have the profoundest respect for the record of John Edrich over the past twenty years and it's a respect that I share."* Tom Graveney, his former England batting colleague, is also a huge admirer of the way in which Edrich went about his cricket. "What a great player. He always appeared as though he was in control. Even when he played and missed twice, he'd hit the next ball for four with the same expression on his face. If I was looking for an opening batsman, I would certainly want John in my side, before Boycott and many other good players."

* Barry Richards, The Barry Richards Story, Faber & Faber (London), 1978

JOHN EDRICH - TEST MATCH STATISTICS   ( ) = As Opener

TESTS: 77   INN: 127 (82)   RUNS: 5138 (3430)
AVERAGE: 43.54 (44.54)   HS: 310* (310*)   50: 21 (16) 100: 12 (9)

OVERALL RECORD   + = Opened in every innings against that country

V AUSTRALIA
TESTS: 32   INN: 57 (36)   RUNS: 2644 (1692)
AVERAGE: 48.96 (48.34)   HS: 175 (175)   50: 13 (8) 100: 7 (4)

V INDIA
TESTS: 10   INN: 14 (5)   RUNS: 494 (111)
AVERAGE: 38.00 (22.20)   HS: 100* (62)   50: 3 (2) 100: 1 (0)

V NEW ZEALAND
TESTS: 11   INN: 15 (10)   RUNS: 840 (725)
AVERAGE: 60.00 (80.55)   HS: 310* (310*)   50: 2 (1) 100: 3 (3)

V PAKISTAN
TESTS: 9   INN: 14 (7)   RUNS: 361 (145)
AVERAGE: 27.76 (24.16)   HS: 70 (54)   50: 2 (1) 100: 0

V SOUTH AFRICA
TESTS: 1   INN: 2 (0)   RUNS: 7 (0)
AVERAGE: 7.00   HS: 7   50: 0 100: 0

V WEST INDIES
TESTS: 14   INN: 25 (24)   RUNS: 792 (757)
AVERAGE: 34.43 (34.40)   HS: 146 (146)   50: 4 (4) 100: 1 (1)

ROY FREDERICKS - PERSONAL FILE

FULL NAME: Roy Clifton Fredericks

DATE OF BIRTH: 11th November, 1942

BIRTHPLACE: Blairmont, Berbice, British Guiana

EDUCATION: New Amsterdam Technical School, British Guiana

PLAYING ROLE: Left Hand Bat, Occasional Slow Left Arm

TEAMS: West Indies; British Guiana (now Guyana) 1963/64 - 1982/83;
       Glamorgan 1971 - 1973

TEST DEBUT: 1968-69 v Australia, Melbourne

TESTS: 59

MOST PRODUCTIVE GROUND - H: Trinidad 896 runs (42.66) in 11 Tests
                         A: Lord's, 312 runs (62.40) in 3 Tests
FIRST-CLASS DEBUT: 1963-64

FIRST-CLASS RUNS: 16,384

FIRST-CLASS WICKETS: 7

HIGHEST SCORE: 250 Guyana v Barbados, Bridgetown, 1974-75

BEST BOWLING: 4-36 Guyana v Trinidad, Port-of-Spain, 1971-72

NICKNAME: Freddo

PERCENTAGE OF TEST INNINGS AS OPENER: 99.08%

FOR THE RECORD: Put on 330 with Alan Jones for the first wicket for Glamorgan against Northamptonshire in 1972, setting a county record; He registered the second-fastest Test century in terms of balls received (71) during his highest Test score against Australia in 1975-76; Played World Series Cricket in 1977-78; Scored 217 and 103 in his last two first-class innings' for Guyana in 1982-83; Became Comrade Fredericks, Guyana government minister.

42

ROY FREDERICKS (West Indies)

This enterprising, often-exhilarating left-hander, had a very defined, attacking technique. He was a player that constantly sought runs with a predatory hunger. Roy Fredericks entertained crowds and was the quintessential, majestic West Indies batsman whose best form of defence was attack. Such an approach may not befit the old-fashioned cliché of how an opening batsman should play, but his attacking game was so natural and so successful that there was no reason to admonish him for his lack of caution. Fredericks played for the West Indies between 1968-69 to 1976-77, while also representing Glamorgan in county cricket from 1971 to 1973, where his offensive game was even more exaggerated than it was in Test cricket. This strength of his could also be his weakness at times, though these moments did not occur regular enough for him to reconsider his game-plan. Alan Jones was Fredericks' opening partner at Glamorgan and recalls one occasion where the opposition discovered just how good he was in attack, particularly to short deliveries. "We were playing Yorkshire and me and Roy had to go in at the end of the day and bat out three overs. Well, typically, Roy got caught hooking at long leg for nought. I got talking to some of the Yorkshire boys that evening and they told me how they fancied getting him out like that every time. I told Freddo this and he said, 'Right then old chap, we'll see about that.' Next innings they continued to bowl short at him, he continued to hook, but this time the ball kept disappearing over the fence and on to the steps. He believed in taking on the bowling from the word go. He loved hooking and he got out to that shot quite a few times, but he also got a lot of runs from it as well. He was a good player of quick bowling because he had plenty of time, quick feet, good reflexes and a great eye." It was never boring for Jones when at the opposite end of the wicket to Fredericks, but his style of constant attack and inability to ignore a chance to cut or hook sometimes frustrated his partner, especially when there was an important cause to battle for. "It used to annoy me at times when he'd get out to the hook shot first or second ball, but that's the way he played. I talked to him about it and asked him to be more patient when the ball's new. Freddo just said, 'Look man, if the ball's short it's got to go, whether it's the first ball of the match or 4.15 in the afternoon'."

There is no better example of just how punishing Fredericks could be at demolishing pace attacks, than his 169 in Perth in 1975-76, when he bludgeoned such respected quick bowlers as Dennis Lillee and Jeff Thomson on a wicket conducive to fast bowling. His fifty came up in 45 minutes off only 33 balls. He then reached his century in 116 minutes off just 71 balls, which became the second fastest hundred scored in Test cricket. It remains one of *the* great Test innings' and was a truly masterful exhibition of batting that oozed confidence, while he treated the Australian quickies with a dismissive contempt. How so many of his batting contemporaries around the cricket world, would have loved to play a similar innings, if only to return hostilities to Lillee and Thomson; but this was not something that could easily be reciprocated. However, Fredericks showed the way, fighting fire with fire and winning out comfortably with his 145-ball innings that included 27 fours and one six. You could say that Dennis Lillee was less than forthcoming with his praise for the West Indian at the time, but now, after having 22 years to reflect, he is considerably more generous with his praise. He said: "When he (Fredericks) was on, he was on; you just couldn't bowl to him. At Perth when he made that big hundred, it didn't matter what we bowled him as he would simply whack you, though we did make the mistake of bowling too short to him and to all their players in that innings, and we paid the penalty." Almost a quarter of Fredericks' Test runs were scored against Australia, and in registering many of those, he had to confront Dennis with the new ball. It was one of the most exciting personal duels of that era. Lillee added: "I had many battles with him and I enjoyed the challenge - he got me a few times and I got him a few times. Although he was a shot-player, he wasn't the kind of batsman that blew hot and cold. He ranks up there very highly in my estimation as an opening batsman He could apply himself for sure, but he did prefer attack, as most West Indians do."

It wasn't until his fifteenth Test that Fredericks made his first century in that arena. His 163 in Jamaica against New Zealand in 1971-72 brought him deserved relief, though he had already exceeded 60 on five occasions. This score combined in a 269 run partnership with Lawrence Rowe (214), who was playing on his home ground, and it became the highest partnership for any wicket for the West Indies against New Zealand. That first Test century for Fredericks, scored in the first of the five-match series, initiated a prosperous period in his career. Following on from that series against the Kiwis where he averaged 54, he then averaged upwards of 40 in his next five series': 42 against Australia in the Caribbean in 1972-73; 50 against England on tour in 1973; 66 against England back home in 1973-74; 40 in India in 1974-75, where he scored hundreds in Calcutta and Bombay, and 45 against Pakistan during that same tour. During the 1973-74 series against England, when he scored 94 in Jamaica, he and Lawrence Rowe (120) set another West Indies batting record as they had done on the same ground two years prior against New Zealand. This time they put on 206 for the first wicket, which became the highest opening partnership for the West Indies against England; a record that is now held by that famous pairing of Gordon Greenidge and Desmond Haynes with 298. Fredericks was out in the nineties again during that same series at Guyana for 98. This, added to his 98 at Barbados against Australia the previous year, and a further eight occasions where he was dismissed between 70 and a hundred, suggests he may have lacked a certain amount of concentration at times. This is always going to be the case though, where a player with the approach of Fredericks is concerned. Still, with more application he could have fared even better. Says Tony Lewis, the ex-England captain who also skippered Roy at Glamorgan. "He was a fine player who could demolish an attack at any time. When he did have problems though, it was certainly more to do with concentration than ability and technique. Although, I felt he did take a more dour approach for the West Indies and worked a little harder than he did in county cricket. You could then see there were two sides to his talent. I think, in county cricket, he found the daily chore quite difficult, with Grace Road on a Tuesday afternoon et cetera."

As a personality, Fredericks was equally admired, particularly in Wales during his stint as overseas player at Glamorgan. "He was good fun; when he laughed his whole body rocked. Freddo fitted in very well," says Tony Lewis. If there were any grudges still held against West Indians in South Wales after Roy's countryman, Gary Sobers, had hit Glamorgan's Malcolm Nash for six sixes in an over in 1968, Fredericks did everything to reverse such feelings. He was well liked by spectators and players alike. Alan Jones comments: "When he first joined Glamorgan we never roomed together, but he went through a bad patch one year and when we played against Kent at Canterbury I got 160 and Freddo got nought. That night, when we travelled down to Southampton to prepare for the next game against Hampshire, I got to the hotel and Roy said, 'You're rooming with me from now on old boy, as I'm hoping some of your good form might rub off on me!' We then shared a room for the next three or four months. It probably helped our opening partnership on the field, although I got used to listening to Calypso music at two in the morning. He was quite a character and a great team man." Jones appreciated Fredericks' style of play as it removed a lot of pressure from him in terms of having to score runs quickly. The only down point for Jones was the calling. "He was probably the worst caller I've ever played with. His favourite saying was, 'Sorry I ran you out old chap'." Despite his lethargic and cavalier exterior, traits so typically Caribbean, anybody under the impression that he was not committed enough to his cricket would be very mistaken. "He was a good competitor who could give the bowler a glowering stare, which was quite thunderous," admits Lewis.

His last Test century was 120 against Pakistan in 1976-77 at Trinidad. This innings brought up four thousand runs for him in Test cricket. The series prior in England, played in conditions that more resembled the Caribbean with the sun burning brightly throughout, the opener scored two centuries that greatly contributed towards his career average against England of 52. He made 138 in the second innings at Lord's and 109 at Leeds. Incidentally, from the three Tests he played at Lord's, only once did he make less than fifty from five innings' - that being a duck in the first innings in 1976. This explains why cricket's HQ is his most successful venue away from his homeland. Given his many successes in England, added to his time in county cricket, Tony Lewis has seen enough to know exactly where Roy Fredericks should rank in Test history. "Although he could be destructive as a county player, he really was a cricketer designed to play in Test cricket. When you talk of Freddo, you're talking about a player of top class, if not the highest class."

ROY FREDERICKS - TEST MATCH STATISTICS   ( ) = As Opener

TESTS: 59	INN: 109 (108)	RUNS: 4334 (4329)
AVERAGE: 42.49 (42.86)	HS: 169 (169)	50: 26 (26) 100: 8 (8)

OVERALL RECORD   + = Opened in every innings against that country

V AUSTRALIA
TESTS: 15	INN: 29+	RUNS: 1069
AVERAGE: 38.17	HS: 169	50: 5 100: 1

V ENGLAND
TESTS: 16	INN: 28+	RUNS: 1369
AVERAGE: 52.65	HS: 150	50: 11 100: 3

V INDIA
TESTS: 13	INN: 23 (22)	RUNS: 767 (762)
AVERAGE: 34.86 (36.28)	HS: 104 (104)	50: 3 (3) 100: 2 (2)

V NEW ZEALAND
TESTS: 8	INN: 15+	RUNS: 537
AVERAGE: 38.35	HS: 163	50: 2 100: 1

V PAKISTAN
TESTS: 7	INN: 14+	RUNS: 592
AVERAGE: 49.83	HS: 120	50: 5 100: 1

SUNIL GAVASKAR - PERSONAL FILE

FULL NAME: Sunil Manohar Gavaskar

DATE OF BIRTH: 10th July, 1949

BIRTHPLACE: Bombay

EDUCATION: St. Xavier's High School & College; Bombay University

PLAYING ROLE: Right Hand Bat, Occasional Right Arm Medium Pace

TEAMS: India; Vazir Sultan Colts XI 1966-67; Bombay 1967/68 - 1986/87;
Somerset 1980

TEST DEBUT: 1970-71 v West Indies, Port-of-Spain

TESTS: 125

MOST PRODUCTIVE GROUND H: Bombay, 1193 runs (54.22) in 12 Tests
A: Port-of-Spain, 793 runs (99.13) in 5 Tests
FIRST-CLASS DEBUT: 1966-67

FIRST-CLASS RUNS: 25, 834

FIRST-CLASS WICKETS: 22

HIGHEST SCORE: 340 Bombay v Bengal, Bombay, 1981-82

BEST BOWLING: 3-43 President's XI v Ranji XI, Jamnagar, 1972-73

NICKNAME: Sunny

FOR THE RECORD: Brother-in-law to G.R. Viswanth (India 1969/70 -
1982/83) who married Gavaskar's sister; His uncle is Madhav Mantri (India
1951/52 - 1954/55); Autobiography "Sunny Days" (1976); Second-highest
scorer in Test cricket. Was top until A.R. Border surpassed him; Holds the
record for the most Test centuries - 34, after beating Sir Donald Bradman's 29
in 1983; Recorded 1,000 runs in a calendar year on four occasions; He is now a
respected TV commentator and newspaper columnist.

SUNIL GAVASKAR (India)

There has never been a more complete batsman than Sunil Gavaskar. The diminutive opener from Bombay was a player of prodigious skill whose batting so often made for a one-sided contest with the bowler. It was inevitable that he would become the first player to top 10,000 runs in Tests. Only Allan Border has scored more. Sunil's unperturbed manner at the crease, coupled with a wide array of strokes, was a combination that frequently frustrated bowlers, almost to the point of submission. He could graft and scrape for runs in the most difficult conditions, but he could also impose his authority on the best of attacks with merciless and aggressive stroke-play. The most impressive aspect from his distinguished career, is the remarkably prolific record he achieved against a West Indies side that dominated world cricket throughout the majority of his Test career: Nobody has scored more centuries against them than Gavaskar, with 13. His average of 65.45 from 27 matches speaks volumes about his ability to play quick bowling. "I always felt against the West Indies that if I could get through the first half an hour when they're trying to knock you out if they can't get you out, then I could score some runs. It was a feeling I never had against any other country," admits Sunny. It was obvious from his initial Test series in the Caribbean in 1970-71, that he had a liking for their offerings; as, in his first four Test matches, he amassed an Indian record series aggregate of 774 runs at 154.80. He remains the only Indian to register four centuries in a rubber; 116 in Guyana, 117 not out in Barbados, while his 124 and 220 in Trinidad meant the precocious 21-year-old became the second player in Test history, after Doug Walters, to score a century and a double century in the same Test. India had appointed a new skipper for that tour - Ajit Wadekar. The fact he was also from Bombay, helped Sunny immeasurably. "I was able to relate to the captain, which I think is very important. He had the kind of leadership that brought the best out of you."

Farokh Engineer was soon to observe India's new starlet from close quarters, when he became his opening partner in the early seventies. The wicketkeeper-batsman immediately noticed star quality in Gavaskar: "The first thing that really impressed me about Sunny early in his career when he opened with me, was his patience and his temperament - nothing could ruffle him. He ground the bowlers down and anything loose they bowled, he punished. It was clear that he was going to be something special, even in those days. He had a tremendous defence and was very strong on his back foot through the cover region." Their partnerships were based on an invaluable blend of experience and raw talent. Engineer, the ex-Lancashire player, has fond and insightful memories of the young Gavaskar. "We were a good combination because Sunny really grafted for his runs where as I liked to give the ball a good crack. He was a far better player than I was technically, so I wasn't the greatest of batsmen to educate him, though I'm sure certain bits of our game rubbed off on the other. When I would hit a four with a shot that wasn't too conventional, we would meet in the middle of the wicket and he'd say, 'Bloody 'ell, you did everything wrong and still got four for it!' Where as Sunny was content to see the ball trickle over the rope, I wanted the ball to smash against the fence and come back. We were two totally different players but I certainly admired his skill and temperament. I used to call him a greedy bugger because he was a superb accumulator, and coupled with class, you're bound to break world records. I just wish I had half his defence or half his concentration!"

Although Sunny's early success against the West Indies came at a time prior to their hostile, four-pronged pace attack, he still maintained such standards in later years. In the six-Test series in 1983-84 in India, Gavaskar averaged 50.50 against the likes of Marshall, Holding, Roberts, Davis and Daniel. However, he did make several low scores in the rubber and speculation mounted that he was struggling to come to terms with Marshall's pace in particular, which saw him drop down the order to number four in the 6th Test at Madras. In the event, Marshall ripped out Gaekwad and Vengsarkar without a run on the board and set up the new-ball confrontation with Gavaskar that was supposed to have been avoided. All such talk was eventually ridiculed when Sunny contributed an Indian Test record score of 236 not out. In his autobiography *Marshall Arts*, the fast bowler recalls: "On a personal level, I believed I had won my battle with him and from a psychological point of view, they could have boosted mine further by leaving him out of the team altogether. Here was the 'little master', hero of all India, opting out of a clash with what I will concede was still very much a young bowler coming to terms with his new role. If ever I needed confirmation of my blossoming skill, I received it here in Madras with that one small change in the batting order. Gavaskar, though, was to have the last laugh. I may have played my part in removing him from having to face the new ball but he was by no means beaten. I should have realised that a batsman of his quality would flourish anywhere, even at number 11." In doing so, he surpassed Don Bradman's 29 Test hundreds, to set a new world record; one which he modestly played down by stating that Bradman had scored his in 52 Tests, while it had taken him 95. He also became the first batsman to score 13 hundreds and three double centuries against the West Indies. Former England and Somerset player, Brian Rose, captained Gavaskar in county cricket in 1980 and he soon discovered why the pint-sized opener was so adept at facing the quick stuff. "He was tremendously light on his feet which enabled him to get behind the ball very quickly and into position to either go forward, back or leave it alone. He played the quick bowlers exceptionally well, who generally pitched it in short at him, and he hooked and pulled with great confidence. I think his lack of height helped him with the short-pitched deliveries."

The way in which Sunil adapted to differing conditions was a great strength of his. Most batsmen favour a certain environment and are more comfortable on either fast wickets, slow wickets or maybe spinning wickets; but the fact that Gavaskar scored hundreds in England, the Caribbean, New Zealand, Australia, Pakistan and in India, against all kinds of attacks, clearly shows that he was at home in any country, whatever the conditions. While he played fast bowling with composure, spin also had a similar affect on him. Farokh Engineer notes: "His game against spin bowling was also very strong because of the way he was brought up, facing a lot of spinners and a lot of very good ones. Indian batsmen get so used to facing spinners that they feel there is no room in the game for them!" Sunny's experience of county cricket in 1980 was another example of how versatile a batsman he was. With Viv Richards touring England with the West Indies, there were not too many players around who were qualified to replace the explosive Antiguan - though the 'Little Master' certainly was. During a particularly wet summer when batting conditions were frequently treacherous, Sunil wasn't prolific, but he did enough to prove himself a more than worthy acquisition to the West Countrymen. Says Brian Rose: "He was very unlucky that season with the conditions. 1980 was a very rainy season and it wasn't easy to get runs as we played on a lot of green and soft wickets. His figures don't honestly reflect just how well he played. One day at The Oval, he scored a century when Sylvester Clarke was near unplayable; other than Sunny, nobody else could handle him." This was an environment that Gavaskar had experienced on previous tours with India: In 1971, he scored 57 on a wet, green-top at Manchester against England with John Price bowling very sharp on an extremely helpful wicket. He rates the innings as one of his best. Although, his 101 on the same ground in 1974 was more significant to him. It was the turning point of his career, because after the four centuries he got in the West Indies in 1970-71, he hadn't scored another since then. He recalls: "I never looked like getting a hundred so I was at a point in my career when I began to doubt my ability and wondered whether the 1970-71 West Indies tour was a fluke; so that hundred came at just the right time and made me feel a lot more positive towards my cricket career."

Brian Rose thoroughly enjoyed his experience of opening the batting with Gavaskar and was pleased to strike up an immediate understanding with the Bombay legend. He was impressed by the way Sunil conducted himself - on and off the field. "He had a nice sense of humour and a soft nature and was very conscientious in terms of his practise - he liked to have a net. His mind was always on the job, his concentration was superb, as nothing whatsoever diverted him from doing his job. With regard to his batting, he had wonderful technical ability, particularly his judgement to leave balls that most other batsmen would be playing at, and I think that was why he was such a great player. His eye was so good that he knew when to leave balls when they were only marginally missing the stumps." Ironically, given his added experience of playing in England on five tours with India, and with Somerset, Sunil's statistical record shows that of the six countries he competed against in Tests, England were his least successful opponents, though his average of 38.20 from 38 matches is hardly something to be ashamed of. In the 4th Test of the 1979 tour, Gavaskar played one of the greatest innings ever seen in England. His 221 was breathtaking and nearly gave India a remarkable victory. Requiring 438 to win, they eventually fell nine runs short and the match was drawn. Ian Botham rates that innings as one of the best he has ever witnessed. On the rest day before his marathon effort, Sunil had dinner at Mike Brearley's house. In conversation, the England skipper asked him if he had completed all his shopping. Sunny's terse reply was the original truth said in jest: 'No, I haven't scored a hundred yet, which I still intend to do before I leave.' To which, Brearley wished him happy hunting - but on another occasion!

When Geoff Boycott passed Gary Sobers' world record of 8,032 Test runs in 1981-82 in Delhi, Sunny was the opposing captain. As a mark of respect, a reception was held. Gavaskar was asked to give a speech in Boycott's honour and he delighted in congratulating the proud Yorkshireman, before announcing, 'Well done Geoffrey, enjoy it for two years!' It was a prediction that was later proved an extremely accurate one, as Sunil Gavaskar became the new record holder in 1983-84 in Ahmedabad against the West Indies. It had taken Boycott 108 Test matches with 193 innings' to amass his 8,114, while the little Indian master required 96 Tests and 25 fewer innings' to reach the milestone. Sunny's next achievement of similar proportion was his passing 10,000 runs. Allan Border may now hold the record with over 11,000 runs, but nobody will ever forget the fact that Gavaskar was the first to reach five figures. Farokh Engineer believes his old partner became a more adventurous player as he got older, though maintaining the same desire that folk had always identified with him. Says Farokh, "Later on in his career he took far greater risks and had a go more and batted like I used to - maybe I was a bad influence on him. But still, when he'd reach 30 or 40 he'd think 'this is my day here' and then graft thereafter." Maybe rather perversely, one of Gavaskar's most cherished moments was his 34th and final Test century against Sri Lanka. It was scored in Kanpur - a venue where he played eight times and had failed to register three figures; but in the city where his wife hails from, he eventually made 176 at the ninth time of asking. He quipped: "It was very satisfying as the in-laws began to think I couldn't play!" Unthinkable, surely?

<u>SUNIL GAVASKAR</u> - TEST MATCH STATISTICS   ( ) = As Opener

TESTS: 125   INN: 214 (203)   RUNS: 10122 (9607)
AVERAGE: 51.12 (48.76)   HS: 236* (221)   50: 45 (42) 100: 34 (33)

<u>OVERALL RECORD</u>   + = Opened in every innings   against that country

<u>V AUSTRALIA</u>
TESTS: 20   INN: 31+   RUNS: 1550
AVERAGE: 51.66   HS: 172   50: 4 100: 8

<u>V ENGLAND</u>
TESTS: 38   INN: 67 (66)   RUNS: 2483 (2483)
AVERAGE: 38.20 (38.20)   HS: 221 (221)   50: 16 (16) 100: 4 (4)

<u>V NEW ZEALAND</u>
TESTS: 9   INN: 16+   RUNS: 651
AVERAGE: 43.40   HS: 119   50: 3 100: 2

<u>V PAKISTAN</u>
TESTS: 24   INN: 41 (40)   RUNS: 2089 (2074)
AVERAGE: 56.45 (57.61)   HS: 166 (166)   50: 12 (12) 100: 5 (5)

<u>V SRI LANKA</u>
TESTS: 7   INN: 11 (3)   RUNS: 600 (336)
AVERAGE: 66.66 (112.00)   HS: 176 (176)   50: 3 (0) 100: 2 (2)

<u>V WEST INDIES</u>
TESTS: 27   INN: 48 (47)   RUNS: 2749 (2513)
AVERAGE: 65.45 (59.83)   HS: 236* (220)   50: 7 (7) 100: 13 (12)

GRAHAM GOOCH - PERSONAL FILE

FULL NAME: Graham Alan Gooch

DATE OF BIRTH: 23rd July, 1953

BIRTHPLACE: Leytonstone, London

EDUCATION: Norlington High School, London

PLAYING ROLE: Right Hand Bat, Right Arm Medium Pace

TEAMS: England; Essex 1973 - 1997; Western Province 1982/83 - 1983/84

TEST DEBUT: 1975 v Australia, Birmingham

TESTS: 118 (An England Record)

MOST PRODUCTIVE GROUND - H: Lord's, 2015 runs (53.02) in 20 Tests
                         A: Melbourne, 310 runs (38.75) in 4 Tests
FIRST-CLASS DEBUT: 1973

FIRST-CLASS RUNS: 44,841

FIRST-CLASS WICKETS: 246

HIGHEST SCORE: 333 England v India, Lord's, 1990

BEST BOWLING: 7-14 Essex v Worcestershire, Ilford, 1982

NICKNAME: Goochie or Zap

PERCENTAGE OF TEST INNINGS AS OPENER: 84.65%

FOR THE RECORD: Wisden 1979; Benefit 1985; Only player to score a triple century and a century in a first-class match (333 & 123, England v India, Lord's 1990). This broke the record for the best run aggregate in a Test match; OBE 1991; Testimonial 1995 (£269,371); Captained England in 34 Tests; Scored 128 first-class centuries; Holds several records at Essex including: Most runs in a season, most runs in a career, most hundreds in career, highest score in Natwest Trophy, highest score in Benson & Hedges Cup, highest score in Sunday League, best bowling in Natwest Trophy; In 1997 became an England selector.

GRAHAM GOOCH (England)

If ever there was a cricketer whose form dramatically improved with age, Graham Gooch was it. In a Test career spanning three decades, Gooch's initial taste of the big time was a sour one to say the least; registering a pair on debut at Edgbaston and just 6 and 31 in his second match at Lord's, when batting at number five. This experience, against a strong Australian team in 1975, was a tough ordeal for a raw 21-year-old and one that many other cricketers may have failed to recover from. However, Gooch has always been a resilient character and such pugnacious qualities were foremost in the redemption of his Test career. Contrary to inevitable opinion at the time, Graham believes he *was* ready for Test cricket, despite his struggles against a superior Aussie bowling attack led by Dennis Lillee and Jeff Thomson. "I'm a big believer that if you pick a player for a Test match, then he must be ready for that arena. I don't believe anybody can be too young. I was in the right place at the right time as England had been well beaten in Australia and were looking for some young blood and although I had only been in first-class cricket a year, I had scored a few runs for Essex. It was a good experience for me, which took me a while to come back from as I lost form after that for Essex as well, but I could only go up from there."

In that Edgbaston encounter, Mike Denness became the first England captain to elect to field in a Birmingham Test match, against the wishes of all his advisors who said it would rain and make batting second a difficult task. But field he did and an innings defeat was the result after the heavens did eventually open as expected and the uncovered pitch was drenched, creating an horrendous track on which to bat against Australia's quicks. It's not hard to feel sympathy for Gooch, who was confronted by these testing conditions on debut. "In hindsight it could all have been different if we had batted first but that's the way it goes," he reflects philosophically. Mike Denness, who also played with Graham at Essex, admits he never saw a great Test player in the making. "The ability that Graham had in the early days was very noticeable, but I'm not sure whether it was that obvious back then that he would become the player he did and have such a tremendous record as he did. After getting a pair at Edgbaston he came back very well from what was an enormous disappointment for him initially in Test cricket." Although history now informs us that Graham Gooch is England's highest ever run scorer in Tests, he did have to wait three years before he could resume his England career after that sorry beginning. By which time in 1978, his county skipper Keith Fletcher had sent Gooch in to open the innings, which was just one of the major factors that set Graham's successful career into motion. He said: "It had a profound influence on my game. It made me tighten up my game and concentrate a lot harder, which was one of my weaker points. I always had the ability to strike the ball, but the concentration and application wasn't there so opening the batting improved that no end." During his three year sabbatical, his thirst for runs had returned and in the summer of 1978 Gooch averaged 52.80 in five Tests, against Pakistan (2) and then New Zealand (3). His transition to the top of the batting order had brought stark reward.

He was still by no means established but he had done enough to earn a place on the 1978-79 tour of Australia. It was to be a series of mixed emotions for Graham, who played in all six Test matches but averaged just 22.36, while as a team, England won 5-1. Gooch opened the batting with little success in the first two Tests with Geoff Boycott, before batting down the order for the remainder of the series. It may seem unfair to upset his game after a promising comeback the previous summer in the opener's berth, though Gooch was not at all unsettled by this and was happy to comply and replace the injured Clive Radley in the middle-order. Despite 74 at Adelaide in the 6th Test, the tour had been a personal disaster. His technique was found wanting and rather than shy away from the harsh but honest truth, Graham confronted his fallibility's. By watching videos, he discovered drastic changes were required and the net result was the infamous high bat-lift that he adopted for the rest of his career. "I needed to change my technique to stand up straighter allowing me to hit the ball straighter. As well as the move to opener, that change in my technique was probably the one thing that set my career off," he admits. The results were instant. In the 1st Test of 1979 versus India, Graham made 83, and 79 in the 4th Test at The Oval. On the subsequent winter tour, to Australia again and India, he was still to win a permanent role as opener along side Geoff Boycott, but his 99 at Melbourne before running himself out, did much to maintain his name at the top of the England order thereafter.

When a batsman displays obvious potential in Test cricket, however precocious his talent may appear, the pressure will still mount when he has failed to score a century in 21 Tests. This was Graham's scenario; though in his 22nd at Lord's in 1980 against the mighty West Indies, the three figure total was finally posted. His 123 against a West Indies pace quartet in their heyday wasn't easy, although his composed 162-ball innings might have suggested otherwise. He recalled: "It becomes a bit of an issue when you've played twenty-odd Tests and you haven't scored a hundred. I would say the team they had in the late seventies early eighties is the best they've had for the last 25 years, so to get runs against that attack was very satisfying. My particular game has always been well suited to fast bowling and I always managed to cope with fast bowling reasonably well. It was very enjoyable getting runs against the likes of Roberts, Holding, Garner and Croft." His relish at taking on the Caribbean's conveyor belt of quicks was always abundant and it was no surprise when Graham was England's chief antidote to their hostile attack on tour in 1980-81. "The West Indian wickets in those days were a lot quicker and more even to how they are now. They were good batting wickets," says Gooch. He scored two centuries in the series and 83 in Antigua, as

England lost 2-0 in the rubber. The first, 116 in Barbados, carried special significance as England's assistant manager, Ken Barrington, died of a heart attack on the second evening of the Test. Graham remembers sadly: "When Kenny Barrington died it was a great loss to me because he was like a father figure. He was my first real coach at international level, even though he was officially the assistant manager and a selector on the tour. Kenny was liked by everyone and was like a counsellor to us all and it was a great shock when he had the heart attack and died. It was a tragic loss and it became particularly meaningful for me, because I went out to bat thinking what Kenny had done for me and the team and I put a hundred on the board in his memory really - it was a good hundred."

Meanwhile, his second ton of the series was 153 in Jamaica in the fifth Test. This time he was batting against the man whom he comfortably rates as the most difficult bowler he ever faced - Malcolm Marshall, a young man learning a trade he eventually went on to master. Of that series, Joel Garner paid tribute to Graham's steely batsmanship in his autobiography *Big Bird - Flying High*. 'Only Gooch of the English batsmen appeared to be able to handle the conditions. He seemed unmoved by what was going on at the other end. Gooch showed his team-mates that our fast bowling was not completely unplayable.'

Gooch acknowledges there is tremendous hardship involved when opposing such a hostile bowling attack as that West Indian quartet. "There are advantages and disadvantages. The disadvantages are that they're the most feared bowlers and historically the most successful bowlers in Test cricket in recent years, apart from the advent of Shane Warne recently. It can become a war of attrition as scoring opportunities are limited. You've got to concentrate all day long and have your wits about you, not only because you can get bowled out but there is also a lot of physical intimidation as well. A lot of the balls are flying through head high and there's a good chance of getting hurt, so you have to be sharp. The main advantage is that it's the same type of bowling all the time and you can get into a rhythm." Barry Richards, South Africa's Test-starved opening legend who Gooch considers the greatest opener ever, once wrote in his autobiography, 'Sheer speed has never been a shattering problem for me, though any batsman who tells you he really enjoys blistering pace is not telling the truth.' This is an honest admission from Barry though my instincts tell me that Graham Gooch was never more in his element than when he was on strike to a West Indian quickie. He enjoyed the battle and duly appreciates the skill he was up against. "There wasn't just pace, they had bowlers who moved the ball around: Andy Roberts swung the ball, Malcolm Marshall moved the ball off the seam and swung the ball - they all had that ability and they were all intelligent fast bowlers. That attack they had then of Roberts, Holding, Garner, Croft and Marshall - four played out of that five at the same time - would be the best I've ever faced. I would single Marshall out as the best as you won't find a quicker bowler about than him who can also swing it and move the ball about off the seam." Gooch went on to achieve similar heights against the West Indies through his career. As their attack changed shape and introduced new fast-bowling starlets, Gooch's stern ability to keep them at bay continued. His most cherished score ever was against Ambrose, Patterson, Walsh and Marshall as he recalls. "My best innings was at Headingley in 1991 against the West Indies when I scored 154 not out which helped to win the game. I batted all the way through the innings and given the conditions that would definitely be my best innings." He became only the sixth Englishman to carry his bat in Tests.

When Gooch decided to join a tour party to play in South Africa for a 'rebel' England team in 1982, it was an extremely controversial issue back then. But as time heals and people understand the reasons, the more pressing concern in hindsight is, how many more Test runs could Graham have scored had he not suffered the penalty of going on the tour. Devoid of any regret, he said: "It's easy to look back and say if I didn't go I could have had three more years of Test cricket, but that's all hypothetical - the bottom line is that I've never regretted my decision. We didn't think the authorities would turn a blind eye, but we didn't know that we were going to be banned for three years. I don't know whether I would have gone if I had have known the repercussions, but what I can say is that I don't regret going." His return to Test cricket in 1985 against Australia was a joyous occasion for England supporters and the player himself. As soon as the ban elapsed, he resumed his place in the side with immediate effect. England won the Ashes 3-1 and Gooch's greatest moment was his 196 at The Oval in the sixth Test.

From 1986 to 1989, Graham was still scoring heavily for Essex and consistently for England, though he felt his game was technically going astray. All this came to a head in 1989 when swing bowler Terry Alderman caused him massive problems. Although the Western Australian was given the chief credit for Gooch's voluntary absence from the side for the fifth Test and for his general loss of form, Graham feels there was more wrong than a mere phobia against Alderman. "Around the 86, 87, 88 period, my game technically fell into bad repair. I was still scoring a few runs but little faults started to creep in and it took me a while to put them right. In 1989 in particular, my game was in real disrepair; I was falling over and Alderman kept getting me out lbw. I played fast bowling and spin bowling better than I played medium pace. My technique always coped well with those two disciplines where as the military medium swing bowling, which you don't get a lot of in Test cricket, gave me problems. I liked the ball coming on a lot more. In the long run he did me a favour because at the end of that season I had to go back to basics and put things right. Fortunately, with a bit of help from Geoff Boycott, we hit on what was wrong and I was able to put my game back in order. From then on I enjoyed the best years of my career."

One aspect of Graham's career that some will remember him for equally as much as his run-scoring, is the fitness ethic that he so religiously followed. As Mike Denness notes: "At some point I feel he made a conscious decision to make himself more mentally and physically tuned, which, as we all know now, became a large part of his game." His dedication was admirable. He began his personal programme in 1980 when attending football training sessions with West Ham United. As his career progressed, the fitness routine became more punishing and it was no coincidence that it brought about the greatest form of his career, coupled with the extra responsibility of captaincy from 1989-90. He explains: "I stepped my fitness up a gear towards the late eighties. It was important in the fact that you need to be fit to play sport in general, but also there was no way that I could have played until I was 44 and maintain my performance unless I kept myself in shape." The first, emphatic sign that Gooch had eliminated all his technical faults and of his increased fitness, was in 1990 when he scored 1264 Test runs in the year. "In terms of volume of runs, 1990 would be my most favourable year to look back on," he announced proudly. It was the summer, though, where Graham excelled further than he or any pundit could ever have predicted. In two three-match Test series' against New Zealand and then India, he amassed 1058 runs, including four centuries in three consecutive Tests. The irony of his success was that his first score of the summer against New Zealand at Nottingham was nought. How he improved on that! Against India at Lord's, the venue where he scored six Test hundreds in total, Gooch posted a thoroughly breathtaking 333, which became the sixth highest score in Test history. It has since been overtaken by Brian Lara, Sanath Jayasuriya and Mark Taylor. His innings lasted 627 minutes and was scored from 485 balls. He recalled: "I remember batting all day and being really tired because I'd scored 170 against Lancashire the game before at Colchester for Essex. On the second day things went well and my memories are mainly of getting 300, because I'd only been beyond 250 once before when I got 275 for Essex. On that occasion I gave it away so this time I was desperate to get to 300 because the chance of getting that sort of score in any type of cricket is remote, as you rarely have enough time. I consider Lord's the best Test ground in the world and it's a nice place to play with all its history and tradition, so that made it all the more special."

With the exception of South Africa, whom Graham opposed briefly at the end of his Test career, his only statistical blot is against Australia. Although an average of 33 certainly isn't terrible from 42 matches, Gooch was capable of much better. He revealed: "In the early days they were just one of the sides where I didn't click. I got a few decent scores against them but I never scored runs against them consistently. So it was nice to get some runs in the latter part of my career against them, particularly against Shane Warne." Slow bowlers do not come any better than Warne, who has taken his wickets at a phenomenal rate, yet Gooch played him with ease in the 1993 Ashes series when his team-mates were praying for rain - or for the wonder leg-spinner to be struck down with injury. Within a disastrous series for England, Graham scored 673 runs at 56.08 including 133 at Manchester and 120 at Nottingham. "I enjoyed batting against him a lot - it was great fun," Gooch acknowledged, without a hint of a smile. "I always had the philosophy of wanting to bat against the best bowlers in the world - that was one of the things that spurred me on because if you have success against those, then you take more satisfaction from the achievement. A lot of players are happy when Curtly Ambrose isn't playing as it would leave a weaker attack, but I always got more of an edge facing the better bowlers and certainly Shane Warne was one of those and something to be reckoned with."

GRAHAM GOOCH - TEST MATCH STATISTICS   ( ) = As Opener

TESTS: 118   INN: 215 (182)   RUNS: 8900 (7859)
AVERAGE: 42.58 (44.65) HS: 333 (333)   50: 46 (41) 100: 20 (18)

OVERALL RECORD   + = Opened in every innings against that country

V AUSTRALIA
TESTS: 42   INN: 79 (59)   RUNS: 2632 (2021)
AVERAGE: 33.31 (34.25) HS: 196 (196)   50: 16 (13) 100: 4 (3)

V INDIA
TESTS: 19   INN: 33 (28)   RUNS: 1725 (1518)
AVERAGE: 55.64 (58.38) HS: 333 (333)   50: 8 (6) 100: 5 (5)

V NEW ZEALAND
TESTS: 15   INN: 24 (20)   RUNS: 1148 (925)
AVERAGE: 52.18 (51.38) HS: 210 (183)   50: 3 (3) 100: 4 (3)

V PAKISTAN
TESTS: 10   INN: 16+   RUNS: 683
AVERAGE: 42.68   HS: 135   50: 5 100: 1

V SOUTH AFRICA
TESTS: 3   INN: 6 (4)   RUNS: 139 (91)
AVERAGE: 23.16 (22.75) HS: 33 (33)   50: 0 100: 0

V SRI LANKA
TESTS: 3   INN: 6+   RUNS: 376
AVERAGE: 62.66   HS: 174   50: 1 100: 1

V WEST INDIES
TESTS: 26   INN: 51+   RUNS: 2197
AVERAGE: 44.83   HS: 154*   50: 13 100: 5

GORDON GREENIDGE - PERSONAL FILE

FULL NAME: Cuthbert Gordon Greenidge

DATE OF BIRTH: 1st May, 1951

BIRTHPLACE: St. Peter, Barbados

EDUCATION: St. Peter's Boys School; Sutton Secondary School, Reading

PLAYING ROLE: Right Hand Bat, Occasional Right Arm Medium, Slip or Gully Fielder

TEAMS: West Indies; Hampshire 1970 - 1987; Barbados 1972/73 - 1990/91

TEST DEBUT: 1974-75 v India, Bangalore

TESTS: 108

MOST PRODUCTIVE GROUND - H: Kingston, 794 runs (56.71) in 9 Tests
A: Manchester, 503 runs (75.80) in 3 Tests

FIRST-CLASS DEBUT: 1970

FIRST-CLASS RUNS: 37, 354

FIRST-CLASS WICKETS: 18

HIGHEST SCORE: 273* D.H. Robin's XI v Pakistan, Eastbourne, 1974

BEST BOWLING: 5-49 Hampshire v Surrey, Southampton, 1971

NICKNAME: Hopalong or G

PERCENTAGE OF TEST INNINGS AS OPENER: 98.37%

FOR THE RECORD: Was the first West Indian to score a Test century overseas on debut, at Bangalore in 1974-75; Wisden 1976; Has scored the most runs in first-class cricket by a West Indian; Autobiography "The Man in the Middle" (1980); Benefit with Hampshire 1983 (£28,648); Holds three batting records at Hampshire: Highest score in Natwest Trophy, Benson & Hedges Cup and the Sunday League; MBE 1985; Scored a century in 100th Test match in Antigua

GORDON GREENIDGE (West Indies)

When you talk of great players, as this stylish West Indian certainly was, there is usually a particular trait that he is best remembered for: David Gower for his elegance, Javed Miandad for his determination, Ian Botham for his heroic unpredictability, Viv Richards for his superb eye and ability to see the ball early. In the case of Gordon Greenidge, not only was he one of the most prolific and skilful batsmen to grace the sport, but he also had power in his strokes that fielders were often helpless to prevent reaching the boundary fence. When this man drove, pulled or cut the cricket ball, it stayed hit. As former England bowler, Mike Hendrick, commented: "Whenever you bowled a bad ball at Gordon, or even an average ball, more often than not he would hit you for a boundary. There was very little room for error. I've never known a batsman hit the ball harder; it was almost as if it was personal." Greenidge was at his best when he was attacking. His aggression was merciless. Although he had an excellent all-round technique and could be as solid in defence as he could dangerous in attack, he was a player that profited more from a predominantly offensive game than anything else. When he was under pressure, whether against spin or pace, you always had the feeling he was boiling inside waiting to explode into a more punishing level of shot-play. Dennis Lillee is one of the greatest fast bowlers to have played Test cricket, and he enjoyed his battles with Gordon, in the knowledge that it was an open contest with the minimal thought of defence from either party. "Greenidge always took you on and was prepared to whack you as hard as he could - and often he did. He also had a very deft touch; he could just as easily drop it by his feet or around the corner for a single. Gordon was a very fine opening batsman and certainly one of the best I ever bowled to. I enjoyed bowling to him because he was always prepared to take you on, rather than play for the day. Anyone that's prepared to take you on like Gordon, gives you a chance at the same time."

Greenidge played the short ball in a dismissive, comfortable way that many West Indies batsmen through the generations have become famous for. Whether square cutting, pulling or hooking, he treated that kind of short delivery with a contempt that said, "Don't you dare bowl that to me again." No one has ever played the square cut with more conviction, or power than this man; who's not an obvious-looking muscle man in any way but has the kind of physique and physical fitness that most middle-weight boxers would be proud of. The only deficiency he seemed to suffer from was a recurring knee injury, which, it is said, brought the best out of him. Like a wounded animal, his knee trouble merely resulted in him adopting an unrelenting hunger for boundaries, rather than running singles. Although, when on top of his fitness, Gordon ran the quickest of singles with his regular West Indies and Barbados opening partner, Desmond Haynes. The pair had such an understanding it was relatively telepathic. Haynes has admitted it was not unusual for them to run singles without so much as a 'yes' or a 'one' being muttered; their team within a team partnership was that good. "To me, Gordon was a fantastic player and one of the best opener's the world has ever seen," Haynes said. "I learned a lot from him; his vast experience, especially of English conditions, helped me a great deal. It was a joy to open the batting with him because I thought he was a damn good player, and one of *the* great openers who was complete as a batsman: Not only did he handle the quicks very well, but he was also a very good player of spin."

Gordon had his technique against spin bowling comprehensively examined in his very first experience of Test cricket in 1974-75 on tour in India. While Bangalore was hosting its first Test, Greenidge celebrated both debuts with 93 in the first innings and 107 in the second, becoming the first West Indies player to score a century on debut in an overseas Test match. This, against Chandrasekhar, Prasanna and Venkataraghavan - the infamous spin attack that, along with Bishan Bedi, made up one of the most feared bowling line-ups of that era. It was a fascinating series that West Indies won 3-2. Following his dream beginning in the first Test, Greenidge struggled to maintain that momentum and managed just one other score over fifty for the remainder of the rubber. After missing the Bangalore Test, Bedi played in the rest of the series, and he was instantly impressed with Greenidge, though felt he still had a lot to learn. "He was a tremendous striker of the ball; bloody hell could he hit the ball hard. He had a terribly firm grip and although he got runs in Bangalore on his debut, that grip prevented him from playing the turning ball well, and he never really scored any more runs in the series. In those days, he looked slightly uncomfortable facing spin early on in an innings, but as he progressed his bottom hand on the bat became nice and loose and he developed into a very good player of spin." The development of his ability against spin was emphasised more than a decade later in 1987. Representing an MCC XI against a Rest of the World XI at Lord's, commemorating 200 years of cricket, he played the off-spin of his countryman Roger Harper and the prodigious leg-spin of Pakistan's Abdul Qadir with an ease that bordered on arrogance; indeed, his reverse sweeps against Qadir (his eventual scalphunter) showed an opening batsman that was equally at home facing top-class spinners as he was against raw pace.

The barren spell Greenidge endured in India continued in 1975-76 against Australia for the two Tests he played in, making a pair at Brisbane and three and eight at Melbourne. This was probably due to playing county cricket and his failure to adapt straight away to the quicker surfaces in Australia. It wasn't until he toured the familiar territory of England in 1976 that the runs returned for him. After scoring 84 at Lord's (from 182), he went to Manchester for the third Test and registered a century in each innings. His 134 and 101 made him the second West Indies player, after G.A. Headley, to achieve the feat against England. The statistical milestones continued in the next Test at Leeds, when Gordon struck another hundred (115) to become the first to score three consecutive centuries against England since Alan Melville of South Africa in 1947. He toured England on four occasions in his Test career, though his experience of English conditions went much further than West Indies tours: He began his first-class career with Hampshire in 1970 after arriving in England as a 12-year-old. He was brought up and educated in Reading, Berkshire. Initially, he found it difficult to adapt to the brutally cold English winters, when compared with St. Peter, Barbados. Gordon later had trials at Hampshire, before eventually breaking in to the full XI. It was here, in Southampton, where he really learnt his trade, benefiting particularly from his opening partnership with South Africa's Barry Richards. Greenidge has admitted to being fortunate in his career with having the opportunity to partner three of the greatest opening batsmen in cricket - Desmond Haynes, Roy Fredericks and Richards, who was sadly deprived the long Test career he deserved due to politics. Gordon's county career with Hampshire spanned 17 years, and it is a significant factor in his success against England throughout his career. It seemed he was at his best in English conditions.

His most successful tour of England came in 1984, when he scored two double hundreds in a series the West Indies emphatically won 5-0. Gordon's 214 not out at Lord's was scored from just 241 balls in 300 minutes and has been widely credited as one of the most exhilarating exhibitions of batting ever witnessed on the ground. The innings took him past 4,000 runs in Tests. In *Botham: My Autobiography*, the former England all-rounder commented: "Greenidge had a wonderful eye. The power of some of his shots left you in awe. A good player when physically sound, devastating when he limped because he was only interested in hitting boundaries. His double hundred to win the Lord's Test of 1984 was a staggering innings and turned what should have been a difficult task into a stroll." In *Clive Lloyd - The Authorised Biography*, the then-West Indies skipper said of Gordon's innings: "It was a tremendous performance. He paced it well, concentrated well, went after the loose deliveries and played the innings of his life. Gordon is a great player and it was a pleasure to see him come good when we needed it." After England had declared their second innings, a magnificent blend of aggression and skilful batting from Greenidge, and Larry Gomes, who made an unbeaten 92, meant the West Indies cruised to the victory target of 344. This became the fifth highest total in a Test for a side batting fourth to win the match. His 223 at Manchester in the fourth Test was slightly more circumspect, lasting 588 minutes and 425 balls. It was the first double century for a West Indies player at Old Trafford. Greenidge was a consistent thorn in England's side throughout his playing days, and it was no surprise at the Recreation Ground,

Antigua in 1989-90, that he should mark his 100th Test match with a century (149) - against England. Here, he shared an opening partnership of 298 with Haynes - their highest stand in Tests.

Throughout his county career, Greenidge consistently applied himself to a demanding task that so many overseas players have failed to succeed at down the years. They are known as the mercenaries of English cricket who take a lot of money and don't always deliver the required performance and attitude. In the case of Gordon, Hampshire can be extremely proud of the service he gave them. His professionalism and his batting was exceptional and certain performances will never be forgotten. Former team-mate, Mark Nicholas, recalls one specific match where Greenidge excelled. "We played Surrey at The Oval in 1982 on a relayed wicket, which was hazardous to say the least. The ball would regularly fly past your nose and this was at a time when Sylvester Clarke was bowling at the speed of light. Well, on the second day (after 19 wickets had fallen the day before), Gordon is about to go out for the second innings - without a helmet! We said, 'What are you doing, you'll get yourself killed out there.' He just replied, 'No man, I just want to sharpen myself up.' He then played one of the greatest innings' I've ever seen." Greenidge scored 84 from his side's 170 total, and it gave Hampshire a lifeline in the match. Surrey required 105 to win, but Gordon's courageous knock allowed his countryman, Malcolm Marshall, the chance to bowl Surrey out with 7-38 and win by three runs.

The West Indies were the indisputable kings of cricket from the mid-seventies to the early nineties and Gordon Greenidge was a significant part of that monopoly. Their four-pronged pace bowling attack was always given chief credit for this prolonged domination, and I wouldn't disagree with that, but the contribution from Greenidge at the top of the order was of equal importance. The regular sound beginnings that he and Desmond Haynes gave them, allowed the likes of Richards, Kallicharran, Richardson, Gomes and Lloyd, to play their natural, flamboyant games; when things may have been different if exposed to more precarious situations more often. Fast bowler Joel Garner wrote in his book *Big Bird - Flying High*: "Greenidge is a totally professional player who approaches every batting situation as if he had made detailed plans. He is a capable, tight player who is not in the habit of giving bowlers a chance to get him out." Such illustrates the organised manner in which this methodical but immensely exciting player approached his cricket. Unlike his batting, Greenidge is not majestic by character like many of his former team-mates, Haynes in particular; he is more of a relaxed person who relies on his dry humour. Desmond Haynes comments: "He was very much a professional, he does everything by the book, he's very tidy in all regards and always well organised. It was an education to play with him and see how he went about his game." Michael Holding was a colleague of Gordon's for many years in the West Indies team and he reveals how Greenidge was a very introverted character in what was a very extrovert dressing room. "He was a bit reserved. Gordon didn't volunteer a lot in team meetings; he just used to sit back and listen to what was being said. He was a naturally reserved person, though in later years he would contribute a bit more to meetings and generally became a lot more open."

Against the five countries he opposed in Tests, Gordon fared well against them all, though his career average of 31.88 versus Pakistan is one record he may consider below average. After scoring his only century against them of 100, and 82 in the second innings at Jamaica in 1976-77, he later failed to advance on the 75 he made at Lahore in 1986-87. However, this minor blip is not something we can attribute to the conditions, given his excellent record in India where pitches are relatively consistent with those in Pakistan, so too the bowling. At the end of his career, he remained the tough competitor he had been throughout and even suggested that there was still a lot more to come, on the evidence of his 226 against Australia in his penultimate Test match at Barbados; and fitting that he should register his highest Test score on his home ground so near to the end of his career, like a farewell thank you message to his adoring home supporters. That certainly ensured his disciples would never forget his sublime batsmanship in a hurry, but I'm sure there was never any real danger of that. To think this guy could have played for England after his upbringing; how thankful West Indians must be that Gordon Greenidge chose to stay loyal to the country of his birth.

GORDON GREENIDGE - TEST MATCH STATISTICS   ( ) = As Opener

TESTS: 108	INN: 185 (182)	RUNS: 7558 (7488)
AVERAGE: 44.72	HS: 226 (226)	50: 34 (34) 100: 19 (19)

OVERALL RECORD   + = Opened in every innings against that country

V AUSTRALIA
TESTS: 29	INN: 52+	RUNS: 1819
AVERAGE: 40.42	HS: 226	50: 8 100: 4

V ENGLAND
TESTS: 32	INN: 48+	RUNS: 2318
AVERAGE: 50.39	HS: 223	50: 8 100: 7

V INDIA
TESTS: 23	INN: 39+	RUNS: 1678
AVERAGE: 46.61	HS: 194	50: 8 100: 5

V NEW ZEALAND
TESTS: 10	INN: 19+	RUNS: 882
AVERAGE: 55.12	HS: 213	50: 5 100: 2

V PAKISTAN
TESTS: 14	INN: 27 (24)	RUNS: 861 (791)
AVERAGE: 31.88	HS: 100 (100)	50: 5 (5) 100: 1 (1)

HANIF MOHAMMED - PERSONAL FILE

FULL NAME: Hanif Mohammed

DATE OF BIRTH: 21st December, 1934

BIRTHPLACE: Junagadh, India

EDUCATION: Suid Madarasa School, Karachi

PLAYING ROLE: Right Hand Bat, Occasional Wicketkeeper, Off Break
Bowler

TEAMS: Pakistan; Bahawalpur; Karachi; Pakistan International Airlines

TEST DEBUT: 1952-53 v India, Delhi

TESTS: 55

MOST PRODUCTIVE GROUND H: Karachi, 551 runs (39.35) in 9 Tests
A: Bridgetown, 354 runs (177.00) in 1 Test
FIRST-CLASS DEBUT: 1951-52

FIRST-CLASS RUNS: 17, 059

FIRST-CLASS WICKETS: 53

HIGHEST SCORE: 499 Karachi v Bahawalpur, Karachi, 1958-59

BEST BOWLING: 3-4 Commissioner's XI v Fazal Mahmood's XI,
Hyderabad, 1959-60

NICKNAME: Little

PERCENTAGE OF TEST INNINGS AS OPENER: 71.13%

FOR THE RECORD: Brothers Wazir, Mushtaq and Sadiq all played for Pakistan in Tests, while remaining brother Raees played for Karachi; Son is Shoaib who has played 45 Tests for Pakistan; Nephews Asif and Shahid both played for PIA; First Pakistani to score 1,000, 2,000 and 3,000 Test runs; Wisden 1968; His 337 against West Indies is the fifth highest score in Test cricket; Most recently, he has been editor of a Pakistan cricket magazine.

HANIF MOHAMMED (Pakistan)

Statistics reflect the memory of Hanif Mohammed harshly, a diminutive batsman of immense talent who played with an ease so befitting a player that once held the world record for the highest first-class innings. He was a lot better than his Test average of 43.98 suggests. His younger brother Mushtaq, who represented Pakistan in 57 Tests, believes Hanif's natural aggression and sublime strokeplay was suffocated by the weight of responsibility on him. As a member of the first Pakistan Test team in 1952-53, it wasn't long before everyone realised just how significant Hanif's contributions were towards the destiny of Pakistan. "He carried the burden of the team," Mushtaq claims. "Every time before he went out to bat, the captain Abdul Hafeez Kardar would say, 'Little', which was the name he used to call him, 'You don't have to get out, stay there until the last ball.' Then he became a defensive batsman unfortunately, though he possessed all kinds of shots. He was quite an attacking player but the situation didn't allow him to be flamboyant and he played the way he was forced to play, in the capacity of having to take the responsibility of the whole side." Hanif paved the way in Test cricket for his countrymen to follow. He was a fine ambassador for his nation as 'Mushie' relates. "There were two or three players in that era of Pakistan cricket (of any real quality). Hanif was well known for his batting, Fazal Mahmood was a great fast-medium bowler and Saeed Ahmed was a very good batsman; these are the people who have done wonders for Pakistan cricket in the early fifties. They played for sheer enjoyment, honour to represent their country and loyalty to their nation. They did it for nothing, as there was no professionalism. They just turned up on their bicycle, chained it up, got into their whites and on to the ground to play. Pakistan cricket was just emerging then and it was these players that gave us an identity in world cricket."

His father was a member of the Indian military and only occasionally played club cricket. Sadly, he died when Hanif was still a small child. It was then left to the two eldest brothers, Wazir and Raees, to instil the love of cricket into the family, which they did with great success. It became evident quite early on amongst the Mohammed brotherhood, that Hanif was the most talented of them all. Mushtaq admits: "We always knew he was the best in our family, in fact he was an icon as far as we were concerned. We looked up to him." It is not only batting skills that counts for his status as Pakistani cricket legend, it is also his mild-mannered attitude that endears him to so many. "He is a very modest guy and very reserved and likes to live in his own world. He is a very quiet person by nature and he's not bothered about what is going on around him," says his younger brother, Mushtaq.

In his first three Tests, Hanif was classed as a wicketkeeper-batsman, but they soon discovered the potential in his batting which was far greater than his wicketkeeping. Fortunately there was another keeper in the side, Imtiaz Ahmed, so a decision was made for the good of the team to play Hanif just as a batsman and allow Imtiaz to keep wicket. From a young age Hanif modelled his game on that of an opener, which was the position he occupied during the prime of his career. It was only in the latter years when his reflexes against the quick bowlers reduced, that he lowered himself down the batting order. Mushtaq, one of five brothers that played first-class cricket, feels Hanif was well suited to opening. "The strength in his batting was sheer concentration, his temperament was so good with a strong will to stay at the crease and he played very correct. This combination made a superhuman opening batsman. He also had a lot of patience and never became anxious. Hanif always believed in his partner to stay there and give him support, while he scored runs from the other end. Watching him bat was sheer poetry. He was born to bat. The only bad luck as far as the Pakistan cricket team is concerned is that Hanif was born too early. If he would have played in the seventies and eighties with a better side, he would have been phenomenal and would not have had to worry about getting out, as there would have been other terrific batsmen in the team." As far as rating him among the Pakistan greats goes, Mushtaq is in no doubt where his brother ranks. "I would say even now, there hasn't yet been another batsman born in Pakistan with the same class as Hanif. The likes of Miandad and Zaheer were very good players, though different types; Hanif was head and shoulders above them. He is up there with the greatest batsmen along side people like Bradman, Hutton, Gavaskar and Boycott."

The legend of Hanif Mohammed began in 1958-59, when playing for Karachi against Bahawalpur. He scored 499, eclipsing the world record set by Don Bradman in 1929-30. This achievement stood alone at the top until Brian Lara made 501 not out for Warwickshire against Durham in 1994. Mushtaq Mohammed was in that Karachi side and can recall his brother's innings with delight, but tinged with sadness at the nature of the dismissal. "The one significant thing that I remember about that innings was how he went from session to session. He paced himself and set targets for each session. He wanted to be on 45 or 50 at lunch, 95 to 100 by tea and 150 by the close. He finished on 170 odd in the end. Then he batted all through the next day and was close to Don Bradman's record of 452. The word went around the surrounding district that he was going to break the record and all the other matches in the area stopped. They all came to watch Hanif break the record which he obviously did, but the only reason he got out - run out - was because the man in the scorebox got it wrong. His score said 497 instead of 498, so when he hit the penultimate ball of the day, he was scampering back for two to keep the strike when he could have took his chance and faced the last ball.

There were speeches after the game in his honour and the opposing captain congratulated him on breaking Don Bradman's record but said, 'Thank god we got you out, nobody scores 500 against us'!"

From his first 18 Test matches, Hanif was averaging under 30 - a gross under-achievement for such a talent; but in his nineteenth Test and his first against the West Indies in Barbados in 1957-58, Hanif turned his form around. He scored 337 in Pakistan's second innings, which was the perfect response after his side had followed on, still trailing by 473 runs, to eventually earn a draw. It became the longest ever innings in Test cricket at 16 hours and ten minutes and was then the second highest Test score behind Len Hutton's 364, but it still remains the highest score by a Pakistan player in Tests. Hanif's other leading achievements include his 187 not out at Lord's in 1967 while captaining the side; scoring a century in each innings (111 & 104) at Dacca in 1961-62 also against England and the unbeaten 203 in Lahore against New Zealand in 1964-65. As his brother has suggested, how interesting it would have been to see Hanif Mohammed in the same batting line-up as Zaheer Abbas, Javed Miandad, Asif Iqbal, Majid Khan and Mushtaq. Without the fear of his wicket costing defeat, partnering other strokeplayers of great skill, Hanif might have flourished even further in such an environment. However, the conditions he did bat in extracted application of the highest order, which may not have existed so prominently in a more powerful unit.

HANIF MOHAMMED - TEST MATCH STATISTICS   ( ) = As Opener

TESTS: 55   INN: 97 (69)   RUNS: 3915 (2726)
AVERAGE: 43.98 (40.68)   HS: 337 (337)   50: 15 (12) 100: 12 (7)

OVERALL RECORD   + = Opened in every innings against that country

V AUSTRALIA
TESTS: 6   INN: 12 (8)   RUNS: 548 (232)
AVERAGE: 49.81 (29.00)   HS: 104 (66)   50: 3 (2) 100: 2 (0)

V ENGLAND
TESTS: 18   INN: 33 (23)   RUNS: 1039 (755)
AVERAGE: 33.51 (32.82)   HS: 187* (111)   50: 3 (3) 100: 3 (2)

V INDIA
TESTS: 15   INN: 26 (24)   RUNS: 970 (942)
AVERAGE: 40.41 (40.95)   HS: 160 (160)   50: 6 (6) 100: 2 (2)

V NEW ZEALAND
TESTS: 10   INN: 15 (6)   RUNS: 622 (208)
AVERAGE: 47.84 (34.66)   HS: 203* (103)   50: 0 100: 3 (1)

V WEST INDIES
TESTS: 6   INN: 11 (8)   RUNS: 736 (589)
AVERAGE: 73.60 (84.14)   HS: 337 (337)   50: 3 (1) 100: 2 (2)

DESMOND HAYNES - PERSONAL FILE

FULL NAME: Desmond Leo Haynes

DATE OF BIRTH: 15th February, 1956

BIRTHPLACE: St. James, Barbados

EDUCATION: Federal High School, Barbados

PLAYING ROLE: Right Hand Bat; Occasional Right Arm Medium Pace,

TEAMS: West Indies; Barbados 1976/77 - 1994/95; Middlesex 1989 - 1994; Western Province

TEST DEBUT: 1977-78 v Australia, Port-of-Spain

TESTS: 116

MOST PRODUCTIVE GROUND H:Bridgetown 1210 runs (60.50) in 13 Tests
A: Sydney 343 runs (49.00) in 4 Tests
FIRST-CLASS DEBUT: 1976-77

FIRST-CLASS RUNS: 26,030

FIRST-CLASS WICKETS: 8

HIGHEST SCORE: 255* Middlesex v Sussex, Lord's, 1990

BEST BOWLING: 1-2 West Indies v Pakistan, Lahore, 1980-81

NICKNAME: Desi or Comedian

PERCENTAGE OF TEST INNINGS AS OPENER: 99.50%

FOR THE RECORD: Played World Series Cricket in 1978-79; Became the fourth man to be dismissed 'handled the ball' in 1983 against India in Bombay; Captained West Indies v England in Port-of-Spain in 1989-90 and on tour of Pakistan in 1990-91; Wisden 1990; Played in 238 limited overs internationals - a record for a West Indian; He has scored the most runs in limited overs internationals with 8,648; Coach at Sussex C.C.C. 1996-97; Batting coach at Hampshire C.C.C. 1998; Batting coach at Northamptonshire C.C.C. 1999.

DESMOND HAYNES (West Indies)

There was something so typical about the way in which Desmond Haynes played that could only be accredited to the bat of a West Indian. Many teachers of the game would cringe at the thought of youngsters being encouraged to attack bowlers from the outset, preferring the normal, cautious game that openers are so often born into, but the cavalier, free-flowing Haynes suffered little with his own personalised game-plan. In fact, he and his regular partner Gordon Greenidge, revolutionised the role of the opening batsmen. They immediately set out to punish anything wayward, when their contemporaries may have left well alone early on. Although the likes of Washbrook, Stackpole and Fredericks had employed similar tactics prior to this era. When required, Desmond also displayed a solid defence, but that was secondary to him. Scoring runs was always his primary concern. He explains: "It is good to put the pressure on the bowlers straight away. The majority of openers will admit how they are under pressure early, so it is important to create a system where you are transferring the pressure off you and on to the bowler. You're making him become very accurate very early; he knows he can't get away with any loose deliveries. The one thing you find with a lot of openers is the fact that just because the intention is to bat for long periods and build an innings for the team, they then lose out on the bad ball and allow the bowler to get on top. Once he is in the groove after a couple of overs, life then becomes a lot more difficult for the batsman." It was never a surprise when Haynes dispatched his first ball in a Test to the boundary, however wide or short the delivery. To so many others the sensible thing would be to let the ball go by until the eye has adapted to the pace and behaviour of the wicket, though Desmond would consider such an action criminal. This is partly due to the confidence he had in his ability. "One of the things that we are brought up on in the Caribbean is the fact that if you're going to hit the ball, you've got to believe that you *are* going to hit it," says Desi. "If you keep leaving it alone all day, you probably will not get any runs. I just thought, well okay people are going to give you some stick when you go at the wide ball and it doesn't come off, but you've got to say to yourself 'I'm going to hit this thing, I'm not going to miss it, I'm not worrying about what people are going to say, because I'm going to hit it.' You've got to be positive. Although we (he and Greenidge) played some extravagant shots and took some chances - we all know there's not a perfect cricketer - we all take chances every day in our lives."

Haynes opened the batting throughout his first-class career, but first he had to make the transition from a middle-order player in amateur cricket. Playing for Carlton in the First Division of the Barbados League, Desi was batting at five most weeks, but when a team-mate refused to open again, the cocky youngster was first to volunteer. It was a change that sparked a great career into motion. The runs came instantly as he made 60 in his first knock as an opening batsman. It was a scenario where player and position fitted one another instantly. He recalls: "At the time it was a position for me to maintain my place in the side, but then I started to feel very comfortable. I'd heard the stories that you always get two bad balls before the bowler has warmed up, but I soon realised that was not the case." In a meteoric rise to fame, Desi had barely made his first-class debut when he was suddenly drafted in to face the touring Pakistanis for Barbados in February 1976-77. His precocity and Test match potential was there for all to see when he scored an assured 136 in the game. Pakistan's hapless captain Mushtaq Mohammed recalls: "I went out for dinner that night with Garry Sobers and as we were sitting at this table chatting, the waiter comes over to serve us. When he left, Garry asked me, 'Do you not recognise him?' Of course, I didn't and wondered who he was. Garry then told me he was the guy that had smashed us round the park a few hours earlier - it was Desi." Another man to witness that innings, though with greater satisfaction, was the West Indies skipper Clive Lloyd. He remembers: "It was customary for the West Indies captain to watch the game involving the host nation before it staged a Test and David Holford had told me that he had this precocious young guy in his side with a lot of ability and that I should have a look at him. Roy Fredericks was making noises about retirement and there was no obvious replacement - until I saw Desi. I liked everything about him The style was excellent and he certainly looked to be a good bet for the future. He was very compact, very correct, a hard worker and clearly very ambitious. From that day I knew it was only a matter of time before he played for the West Indies."*

With his obvious attacking flair, Desmond was always likely to score runs, though so many batsmen with a similar skill have failed to match his achievements. The reason being, Haynes knew when to attack and when to defend. Shot selection is an invaluable quality to a batsman and Haynes was exemplary in that he could graft in tough conditions, while knowing when to take bowlers apart also. His grounding in the Caribbean helped to shape his game. "I had a very good technique for an opening batsman. Early in my career I developed the checked drive which helped when playing against the swinging ball. I also learned to adapt to different conditions well, because of the way I was brought up, playing with a tennis ball on the rough outfield. This allowed me to play the short-pitched delivery very well." Desmond rates his obdurate 143 at Sydney in 1988-89 as his greatest innings. It was a fighting

*Rob Steen, Desmond Haynes - Lion of Barbados, H. F. & G. Witherby (London), 1993

effort and a good example of his versatility to adapt to adverse conditions. Sixty-five percent of the bowling in the match was spin - an indication of how the wicket behaved. Up against Australia's spin triplets Peter Taylor, Trevor Hohns and Allan Border (11-96 in the match), West Indies crumbled and were defeated comfortably. Haynes, though, fought a lone battle and showed how far he had come from the player that once struggled against the spinning ball. He remembers: "I've had some good ones but that one in Sydney would be the best innings I've played. It was a turning wicket and everyone was getting out, but I stayed there. Early in my career I wasn't as fluent against spinners as I would have liked; I tried to accumulate and work the ball around, but later on I became more positive against them and wasn't afraid to hit them over the top if I thought it was possible." With 75 in the first innings added to that century in the second, he proved what a combative batsman he could be, as well as a majestic stroke-maker.

His Test career began with promise when he registered three fifties in his first three innings' in Australia. This led to an invitation from Kerry Packer to play World Series Cricket after just two Tests. Although the Aussie bowling attack had lost some leading names to Packer, the ferocious Jeff Thomson was there and still bowling as fast as ever. "Thommo was very, very sharp - probably the quickest thing that I ever faced," Haynes admits. "It was a pleasing start because from childhood it was my dream to play cricket for the West Indies. Just making the West Indies team with people like Clive Lloyd, Viv Richards and Gordon in the side was a marvellous feeling; and to start like that was tremendous. I just thought if I get into the side I've got to be fairly consistent to hold my place because I'm around some of the greatest cricketers in the world, I knew I had to be up to it so I was very pleased with those first three innings." With Gordon Greenidge more than established in one opening position, several players were hungry to fill the other role vacated by Greenidge's long-term partner Roy Fredericks. When Desi had the first opportunity it was vital he scored runs straight away and although he did just that, he felt a great deal of strain on him. "It was tremendous pressure. Every island in the Caribbean was trying to push their player to take Fredericks' position. There were guys like Faoud Bacchus, Alvin Greenidge, Richard Gabriel, Basil Williams - they were all pushing. What helped me, on top of those fifties I got, was a hundred in the one-day games against Thommo."

Opening batsman in particular have to be mentally strong and possess a great deal of courage, as it is they who must blunt the initial pace threat of the opposition. Desmond's early experiences with Jeff Thomson prove that he was more than capable of handling the quick stuff. This quality of his never came into question throughout his career and he is wholly convincing when admitting that pace never once frightened him. "I never really had fear for a bowler, but I was cautious of all of them. At the end of the day there were some that were more accurate than others and those who were more quicker than others. Even though I found some were not that quick, I was still a bit worried of them because they're the ones, if you're not careful, who can make you fail. You don't really get scared of pace, but obviously if you get one that goes past your nose it makes you wonder 'Suppose that'd hit me flush on.' Even if you are a little apprehensive, you've got to make sure that you don't show it. Your body language speaks a hell of a lot about the way you feel." He may not have been scared, but he certainly had a lot of respect for many of his fast bowling adversaries like Thommo, Dennis Lillee, Richard Hadlee, Geoff Lawson, Craig McDermott, Bob Willis and Ian Botham. "Their records prove they were a force to be reckoned with without my saying so," Desi acknowledged.

Cynics have questioned how the likes of Haynes would have coped against his own bowlers in a Test match atmosphere. Playing in an era where the West Indian fast bowlers dominated world cricket, it is a fair debate. Marshall, Patterson, Roberts, Garner, Holding, Ambrose, Walsh and company, have all imparted their fair share of cuts, bruises and broken bones between them on many hapless batsmen the world over. However, Desmond is confident that his ability would have prevented any tears on his part. "I don't think it would have been a great problem because I grew up on facing a lot of quick bowlers. I learnt my cricket with the fast stuff. As a boy I soon learned what a leg-break and what a googly was and I knew what pace was. Those were two things I relished and that experience helped me in my career. I played in Australia when they had four very good fast bowlers and I felt you needed to be aggressive to at least one - that was the secret, I think."

One of the greatest strengths that Desmond gave the West Indies team was consistency. He and Gordon Greenidge were so often responsible for laying the foundations of victory. On run-friendly pitches they ripped in to the heart of bowling attacks with merciless vigour, while they could also be depended on to produce runs on the more treacherous of wickets. They shared 16 century partnerships as an opening team. Desi regards his partnership with Gordon as a vital component in his own success. "I don't think I could ever have achieved what I did if it wasn't for the partnership I shared with Gordon, though you never really know. We were so together and understood each other so well. We were different in a lot of ways, but when we got on to the field we tried to assist each other and work as a team." Haynes gave the impression he was literally 'at work' when he was at the crease, with his workmanlike way; though Greenidge appeared more the entertainer who was forever the aggressor. Desmond was an elegant-looking batsman. He played the hook better than anyone, always looking in control of what is so often a dangerous shot; while his cover drives were another feature of his game that was always a treat to onlookers - even to the envious eyes of opposing spectators. It is sad to think his Test career was ended prematurely when he still had much more to offer his country. After plying his trade in South Africa for Western Province, he narrowly failed to meet the prescribed number of Red Stripe Cup games that the West Indies Cricket Board say their cricketers should participate in. The net result was the end of a great international career. Haynes is a cheerful, friendly character who was a good team man and always appears to enjoy life to the full. After representing the West Indies in 116 Test matches and in a record number of one day internationals (238), he deserved better. Haynes was justifiably bitter at the treatment he received, which prevented him from achieving milestones that he had always been determined to conquer. With 7487 Test runs, including 18 centuries and a top score of 184 against England at Lord's, he fell short of his statistical targets. Desi admits: "I always said that I wanted to finish my Test career after making a double hundred and scoring 20 Test centuries in total. I badly wanted those 20 centuries. I also wanted to score more runs than Sir Garfield Sobers (8032). I was disappointed with the way everything happened; it could have been handled differently. I would like to have ended my career with the tour of England in 1995. However, I'm very happy with my career and with the way I batted and the record speaks for itself. I never batted down the innings in a Test match - just once when I was injured - even when I was failing I was always up front, battling for the team."

DESMOND HAYNES - TEST MATCH STATISTICS   ( ) = As Opener

TESTS: 116   INN: 202 (201)   RUNS: 7487 (7472)
AVERAGE: 42.29 (42.45)   HS: 184 (184)   50: 39 (39) 100: 18 (18)

OVERALL RECORD   + = Opened in every innings against that country

V AUSTRALIA
TESTS: 33   INN: 59+   RUNS: 2233
AVERAGE: 42.13   HS: 145   50: 14 100: 5

V ENGLAND
TESTS: 35   INN: 59 (58)   RUNS: 2392 (2377)
AVERAGE: 46.90 (47.54)   HS: 184 (184)   50: 13 (13) 100: 5 (5)

V INDIA
TESTS: 19   INN: 32+   RUNS: 990
AVERAGE: 34.13   HS: 136   50: 4 100: 2

V NEW ZEALAND
TESTS: 10   INN: 20+   RUNS: 843
AVERAGE: 49.58   HS: 122   50: 5 100: 3

V PAKISTAN
TESTS: 16   INN: 29+   RUNS: 928
AVERAGE: 37.12   HS: 143*   50: 2 100: 3

V SOUTH AFRICA
TESTS: 1   INN: 2+   RUNS: 81
AVERAGE: 40.50   HS: 58   50: 1 100: 0

V SRI LANKA
TESTS: 1   INN: 1+   RUNS: 20
AVERAGE: 20.00   HS: 20   50: 0 100: 0

SIR JACK HOBBS - PERSONAL FILE

FULL NAME: John Berry Hobbs

DATE OF BIRTH: 16th December, 1882 Died 21st December, 1963

BIRTHPLACE: Cambridge

EDUCATION: Bedford School

PLAYING ROLE: Right Hand Bat, Right Arm Medium, Cover Point Fielder

TEAMS: England; Surrey 1905 - 1934

TEST DEBUT: 1907-08 v Australia, Melbourne

TESTS: 61

MOST PRODUCTIVE GROUND - H: The Oval, 619 runs (56.27) in 7 Tests
                          A: Melbourne, 1178 (69.29) in 10 Tests
FIRST-CLASS DEBUT: 1905

FIRST-CLASS RUNS: 61, 237

FIRST-CLASS WICKETS: 113

HIGHEST SCORE: 316* Surrey v Middlesex, Lord's, 1926

BEST BOWLING: 7-56

NICKNAME: Jack or The Master

PERCENTAGE OF TEST INNINGS AS OPENER: 95.09%

FOR THE RECORD: In 1920 he topped the first-class bowling averages with 17 wickets at 11.82!; He holds the records in first-class cricket for most runs and most centuries (197); Received three benefits from Surrey; On his retirement from cricket, he was made an honorary member of the MCC and also at Surrey; Served on Surrey's committee until his death; Received a knighthood in 1953 for his services to cricket and became the first professional to be so honoured; After his cricket career, he owned a sports outfitters business, funded mostly by his benefit rewards.

JACK HOBBS (England)

Cricket is a great game for nostalgia. Whether analysing statistics, musing over the general state of the sport and drawing parallels to years before, or discussing the greats of yesteryear, cricket will always breed tremendous conversation and unearth new debates. However, at whatever rate the sport continues to advance and irrelevant of the constant turnover of fresh, exciting talent, cricket will never see another like Sir Jack Hobbs, who served the game so professionally and so loyally. The sport has projected many players to superstardom through the years of its history, and though recent times have ensured even greater exposure with the rapid progression of media coverage, the like of Sir Jack will forever remain one of cricket's most famous sons, if not the number one son. Along with W.G. Grace and Sir Donald Bradman, Hobbs has legendary status that will never fade. Cricket has always honoured its immortals and Hobbs is one of them. In fact, given the value of nostalgia to cricket, his memory will probably grow stronger. He was known as 'The Master' and he sincerely earned such a title. From his first-class career he holds the record for scoring the most centuries - a record 197; that's 27 more than his nearest rival. He also tops the list for scoring the most runs in first-class cricket with 61,237, during his career from 1905 to 1934. He is the only man to ever reach the 60,000 figure. What's more is the fact that he lost four years of his career to the Great War. Furthermore, by the close of his first-class career, he was aged 52! Sir Jack was able to carry on playing to such an age because he was so in love with his craft, and age was not an issue that concerned him.

The late John Arlott, one of cricket's most celebrated writers, said of Hobbs. "In play, the salient feature of his cricket was that it seemed so unspectacular; he batted perfectly because he was the perfect batsman. His strokes did not seem startling, but inevitable. So, to a schoolboy, watching the famous cricketer for the first time, an immediate impression was of disappointment. He moved so unhurriedly, easily, forward or back, placing a single, smoothly putting away a four, recognising the good ball early and meeting it with impeccable defence. No violence, no hurry: the stroke rolled away like a well-cued billiard ball. It was only when the watcher perceived that his partner - a Test player of some standing - was in genuine difficulties that the utter perfection of Jack Hobbs's batting was borne in upon him. Others have hit greater distances, scored faster, played longer innings; but no one ever batted with such consummate mastery over every type of bowling as this man who loved to bat but cared little for records."*

* John Arlott, John Arlott's Book of Cricketers, Sphere Books (London), 1982

Jack Hobbs made his bow in Test cricket in Australia in 1907-08. On debut at Melbourne he made impressive totals of 83 and 28. These scores typified his cricket in the early stages of his Test career. Although he was scoring consistent runs, he was still devoid of a three-figure total by his twelfth match, though he was averaging a respectable 41. That all changed at Cape Town in 1909-10 when he scored 187 against South Africa. Strangely, he was dismissed hit wicket here for the only time in his 102 Test innings. This century sparked off his run-making in Tests that soared thereafter: His next Test match was at the beginning of the 1911-12 Ashes series at Sydney, where he scored 63 and 22; contributions that pale into insignificance throughout the remainder of that series, given his further scores of 6 and 126 not out in Melbourne, 187 and 3 in Adelaide and 178 in Melbourne once more. Those three centuries scored in consecutive Test matches, were all connected with some notable achievement: The match-winning unbeaten 126 was made in 227 minutes and was his first hundred versus Australia; the 187 was the highest of his 12 centuries against Australia and became England's highest score at Adelaide; while the 178 was made in a first-wicket partnership of 323 with Wilfred Rhodes that remains England's second highest opening partnership after the 359 by Len Hutton and Cyril Washbrook. In 1924 against South Africa, Hobbs registered the highest Test score of his career when he made 211 at Lord's. He combined with Herbert Sutcliffe to put on 268 for the first wicket, which became England's highest opening partnership at the home of cricket. His is a career that's littered with records and outstanding achievements, so it was no surprise when on tour in Australia in 1924-25 at Melbourne, that he became the first player to score 2,000 Test runs against the Australians. That series was another of his *particularly* successful ones. At Sydney in the first Test he made 115 in the first innings, and he followed this by adding a further two hundreds to his tally in the next two Tests at Melbourne (154) and Adelaide (119).

Hobbs played only two games against the West Indies, in 1928, but he sincerely made the most of his brief encounter by averaging 106.00. This statistic includes 159 at The Oval, which was the last of his five hundreds scored in England. Such a fact tells us that he was equally at home on the harder, faster wickets in Australia and South Africa as he was in England on batting tracks that were far more unpredictable in behaviour. The last of his 15 Test centuries was made at Melbourne in 1928-29, when he scored 142. In making that century, he achieved another milestone: At the age of 46 years and 82 days, he became the oldest batsman to score a century in Test cricket and it was also his 12th hundred against Australia. Throughout his Surrey and England career, he shared many fruitful opening partnerships. In total, he combined in 166 partnerships over a hundred, most of them with his Surrey opening partner Andrew Sandham (66), 40 with Tom Hayward and 26 with Herbert Sutcliffe.

Although Sir Jack Hobbs will be remembered for his record-breaking achievements and his mastery of his craft, there were further elements to his personality that should not be forgotten. Yes, he was widely respected as a great player and by some, the best ever, but also his honesty, natural dignity, charm, modesty and humour were other aspects that many admired him for equally as much as his run-scoring. Hobbs was an infamous practical joker and leg-puller in the dressing room, and his mischief was always received warmly: Like when he picked lighters out of colleagues' pockets without their knowledge and returned them later when they were unaware of its disappearance; and when he substituted water for gin in the flask of an England captain, these were things that his team-mates all saw the funny side of and appreciated for the humour. I, like many in this generation, consider myself unfortunate to have never seen him play and so, must believe the stories repeated of his genius throughout the history of cricket. The great John Arlott, however, did witness the skill of Sir Jack Hobbs's batting and recalled: "It is one of the riches of cricket to have watched him bat. Those who never saw him may find it difficult to imagine such skills as made all bowling see easy; the unforced movement, on neat feet, into a flow of stroke which sent the ball away placed to inches, and at the high pace of perfect timing. Here every man who had ever striven to bat could see the flowering of his craft, through perfect execution, into an art."

<u>SIR JACK HOBBS</u> - TEST MATCH STATISTICS   ( ) = As Opener

TESTS: 61   INN: 102 (97)   RUNS: 5410 (5130)
AVERAGE: 56.94 (56.37) HS: 211 (211)   50: 28 (27) 100: 15 (14)

<u>OVERALL RECORD</u>   + = Opened in every innings against that country

<u>V AUSTRALIA</u>
TESTS: 41   INN: 71 (69)   RUNS: 3636 (3483)
AVERAGE: 54.26 (53.38) HS: 187 (187)   50: 15 (15) 100: 12 (11)

<u>V SOUTH AFRICA</u>
TESTS: 18   INN: 29 (26)   RUNS: 1535 (1408)
AVERAGE: 59.03 (58.66) HS: 211 (211)   50: 12 (11) 100: 2 (2)

<u>V WEST INDIES</u>
TESTS: 2   INN: 2+   RUNS: 212
AVERAGE: 106.00   HS: 159   50: 1 100: 1

CONRAD HUNTE - PERSONAL FILE

FULL NAME: Conrad Cleophas Hunte

DATE OF BIRTH: 9th May, 1932

BIRTHPLACE: St. Andrew, Barbados

PLAYING ROLE: Right Hand Bat, Occasional Right Arm Medium Pace

TEAMS: West Indies; Barbados 1950/51 - 1966/67

TEST DEBUT: 1957-58 v Pakistan, Bridgetown

TESTS: 44

MOST PRODUCTIVE GROUND H: Port-of-Spain 582 runs (44.76) in 8 Tests
A: Manchester 318 runs (159.00) in 2 Tests
FIRST-CLASS DEBUT: 1950-51

FIRST-CLASS RUNS: 8,916

FIRST-CLASS WICKETS: 17

HIGHEST SCORE: 263 Barbados v Jamaica, Georgetown, 1961-62

BEST BOWLING: 3-5 West Indians v President's XI, Nagpur, 1966-67

EDUCATION: Alleyne School, Barbados

PERCENTAGE OF TEST INNINGS AS OPENER: 100%

FOR THE RECORD: Scored 142 on Test debut against Pakistan; In that 1957-58 series, he was involved in what became the second-highest partnership (to Ponsford and Bradman - 451) in Test cricket when he put on 446 with Gary Sobers for the second wicket. It is now the third-highest second wicket partnership in Tests; Took a wicket in his last Test match in 1966-67 against India (D.G. Borde for 125). His only other Test wicket was that of M.J.K. Smith in 1959-60, dismissing him for 96; Autobiography "Playing To Win" (1971); Became a full-time worker with the Moral Rearmament after retiring from cricket; He is now working in South Africa and furthering the development of young black cricketers of the future.

CONRAD HUNTE (West Indies)

There can be few better ways to launch a Test career than the way Conrad Hunte did. Following a seven-year wait to play in the greatest arena of all, Hunte then accepted his opportunity with a hunger that more befitted a beggar being handed fillet steak; there was no way he was ever going to allow himself to miss this chance of the big time, and he promptly embraced Test cricket as if he was taking up an old hobby. On debut in his native Barbados against the touring Pakistanis, he struck a marvellous 142 followed with two more hundreds later in the series, though he had to iron out some technical flaws beforehand. He said: "I had just come back from playing league cricket in England and by the time I got back home my timing was all out. Herman Griffith, the former West Indies Test player, saw me struggling in the nets and he suggested that I stop batting from the full 22 yards and that I bat from half the distance to sharpen up my reflexes. That did the trick. I then got 77 for Barbados against the Pakistanis and went into the first Test full of confidence to make my debut. It really was a fairytale beginning, getting a century on debut in my home town; and Pakistan had some real good bowlers like Fazal Mahmood."

His local celebrity status after that debut grew world-wide after the third Test at Jamaica: He scored 260 and shared a second-wicket partnership of 446 with Garfield Sobers, failing by just five runs to break the world record partnership for any wicket in Tests, set by Don Bradman and Bill Ponsford at The Oval in 1934. The enterprising way in which Conrad went about his innings was evident instantly when he put on an opening stand of 87 with Rohan Kanhai, before Kanhai was dismissed for just 25. The partnership with Sobers was as entertaining a display of batting that spectators will ever see throughout a day's cricket. As Hunte compiled his own mammoth total, which was ended by a run out, Sobers beat Len Hutton's world Test record with his 365 not out. "Gary and I always played well together," admitted Hunte. "He gave you confidence when he was at the other end. It was one of those times when everything just came off, and we'd still be batting today if I hadn't have got run out because it was a batting paradise. When we were five runs away from beating the record, I played one to midwicket thinking it was a comfortable single, but I never realised it was Ejaz Butt who was on to it. He had come on as substitute fielder and was the only one that wasn't leaden-footed after spending two days in the field. I was so upset to be run out after getting so close to the record that I didn't even recognise the standing ovation as I walked off. When I got into the dressing room, I put my head in my hands and our manager, Barclay Gaskin, said he'd never seen a player dejected before after getting 200!" The one consolation for Conrad in terms of record-breaking is that it remains a record West Indies partnership for any wicket.

The following Test match in Guyana saw the newcomer score his third century of the series - 114. There were elements of this innings that displayed a rapidly maturing cricket brain in Hunte. He was a renowned leg-side player; he loved to whip balls off leg stump, and the wily Fazal Mahmood tried to exploit this area of Hunte's game, but the young West Indian was equal to it. As opposed to playing through square leg, he made a conscious effort to play straighter, in the V. He knew he had to be wary of Mahmood's fine away swinger that often found the leading edge from right-handed batsmen. Despite this early signal of precocity from Hunte, it proved a deceiving message. In the next series in India, he averaged just 27; figures salvaged somewhat by his 92 at Delhi in the fifth and final Test. "The Pakistan series was very special and a very heady time for a youngster of 25. I then made the fatal mistake of thinking I had made it. I became big-headed and my attitude was all wrong. In India at Delhi, I realised that I had to become a student of the game again. Cricketers must be eternal students. I should have got a hundred in that game, as I was given out LBW when I had snicked it on to my pads. I then showed dissent, and that was the only time I ever questioned an umpire's decision."

After the 1959-60 home series against England, Conrad was touring foreign land once more in 1960-61 - this time, Australia. They lost the series 2-1 against a very strong Australian team, after contesting the first ever tied Test in the first match. Hunte batted consistently throughout the rubber, and he is particularly proud of his fighting 110 (out of 233) at Melbourne as West Indies went down by eight wickets. "That was one of the best innings I ever played, on a turning wicket against Richie Benaud who was the best spinner I ever faced. I was always more comfortable against fast bowlers. When the spinners came on I was not so competent against them, so I had to work on that part of my game. In my view it was a significant achievement." Conrad also considers Richie Benaud the best captain he played against and it is no surprise to hear this when Hunte recalls his dismissal at Melbourne, when he was set for a far bigger hundred. "Richie brought on Norman O'Neill, who hardly ever bowled, and he immediately bowled me a full toss which I tried to hit for six over midwicket, but managed to just edge it to the keeper. That was good captaincy."

When he faced India again in 1961-62, this time in the Caribbean, Hunte failed to score runs of any significance. He feels this was because it was a time when his game was experiencing great, personal change. "I was making a transition from a shot player to an anchor man. If we lost a few quick wickets, there was nobody who would try and stop the rot, so I then tried to become more circumspect and, subsequently, I lost out with my attacking game. It was a change to a new approach which didn't pay off until the England tour in 1963." Hunte had represented Enfield in the Lancashire League from 1957 to 1962, and so was used to the more dull and varying conditions. "My previous experience taught me to hit through the line of the ball and play on the front foot. In England you have to play on the front foot and revert back in the West Indies to a predominantly back foot game." In a series the West Indies won 3-1, Conrad contributed with some weighty scores. His 182 at Old Trafford was made in familiar surroundings, while his 108 not out at The Oval ensured a comprehensive series win for his country in the fifth Test match. Incidentally, both of these centuries were made against the fast bowling duo that Conrad considers one of the best he ever did battle with - Trueman and Statham. Of further significance is the fact that Statham did not play in the second, third and fourth Tests, which meant Hunte's two centuries in the rubber were scored against this infamous, double-headed pace attack. "I'd faced Lindwall and Miller at the end of their careers, and Trueman and Statham were right up there with them, and Alan Davidson was as good also. Brian Statham bowled so tight and accurately that you tended to get out to Fred through frustration." To emphasise the benefit of playing in the Lancashire League, Hunte compiled another century (135) at Manchester on his next England tour in 1966. "I had lived in Lancashire and I felt at home there. It was nice that the English supporters continued to cheer us even when we were winning; they just appreciated good cricket." His 135 combined in another 3-1 series win for the West Indies. However, he admits that the 1963 English tour was his most successful ever when he made 1,367 runs on the tour. "I reckon a tour of England is the most challenging and the most rewarding," he offers.

In between those England tours, Hunte had played a home series against Australia in 1964-65. Initially, it was a troubled time for the opening batsman, as he was expecting to be handed the captaincy ahead of his rival Gary Sobers, following the retirement of Frank Worrell, but events did not evolve as he had hoped. "When Sobers got the captaincy ahead of me, I was angry, bitter and jealous, which is an understandable emotion, but also a destructive emotion. Eventually, I recognised this and I went to Gary to repair the damage, which he appreciated. We then worked well together as captain and vice-captain. I managed to outplay Sobers and Kanhai because I was working on a new energy I had discovered." Hunte's scores were consistency personified, given his totals of 41, 81, 89, 53, 31, 38, 75, 81, 1 and 60 not out. "I should have scored four hundreds in the series," he admits, "but each time I received a very good ball, which can always happen at any time." Still, a 2-1 series triumph was enough to console the run-happy Bajan. Following that series, Conrad was awarded the Karl Nunes Trophy, which is awarded to a West Indies player once in his lifetime, when he is thought to have done the most on and off the field to uphold the traditions of the game and the spirit between the sides.

Given Hunte's previous admission at how much more difficult he found the battle against spinners, it is a tribute to his resilience that he scored 101 at Bombay in 1966-67 against India, in the last Test series of his career. This innings was achieved in combat against one of the game's greatest ever spin bowlers, Bhagwat Chandrasekhar. "It was a very interesting contest," Hunte acknowledges. "He had contracted polio when he was five, so as a result, he had very limp wrists and he himself didn't always know which way he was going to turn it. I tried to play a very patient and watchful game, and give my team-mates enough time to see what he was bowling. In fact, an Indian journalist wrote, 'Hunte would not be tempted, and if Adam had been like Hunte, we would still be playing cricket in the Garden of Eden'."

When aged just 35, still with much to offer the West Indies in terms of runs and knowledge, Conrad had to end his active association with Test cricket, due to injury. This was just prior to the 1967-68 home series against England. He remembers: "I was playing for a Rest of the World side at Lord's in 1967, and I felt a pain in my knee. I went to visit a specialist in London, where I had deep wax treatment and a cortisone injection. After, he informed me that I had the early stages of osteo arthritis, and that it might be okay to play on for another few years, but it could also collapse beneath me at any time. I had never before taken the field without feeling fully fit and I didn't intend to." This brought a very sad and sudden end to Conrad's cricket career. He had always played the game with a smile and it was fitting that on his retirement he set out to further the bond between blacks and whites, ensuring the sport of cricket would always be appreciated, irrespective of colour. "I sent the West Indies Cricket Board a cable telling them that I was retiring due to injury and that I am going around the world to build harmony and to enhance friendly relations between races. On the 1963 tour of England, I had noticed a difference with the way people looked at West Indians since the immigrants had arrived and I wanted to help bridge these gaps."

CONRAD HUNTE - TEST MATCH STATISTICS

TESTS: 44	INN: 78	RUNS: 3245
AVERAGE: 45.06	HS: 260	50: 13 100: 8

OVERALL RECORD   NB - C.C. Hunte opened in every Test match innings

V AUSTRALIA

TESTS: 10	INN: 20	RUNS: 927
AVERAGE: 48.97	HS: 110	50: 8 100: 1

V ENGLAND

TESTS: 15	INN: 26	RUNS: 1005
AVERAGE: 43.69	HS: 182	50: 2 100: 3

V INDIA

TESTS: 13	INN: 21	RUNS: 670
AVERAGE: 33.50	HS: 101	50: 3 100: 1

V PAKISTAN

TESTS: 6	INN: 11	RUNS: 643
AVERAGE: 64.30	HS: 260	50: 0 100: 3

SIR LEN HUTTON - PERSONAL FILE

FULL NAME: Leonard Hutton

DATE OF BIRTH: 23rd June, 1916 Died 6th September, 1990

BIRTHPLACE: Pudsey, Yorkshire

EDUCATION: Pudsey School

PLAYING ROLE: Right Hand Bat, Leg Break Bowler

TEAMS: England; Yorkshire 1934 - 1955

TEST DEBUT: 1937 v New Zealand, Lord's

TESTS: 79

MOST PRODUCTIVE GROUND H: The Oval, 1521 runs (89.57) in 12 Tests
                        A: Adelaide, 456 runs (91.20) in 3 Tests

FIRST-CLASS DEBUT: 1934

FIRST-CLASS RUNS: 40,140

FIRST-CLASS WICKETS: 173

HIGHEST SCORE: 364 England v Australia, The Oval, 1938

BEST BOWLING: 6-76 Yorkshire v Leicestershire, Leicester, 1937

NICKNAME: Len

PERCENTAGE OF TEST INNINGS AS OPENER: 94.92%

FOR THE RECORD: Son R.A. Hutton (Yorkshire & England); His 364 at The Oval in 1938 was then the highest score in Test cricket, beating Wally Hammond's 336*. It is still the third highest behind Sobers and Lara, though remains the top score by an Englishman in Tests; In June 1949 he scored 1294 runs in one month at an average of 92.42 - still the most runs ever scored in a month in first-class cricket; Scored 129 hundreds in his career; Knighted in 1956; After his cricket career, went into business; Sir Leonard was also an England selector and a respected newspaper columnist.

LEONARD HUTTON (England)

When you talk of the genuine all-time greats, Leonard Hutton is firmly amongst them. There have been few more organised batsmen than Sir Len. He knew his own game so well that he played within the boundaries of his limitations - which, although sounds derogatory, is actually quite a compliment. How many players do we know that often succumb to ambitious strokes? Quite a few I would say. Hutton made bowlers earn his wicket; it really was a prize to boast about. He has occasionally been likened to fellow Yorkshireman Geoffrey Boycott - another batsman who flourished through employing the workmanlike ethic. Although, two former Test stars that have seen both players at close range feel this is a comparison with few similarities. "Like Boycott, Len was a very sound player with a good technique and wasn't exhilarating to watch, but he had more shots," Sir Alec Bedser says. Following on with those sentiments, Tom Graveney echoed: "Len was a wonderful player. Without being unkind to Boycott, to compare the two is ridiculous. Len was streets ahead of him. When the situation called, Len was able to up the anti and play a few shots and knock it about if he was on a good wicket. Where as Geoffrey was the same pace most of the time. People associate the word 'great' with far too many players for my liking. Len, however, really was 'great'. As a technician, he would have to be the best there has ever been; and the amazing thing is that his left arm was an inch and a half shorter than his right arm, due to an accident in the war when he was a physical training instructor."

Len was not a player who significantly improved with age like Graham Gooch or John Wright; on the contrary, he soon proved himself an extremely precocious Test match batsman. Despite a disappointing debut at Lord's against New Zealand in 1937, scoring nought and one, his next performance at Manchester in the following Test match, more than compensated for his bleak start; he registered exactly a hundred. He repeated that score in his fourth Test at Nottingham against Australia in 1938. However, it was during that same Ashes series at The Oval that he really announced himself. In his sixth Test and still only 22 years of age, he broke the world record for the highest individual Test score, beating Don Bradman's 334. On that innings, Wisden wrote in 1939: "No more remarkable exhibition of concentration and endurance has been seen on the cricket field than that of Leonard Hutton in a match which ended in the defeat of Australia by an innings and 579 runs. Record after record went by the board as Hutton mastered the bowling in calm, methodical fashion for the best part of two and a half days. At the end of 13 hours, 20 minutes the batsman of only twenty-two passed the highest individual score in Test history and had taken part in two record stands - 382 with Maurice Leyland for the second wicket, the best for any wicket by England, and 215 with Joe Hardstaff for the sixth wicket. This Test, which enabled

England to share the series, will always be remembered as Hutton's match."

One would think that after such a phenomenal beginning to a Test career, the player would be so full of confidence that his personal attitude would change with the sudden euphoria cast upon him from the media, though not with the same impact as today. It is easy for a professional sportsman to forget the fundamentals of his trade, when such complimentary treatment is frequently bestowed on him. Many players have suffered from premature star status, in failing to keep their feet on the ground and allowing the attention to hamper their performance. Although, with Len, this was hardly the case. In his autobiography, *Fifty Years in Cricket*, he explained: "I sometimes wonder if it wasn't the second worst happening of my career to become a record-breaking national celebrity at an age when I had just qualified to vote. It wasn't that I lost my head in the clouds; quite the reverse. Proud as I was to have scored 364 against Australia and to have overtaken Don Bradman's record, which I had watched spellbound as a schoolboy at Headingley eight years before, I was still capable of being overwhelmed by the suddenness of fame and worried by its penalties. No doubt some might deem it highly implausible that a young batsman able to stay for almost fourteen hours in a Test match could be vulnerable to pressures and private misgivings. The public might have seen me as a dedicated, single-minded, perhaps even ruthless, scoring machine, but the truth was that I was shy and retiring by nature. By upbringing and instinct I was highly practical, a Yorkshireman in heart and soul, but reluctant to voice an opinion. There was never any danger of my feet leaving the ground. Indeed the more praise to come my way the more I fretted that I might not be able to live up to my reputation as a record-breaker."*

Hutton's initial retiring nature was reflected through his attitude in the dressing room. He may have appeared a confident, dominant figure in the middle, but when back in the pavilion, things were much different. He admitted to being an unashamed hero-worshipper who could never bring himself to believe he could enter the world of Hobbs, Bradman and the entire Yorkshire team of the thirties. His first meeting with Sir Jack left him literally tongue-tied. He recalled: "I gaped and no words came. I shudder to imagine what he must have thought of me. When I went into the Yorkshire dressing room I felt like a youthful interloper, a boy among men, and I can say with honesty that when I opened the batting for Pudsey St. Lawrence in the Bradford League at the age of fourteen, I did not think I was anything better than above average for my years."*

* Len Hutton, Fifty Years in Cricket, W. H. Allen (London), 1984

MICHAEL ATHERTON (England)

GEOFF BOYCOTT (England)

AAMIR SOHAIL (Pakistan)

DENNIS AMISS (England)

As all opening batsmen have to be, Len was particularly sound against fast bowling. His greatest test in handling the quick stuff came from Australia's well-respected opening duo, Keith Miller and Ray Lindwall. Tom Graveney said: "Strangely enough for an opening batsman, he used to like to get on the front foot quite a lot, although he could also play the short stuff comfortably. After the war, he had people like Lindwall and Miller to contend with and he coped *so* well it was unbelievable. People talk about how much quicker the likes of the West Indies quicks were in the seventies and eighties than fast bowlers in our era, but they forget bowlers got much closer to us in those days with the front-foot rule."

World War II prevented Hutton from compiling many more runs to his career total, but the remainder of the forties was a fruitful period in his playing days. None more so, though, than his captaining England to a 1-0 series win over Lindsay Hassett's Australians in 1953. England's regaining of the Ashes meant they held them aloft for the first time in just short of 19 years of Aussie dominance. It was the controversial series in 1953-54 in the West Indies, though, that merits the greatest amount of column inches, as Hutton's skill, temperament and demeanour were characteristics exhibited with true professionalism. As England's first professional captain, he led from the front throughout the tour. England got off to a disappointing start in the five-Test series, losing the first two matches. However, the third Test in Guyana sparked an England revival. Tom Graveney, a tour member, recalls: "The thing I remember most about Len was his attitude during that 1953-54 tour of the West Indies. We had a lot of trouble off the field, even from our own broadsheet press who were anti-Hutton because he was a *professional* England captain, but Len still did the job with the bat despite these other burdens. After losing the first two matches, we knew we had to win in Guyana, as the fourth Test was on the matting in Trinidad where you got out when you was tired." As it happened, Len batted beautifully for a superbly crafted 169 to help win the game.

True to form, Trinidad in the next game was a draw, so it was on to Jamaica for the final match, where England had to win to square the series. Graveney continues: "When we got up to Sabina Park, the groundsman said to us, 'This is the best pitch I've ever prepared in my life,' so we thought we've got to win the toss. Len went out and lost the toss. We thought it was going to be an uphill struggle, but as we took the field, there was a little bit of juice in the wicket and we bowled them out for 130 odd. Len then went out to bat, set his stall from the outset and got a double century (205). He'd still have been batting now if he hadn't have had a slight ruction with the Chief Minister in Jamaica at tea-time. It broke his concentration and he got out." The ruction was something that developed into quite a storm, from which should have been only of the tea cup variety. Apparently, Hutton was congratulated after coming off the park at tea by the government official, who took offence that Len did not acknowledge his praise. Quite rightly, Hutton explained that he was not to know who was tapping him on the back, however, the situation still became ugly. His tremendous 205, though, did earn an England victory. Hutton said: "If I am permitted one satisfaction, it was in my refusal to be side-tracked from my duty to lead England to the best of my ability and to score as many runs as I could for England." He averaged 96.71 in the series. In normal circumstances, there was nothing that could ever distract him from concentrating on scoring runs, as Tom Graveney says. "He was a very quiet man and he kept things inside. When he was batting a long innings, he used to go into a daze, in a little cocoon all of his own. Even at tea-time, he would come in, have his cuppa and hardly say a word to anyone."

Despite an incredible beginning to his Test career, Len's conclusion was not quite as spectacular, on the contrary in fact. But by 1954-55, when he played his final Test against New Zealand, he had severe back pain and it was impossible for him to continue. He felt it was a good time to bow out. "At the time I did not know it was to be my last Test, but, in retrospect, it was not a bad time to go. Right at the top. And I was spared the emotional upset of a sentimental farewell. Who could forget Bradman's last Test at The Oval in 1948 when the whole ground stood and cheered him all the way to the wicket. I am not suggesting I would have had - or deserved - a similar tribute, but as I watched Bradman take guard I could see the warmth of his reception and the occasion had got to him, and he was bowled second ball by Eric Hollies. As he said, 'It's not easy to bat with tears in your eyes'." Shortly after the completion of his Test career, in 1956, he became Sir Leonard Hutton - a fitting tribute to one of cricket's great performers.

SIR LEONARD HUTTON - TEST MATCH STATISTICS   ( ) = As Opener

TESTS: 79   INN: 138 (131)   RUNS: 6971 (6721)
AVERAGE: 56.67 (56.47)   HS: 364 (364)   50: 33 (31) 100: 19 (19)

OVERALL RECORD   + = Opened in every innings against that country

V AUSTRALIA
TESTS: 27   INN: 49 (45)   RUNS: 2428 (2306)
AVERAGE: 56.46 (56.24)   HS: 364 (364)   50: 14 (13) 100: 5 (5)

V INDIA
TESTS: 7   INN: 11+   RUNS: 522
AVERAGE: 58.00   HS: 150   50: 2 100: 2

V NEW ZEALAND
TESTS: 11   INN: 17 (16)   RUNS: 777 (724)
AVERAGE: 45.70 (45.25)   HS: 206 (206)   50: 4 (3) 100: 3 (3)

V PAKISTAN
TESTS: 2   INN: 3+   RUNS: 19
AVERAGE: 6.33   HS: 14   50: 0 100: 2

V SOUTH AFRICA
TESTS: 19   INN: 34+   RUNS: 1564
AVERAGE: 52.13   HS: 158   50: 7 100: 4

V WEST INDIES
TESTS: 13   INN: 24 (22)   RUNS: 1661 (1586)
AVERAGE: 79.09 (79.30)   HS: 205 (205)   50: 6 (6) 100: 5 (5)

SANATH JAYASURIYA - PERSONAL FILE

FULL NAME: Sanath Teran Jayasuriya

DATE OF BIRTH: 30th June, 1969

BIRTHPLACE: Matara

PLAYING ROLE: Left Hand Bat, Slow Left Arm, Slip Fielder

TEAMS: Sri Lanka; Bloomfield (Colombo)

TEST DEBUT: 1990-91 v New Zealand, Hamilton

TESTS: 38

MOST PRODUCTIVE GROUND - H: Colombo (SSC), 639 runs (53.25) in 7
                                   Tests
                                   A: The Oval, 237 runs (237.00) in 1 Test
FIRST-CLASS DEBUT: 1988-89

HIGHEST SCORE: 340 Sri Lanka v India, Colombo (RPS), 1997-98

BEST BOWLING:

NICKNAME: Sanna

PERCENTAGE OF TEST INNINGS AS OPENER: 64.06%

FOR THE RECORD: Played in the 1992 World Cup in Australia & New Zealand, and in the 1996 World Cup in India, Pakistan & Sri Lanka, where he was a significant member of the Sri Lankan team that won the cup; Took 6-29 against England in a one-day international at Moratuwa in 1992-93; His score of 340 against India at Colombo in 1997-98, became the fourth-highest individual total ever in Test cricket behind Brian Lara (375), Gary Sobers (365*) and Leonard Hutton (364). In that match he featured in the second highest partnership in first-class cricket with R.S. Mahanama of 576; During his 213 at The Oval in 1998, he shared a record Sri Lankan third-wicket partnership of 243 with P.A. De Silva.

SANATH JAYASURIYA (Sri Lanka)

The situation of a game or it's format, would appear to be of no consequence to this man. Whether playing Test cricket or one day internationals, Sanath Jayasuriya will always bat in the same exciting and exhilarating manner - it's the only way he knows how. This judgement should not be taken as a smear on his ability or an accusation of inflexibility; more a compliment of how natural is his talent, able to destroy any attack on any wicket. His type is not exactly non-existent, though not in abundance to say the least. Past masters who appeared to know no other way to bat than to dominate bowling attacks in either the short or long form include Viv Richards, Ian Botham and Kapil Dev. The modern-day posse is led by Sanath along with Sachin Tendulkar and Brian Lara. Such company is exclusive. It would be easy to hang a label on him like 'pinch-hitter', especially in limited-overs cricket, but he is much, much better than that. His superior batting in one day cricket, that originally launched him to great heights in the 1996 World Cup, has almost been a hindrance as far as his reputation goes. He is a calm, unassuming and undemonstrative individual - rather unlike his batting - but his aggressive and impetuous stroke-play does not come at the expense of elegance, contrary to the thoughts of some: His shots are nearly all of the text book form; it's just that his hunger for runs and impetuosity to 'get on with it' is so great that he bats with a constant scavenger-like prowess to keep the scoreboard ticking. In that 1996 World Cup, he scored 82 off just 44 balls against England in the quarter-finals at Faisalabad. Such a breathtaking exhibition of offensive batting from an opening batsman who took advantage of the early fielding restrictions, whether against poor bowling or not, was just brilliant. However, some seemingly jealous Englishmen had the temerity to call this man a slogger. If it had been scored on a village green or in a parks game then the accusation may have had some substance, but against an experienced international attack, you can't bat like that so successfully and so consistently if you're merely a slogger. Added to his useful bowling and fielding ability, it's no wonder he was voted the most valuable player of the World Cup! After the tournament, many more cricket followers were so much more aware of Sanath Jayasuriya, and his form in Test cricket as opener thereafter did not belie his previous displays in 50-over cricket. Moreover, his reputation as a world-class opening batsman gained momentum.

It wasn't until his 15th Test match against Pakistan that Jayasuriya first opened in Test cricket. With scores of nine and one, it wasn't the auspicious beginning he would have liked in the role, but he never had to wait too long until his initial major breakthrough came in that opening position. Against a strong Australian side at Adelaide in 1995-96, he scored 48 and 112 not out. "The hundred in Adelaide was a big moment in my life. I proved to myself that I could play," he said. And *can he play*? His honest admittance smacks of a man that once suffered from a lack of confidence mentally, though his batting may have suggested otherwise. From here on, his transition to the batting up front suited him perfectly. His current Test average of 45.82 proves he is a player of immense ability, though he averages 51.56 as opener, which adds further weight to the fact he is far better when opening. His Test match figures, when analysed, do tell a curious story given the topsy-turvy results. Against the two weakest Test nations due to current form, he averages just 22.63 versus New Zealand and 21.14 versus Zimbabwe from 12 matches in total. However, against Australia he averages 45.50, 38.40 against the West Indies, 58.44 against Pakistan, 78.00 against India and 81.00 against England. He does remain unperturbed, though, realising that every innings cannot be a big one. "Some days you see the ball early; other days you struggle to time the ball at all. You can't hit every ball for four," Sanath reasons. It may be that his previous exhibitions have raised the level of expectancy on him too highly, but if statistics are anything to go by, it seems that he is better when the competition and the match is tougher.

After posting his first Test match century in that Adelaide game, he further strengthened his position in the team and as a blossoming opener, when he made two fifties and a hundred in the home series against Pakistan in 1996-97. From here Sri Lanka toured the West Indies to play two Test matches, where in Antigua Jayasuriya scored 85 and in St. Vincent he made 90. The series was won 1-0 by the West Indies but was still hugely competitive. It was the very next Test match, though, that really blew the lid off the success story of Sanath Jayasuriya. At the Premadasa Stadium in Colombo, he scored a colossal 340 against India in a match that rewrote the record books. On a flat wicket, lifeless wicket, Sanath took full advantage of the conditions to greedily amass his highest score and the fourth-highest in Test match history. This contributed towards the highest-ever team total in Tests. Sri Lanka's first and only innings of the match was 952-6 declared, which superseded England's 903-7 declared in 1938 at The Oval. The partnership of 576 between Jayasuriya and Roshan Mahanama for the second wicket also made history, becoming the second highest partnership in first-class cricket. After India had already scored 537-8 declared, it was always likely to be a game of milestones and comfort rather than wickets and fierce competition. Jayasuriya's innings spanned 799 minutes and was made from 578 balls. The thought of breaking Brian Lara's record of 375 only occurred to him near the end of his innings, he admitted: "I was happy to go all that way. I wasn't going after the record - at least not until the end of the fourth day, when someone told me I was only 50 short." By the close of that fourth day he had reached 326 and had become his country's first player to score a triple-century. On the last day the gates were thrown open to the public, and in anticipation of seeing their hero surpass Lara's record, 30,000 locals crowded in to view the proceedings. Sadly, their hopes of mass jubilation were soon thwarted when a ball from off-spinner Chauhan, bounced more than usual and a catch was spooned up to Ganguly at silly point. The moment was bittersweet for the leanly-built Jayasuriya. "I felt a great pressure on me when I came out to bat (on the fifth morning)," he announced, "and obviously I am disappointed now - but at least my country has made a great achievement," he concluded philosophically. There were some interesting Indian bowling figures after that flat-track hammering: Chauhan went for 276 from 78 overs and took one wicket, Kumble took 1-223 from 72 overs while Kulkarni took 1-195 from his 70 overs. Sachin Tendulkar called the pitch 'unfit for Test cricket'. A one-sided contest it undoubtedly was between bat and ball, though Jayasuriya's superb performance should not be undermined. This pitch was nowhere near the first flat, docile wicket to host a Test match, and certainly won't be the last. But still, there haven't been too many scores over the 300 mark in 121 years of Test cricket. It's just that only a minority have the sufficient hunger, temperament and ability to bat for so long - Sanath Jayasuriya is obviously one of them.

If the law of averages is worth believing, you would think he'd have bagged a pair in his next Test after scoring 340. Yet, he scored 32 and 199 in another drawn game against India. At this point, batting was an addiction to him that he couldn't help but feed. I'm sure the Indian fielders must have grew bored of him, while their bowlers must have considered the experience of bowling at him slightly tedious, though his home supporters were less melancholy to say the least. After playing Test cricket for over a decade and being accustomed to defeat, the Sri Lankan people now feel proud of their cricket team, that can compete against the very best and as they proved in the 1996 World Cup, win things. The likes of Ranatunga, De Silva, Muralitharan and Jayasuriya are all world-class players and the side is getting tougher to beat all the time. Just ask Alec Stewart. He captained the England team that was expected to beat Sri Lanka at The Oval in 1998, but eventually lost by ten wickets. The performance of off-spinner Muttiah Muralitharan claimed most of the praise - and I wouldn't argue with that after his 16-220 - but it was Sanath's fluent innings of 213 from only 278 balls that gave Sri Lanka a match-winning position after replying to England's first innings of 445. They gained a 136-run lead, before Murali spun his magic in England's second innings. Right from the start, nearing the close of the second day, Jayasuriya looked in ominous form, easily dismissing anything that was slightly wayward for four. And indeed he continued in this fashion throughout Saturday, linking up with De Silva to register a new Sri Lankan third-wicket record of 243. On this evidence, I think there are many more Sri Lankan victories approaching fast - thanks greatly to Sanath Jayasuriya.

SANATH JAYASURIYA - TEST MATCH STATISTICS   ( ) = As Opener

TESTS: 38   INN: 64 (41)   RUNS: 2610 (2011)
AVERAGE: 45.82 (51.56) HS: 340 (340)   50: 14 (10) 100: 5 (5)

OVERALL RECORD

V AUSTRALIA
TESTS: 3   INN: 5 (2)   RUNS: 182 (160)
AVERAGE: 45.50 (80.00) HS: 112 (112)   50: 0 100: 1

V ENGLAND
TESTS: 3   INN: 6 (2)   RUNS: 324 (237)
AVERAGE: 81.00 (237.00) HS: 213 (213)   50: 1 (0) 100: 1 (1)

V INDIA
TESTS: 7   INN: 11 (7)   RUNS: 780 (726)
AVERAGE: 78.00 (103.71) HS: 340 (340)   50: 2 (2) 100: 2 (2)

V NEW ZEALAND
TESTS: 7   INN: 12 (9)   RUNS: 249 (184)
AVERAGE: 22.63 (20.44) HS: 59 (59)   50: 2 (2) 100: 0

V PAKISTAN
TESTS: 6   INN: 10 (6)   RUNS: 526 (288)
AVERAGE: 58.44 (48.00) HS: 113 (113)   50: 4 (2) 100: 1 (1)

V SOUTH AFRICA
TESTS: 4   INN: 7 (4)   RUNS: 209 (84)
AVERAGE: 29.85 (21.00) HS: 65 (51)   50: 2 (1) 100: 0

V WEST INDIES
TESTS: 3   INN: 5 (4)   RUNS: 192 (192)
AVERAGE: 38.40 (48.00) HS: 90 (90)   50: 2 (2) 100: 0

V ZIMBABWE
TESTS: 5   INN: 8 (7)   RUNS: 148 (138)
AVERAGE: 21.14 (23.00) HS: 68 (68)   50: 1 (1) 100: 0

GARY KIRSTEN - PERSONAL FILE

FULL NAME: Gary Kirsten

DATE OF BIRTH: 23rd November, 1967

BIRTHPLACE: Cape Town

EDUCATION: Rondebosch Boys High School

PLAYING ROLE: Left Hand Bat, Occasional Off Break Bowler

TEAMS: South Africa; Western Province 1987-88 - .

TEST DEBUT: 1993-94 v Australia, Melbourne

TESTS: 45

MOST PRODUCTIVE GROUND H: Johannesburg 409 runs (31.46) in 7 Tests
                         A: Adelaide, 235 runs (78.33) in 2 Tests
                         & Calcutta, 235 runs (117.50) in 1 Test

FIRST-CLASS DEBUT: 1987-88

HIGHEST SCORE: 244 Western Province b Border, East London, 1995-96

BEST BOWLING: 6-68

NICKNAME: Gazza

PERCENTAGE OF TEST INNINGS AS OPENER: 100%

FOR THE RECORD: Son of N. Kirsten (Border 1946 - 1960), Brother of P.N. Kirsten (WP/Border/Sussex/Derbyshire/SA 1973 - 1995), A.M. Kirsten (WPB 1986 - 1989), P. Kirsten (SW/WP,WPB 1992 - 1995); In 1997-98, Gary became only the 5th South African to carry his bat in Tests when he scored 100* against Pakistan in Faisalabad; At Manchester in 1998, he became the first South African batsman to score a double century since isolation, when he registered 210 against England.

GARY KIRSTEN (South Africa)

When Gary Kirsten made his career best score in Test cricket of 210 at Old Trafford in 1998 against England, it typified everything about his game: It was clear that his timing was out initially and that his stroke-play was not as fluent as it should have been for a man who was 98 not out at the close of play. Although he went on to register the first double century for a South African since isolation on the second day, and in good style too, it was the resilience he showed on the first day that was more impressive. Often, when the runs aren't coming as easily as they should, frustration can frequently account for the batsman's eventual dismissal. But in this case, Kirsten defied all the elements that prevented his game from functioning smoothly and exhibited a superior temperament that allowed him to remain unruffled and not only maintain his cool but his wicket as well. This batting display wasn't typical of his true skill, for he is a much better player than spectators were led to witness here; although the mental side of this innings did exemplify Gary Kirsten's approach to Test cricket. "It was a real highlight," he admits. "We get a lot of stick at the fact we aren't the greatest batting side, so in that respect it was satisfying. The likes of Graeme Pollock, Jimmy Cook and Barry Richards have honed in to us just how important it is to score big hundreds - not just small hundreds - so that was another reason to feel pleased."

There are several aspects that have contributed to Gary Kirsten ascending the Test cricket ladder. For he has seized on the opportunities that have come his way, which he knew could only further his education of the game. The lessons he learned from former South Africa captain, Kepler Wessels, were imperative to him, he feels. "It's been a dream to play Test cricket. It takes a lot of hard work and determination. Probably the greatest thing I have ever heard was from Kepler. He instilled into us that success in cricket comes from hard work. Seeing him average fifty every season just proved to us all that his work ethic was so important in his success. His determination and mind-set was an inspiration to me." Add to this the experience and education he received from playing with ex-West Indies opener Desmond Haynes at Western Province, and you have a cricketer that has been lavishly treated with sound advice, though it speaks volumes for Kirsten's professionalism and eagerness to improve in receiving all such advice appreciably. On Haynes he commented: "He's a legend. When we batted together it was almost like chalk and cheese. He was brilliant for my cricket; he was just so experienced as he'd seen it all before and he told me what to expect, from the quicks, spinners, whatever. His presence at the wicket made it easier for me and I benefited so much from the time I played with him, and so did guys like Kallis, Ackerman and Gibbs." These were the greatest influences on Kirsten's Test career, though further words of wisdom from another legend of Test history influenced his batting even more. He revealed: "I will never forget the words that Sunil Gavaskar told me: 'The first hour of the innings give to the bowler, then take the next ten yourself'."

Gary began his Test career at Melbourne in 1993-94 against a strong Australian attack of McDermott, Reiffel, Warne and May, though ironically it was the lesser-threat of Mark Waugh's bowling that accounted for his first dismissal in the arena when he had scored just 16. It wasn't the easiest baptism he could have had; on the contrary. "To make your debut against the best team in the world is not easy. It was a tough tour, but I learnt so much about batting." Kirsten believes Crag McDermott, Shane Warne and later Glenn McGrath have been the toughest bowlers he's ever faced in Tests, added to the left-arm of Wasim Akram; though he acknowledges he has yet to confront the West Indies in Test cricket and realises the challenge of Ambrose and Walsh is likely to be a tough one. In his second Test at Sydney, his scores of 67 and 41 reflected his consistent Test form for a long time to come. It wasn't until his 17th match, though, that he first reached three figures. However, he feels consistency is more important than posting occasional centuries in sporadic fashion. "To stay in the team you have to keep contributing. Everybody talks about getting hundreds, but it's no good getting a century then not scoring for another eight innings. I have made a lot of forties, fifties and sixties and though you could say I should have scored more centuries, at least I am contributing consistently."

When Kirsten did score his maiden Test century of 110 in Johannesburg in 1995-96 against England, it not only relieved the mounting pressure on him to do so, but it answered questions about his own game that he himself wanted to know. The memory of Devon Malcolm's blistering spell of quick bowling of 9-57 at The Oval in 1994 had left physical and mental scars on the South Africans, which they were all eager to remove, especially Kirsten. "It was a great relief because a lot of people were telling me that I needed to get a Test hundred. Although I was still making runs, the hundred was eluding me. It was particularly nice to get back at Devon Malcolm also. When he ripped through us at The Oval, he put doubts in all our minds as to whether we had it in us to hack it at that level. But it was fortunate that it happened at the end of the tour because it gave us time to regroup and prepare for next time. I was glad that Devon played in the game at Johannesburg because I wanted to take him on and prove to myself that I could handle it in Test cricket."

From then on, the centuries became more frequent for Gary, and this was evident in South Africa's following series in 1996-97 in India. At Calcutta in the second Test match, he struck a hundred in each innings (102 & 133) to set up a fine victory for his team while earning the man of the match award, which remains a memory he cherishes. "Apart from the 200 at Old Trafford, that will go down as my best highlight. There were 90,000 people in the ground every day and it was nice to do superbly well. Lance Klusener got eight wickets in the second innings to help win the game and still didn't get man of the match, so that says a lot about my achievement." Deriving from a country that is renowned for its hard, fast wickets, there were plenty of doubters speculating about South Africa's deficiencies in handling the Indian spinners on their home, custom-made pitches. However, Kirsten was fearless about such a proposition. "Initially, as a team, we struggled against the spinners in the subcontinent, but we got better the more we played against them. Personally though, I have always regarded myself as a good player of spin." A comment which can be justified by his performances against Shane Warne, the man he rates as the best spin bowler he has ever faced. From their experiences out in the middle, Warne said of Kirsten: "(He's) an important player around whom the South Africans like to build an innings. He has an excellent temperament and has no trouble concentrating in any situation. With such a long and talented batting line-up there is even more need to take early wickets. If Kirsten can dig in and prevent that then you can be in trouble." Gary said: "I have enjoyed my battles with Shane Warne. I am fortunate that by the time Shane comes on, I have usually got a few runs on the board and set, even if he comes on early. Still, it's a great challenge. He's the best spinner I've played against and it's pleasing to do well against him. I'd say he's got me a few times and I've got him a few times." One of those occasions when Gary 'got him', was at Adelaide on the 1997-98 tour. South Africa needed to win the Test in order to level the series. Kirsten did everything in his power to ensure that happened when he registered 77 and 108 not out, though it took a fighting 169 not out from Mark Taylor to save the match. Says Gary, "They have this honours board there at Adelaide for when you score a hundred and I was determined to get my name on the board, along side some of the great players already listed on it." Past greats like Bradman, Hutton, Compton, Harvey, Pollock and Kanhai are all scrolled on the honours board and Kirsten's determination to achieve the feat, means he now accompanies such an illustrious crop of Test legends.

The series prior to that Australian tour was a hard fought contest with Pakistan in the subcontinent. After two drawn Tests at Rawalpindi and Sheikhupura, the tenacity of the Western Province opener set up a dramatic triumph at Faisalabad in the third Test and helped to give South Africa their first ever series victory on Pakistan soil. In the first innings, the South Africans found themselves in desperate trouble at 99 for seven at lunch. Kirsten stood alone in defying the strong Pakistan attack of Akram, Younis, Mushtaq, Mahmood and Saqlain. He was then joined by spinner Pat Symcox who counter-attacked to score a 94-ball 81 in a 124-run eighth-wicket partnership. Eventually, South Africa were bowled out for 239 with Gary becoming only the fifth South African batsman to carry his bat in Tests with his 100 not out. This was a vital contribution to the victory, though Shaun Pollock's 5-37 was equally important in dismissing Pakistan in their second innings for just 92 when chasing 145. "That would be one of my greatest highlights," says Gary. "Those runs were crucial in the game, though it took a great bowling performance from Shaun Pollock as well." These exhibitions of fight and resilience trademark the game of Gary Kirsten, who can plunder the strongest of attacks in any conditions, but is more familiar battling with a cause. These situations unearth the greatest qualities about Kirsten who modestly admits, though with a cutting honestly: "I play to the best of my limitations. I work hard at my game and I have the ability to stick it out for a long time. I have never regarded myself as a great talent in Test cricket, but I have done well with what I've got."

GARY KIRSTEN - TEST MATCH STATISTICS

TESTS: 45   INN: 81   RUNS: 2895
AVERAGE: 39.12   HS: 210   50: 15 100: 7

OVERALL RECORD   NB - G. Kirsten has opened in every Test match innings

V AUSTRALIA
TESTS: 12   INN: 22   RUNS: 697
AVERAGE: 33.19   HS: 108*   50: 3 100: 1

V ENGLAND
TESTS: 13   INN: 21   RUNS: 750
AVERAGE: 39.47   HS: 210   50: 4 100: 2

V INDIA
TESTS: 6   INN: 12   RUNS: 459
AVERAGE: 38.25   HS: 133   50: 0 100: 3

V NEW ZEALAND
TESTS: 4   INN: 8   RUNS: 318
AVERAGE: 39.75   HS: 76   50: 3 100: 0

V PAKISTAN
TESTS: 7   INN: 12   RUNS: 92
AVERAGE: 49.20   HS: 100*   50: 3 100: 1

V SRI LANKA
TESTS: 2   INN: 4   RUNS: 165
AVERAGE: 55.00   HS: 75*   50: 2 100: 0

V ZIMBABWE
TESTS: 1   INN: 2   RUNS: 14
AVERAGE: 7.00   HS: 13   50: 0 100: 0

BILL LAWRY - PERSONAL FILE

FULL NAME: William Morris Lawry

DATE OF BIRTH: 11th February, 1937

BIRTHPLACE: Thornbury, Melbourne

EDUCATION: Preston Technical School, Melbourne

PLAYING ROLE: Left Hand Bat

TEAMS: Australia; Victoria 1955/56 - 1971/72

TEST DEBUT: 1961 v England, Birmingham

TESTS: 67

MOST PRODUCTIVE GROUND H: Melbourne, 1023 runs (78.69) in 8 Tests
                                  A: Manchester, 379 runs (75.80) in 3 Tests

FIRST-CLASS DEBUT: 1955-56

FIRST-CLASS RUNS: 18,734

FIRST-CLASS WICKETS: 5

HIGHEST SCORE: 266 Victoria v New South Wales, Sydney, 1960-61

BEST BOWLING: 1-3

NICKNAME: Phant (after his childhood addiction to 'The Phantom' comic character)

PERCENTAGE OF TEST INNINGS AS OPENER: 100%

FOR THE RECORD: Wisden 1962; He captained Australia in 25 Tests; Lawry and R.B.Simpson became the first opening pair in Test history to score double hundreds in the same innings, in a stand of 382 against the West Indies. That partnership was just 31 runs short of the world record set by M.H. Mankad and Pankaj Roy in 1955-56 in Madras; Autobiography "Run Digger" (1966); Has a keen interest in pigeon racing; Has worked for Channel Nine in Australia as a TV commentator for many years.

BILL LAWRY (Australia)

Bill was ideal for Test cricket; he was a very tough man," Bobby Simpson comments, on his regular opening partner for nearly seven years in Test cricket. It would appear to be a compliment of great accuracy, as it's an opinion that all those who saw Bill Lawry play would surely agree with. His fierce determination and desire to occupy the crease was as strong as any in Test history. Opening contemporaries Geoff Boycott, Glenn Turner and Bruce Mitchell were all in the same mould as Lawry in terms of their mental approach - and all have excelled in terms of tenacity, application and fight out in the middle. None, though, can boast a greater level of these qualities than Bill. He thrived on denying bowlers his wicket, as much as he did scoring runs off them. It was this gritty, obstinate element of his batting that people mainly identify with him. However, he could be a very capable attacking batsman when he did accelerate the tempo, aided by a good technique. "He wasn't blessed with the greatest natural talent in the world, but he just worked so hard with the ability he did have that he became a very successful player and he deserved his success," Simpson added. "He wasn't known to be a very exciting player, but I think he was very unfortunate to get that reputation, as he could be a very good attacking player as well as a solid and defensive batsman; his performances on the England tour in 1961 prove that. Bill was one of those underrated players who didn't look particularly attractive but his record is sensational. He's also a great character: Bill's just so much fun, he's a larger than life character. You hear his outgoing commentary on television, and he's like that normally as well."

The 1961 Ashes series that Simpson referred to was Lawry's first tour and was as successful as he could ever hoped it to be. Initially, his call-up came when he was still working as a plumber, a job coupled with his career with his state side, Victoria. Lawry was surprised by his selection for the most prestigious of all tours, but after getting the nod to play in the first Test at Birmingham, all his reservations of the big time soon dispersed as he quickly acclimatised to Test cricket with an efficient urgency. His 57 in the first Test reduced the nerves somewhat for when he arrived at Lord's in the second. His eventual score of 130 set up an Australian victory and a 1-0 lead in the series. The 369-minute innings was a hard-earned century on a lively pitch, facing Fred Trueman and Brian Statham. After England had fought back to level the series in the third Test, Lawry struck another fine hundred (102) at Manchester in the fourth Test to help his side to victory and an eventual 2-1 series triumph. His application in difficult conditions was a study of excellence. His skipper on that tour, Richie Benaud, commented: "Lawry played two of the best innings I have ever seen in the Lord's and Old Trafford Tests of that 1961 series in England; both were wonderful knocks on bowlers pitches."

It was at the end of that series when Lawry and Simpson first opened together in Tests, beginning a wonderfully cohesive opening partnership that benefited Australia throughout the majority of the 1960's. "Bill Lawry and I were lucky that we had styles that differed," offered Simpson. "While he was slow against the spinners, I could take my fair share off them, while he used to get off to a good start against the quicks. We were both very, very good judges of a run, quick between wickets, both very fit and we had total faith in each other." Benaud, who saw the Lawry-Simpson opening partnership blossom from its initial stage as skipper, rates the partnership as one of the best in the history of Australian cricket. "Lawry and Simpson were outstanding, the best Australia had as a pair since Brown and Fingleton and, before them, Woodfull and Ponsford. Their running between the wickets was very good." The most rewarding innings that displayed their understanding and ease with one another out in the middle, was at Barbados in 1964-65 when they put on 382 for the first wicket in a run-soaked drawn game. It remains Australia's highest opening partnership and it was the first time that opening partners both registered double centuries in the same innings (Lawry 210, Simpson 201). In total, Lawry and Simpson shared 62 opening partnerships at an average first-wicket dismissal of 60.95. This allowed the more flamboyant shot players like Norman O'Neill, Doug Walters, Ian Chappell and Peter Burge to play their natural, fluent games, seldom with the burden of a pressurised situation early in an innings."

Bill played his first ten Tests all against England in home and away series'. With two centuries and five fifties, including 98 at Brisbane, it was a solid beginning to his Test career. His consistency continued thereafter: First at home against South Africa in 1963-64, when he scored 157 at Melbourne; further lofty totals against the Englishmen in 1964 including 106 at Manchester and 94 at The Oval; then steady contributions on tour in India. His one and only tour of the West Indies in 1964-65 was a bitter-sweet experience for him. Overall, it was a disappointing time for him, playing in an Australia side that lost the series 2-1, and also personally things didn't go his way. Except, that is, in Barbados, where he scored that 210 and 58 not out. It was at a time when the West Indies pace duo of Wes Hall and Charlie Griffith were firing at their peak, though pace was not something that normally worried Lawry. On the contrary, it more likely served as an added hazard that he delighted in battling against. To prove he could handle this West Indian attack, he scored prolifically at home in 1968-69, plundering 667 runs in the five-match series at an incredible average of 83.37. These figures include 105 at

Brisbane, 205 at Melbourne and 151 at Sydney. His marvellous contributions as batsman and captain helped Australia regain the Frank Worrell Trophy, winning the rubber 2-1. Although Hall only played in two Tests and Griffith three, there was still Gary Sobers and off-spinner Lance Gibbs to contend with.

Against England in 1965-66, he registered a further three hundreds in the drawn five-match series. He was then entering the peak of his career and for England fast bowler David Brown, bowling to Lawry was a laborious and heartbreaking process. Indeed, Lawry's time at the crease in that rubber led Brown to comment: "We felt as though we were bowling against him most of the time." He added: "He had tremendous powers of concentration - that was his major attribute. He knew exactly what his game was about and he stuck to it, playing within his limitations. Bill was pretty well equipped all round. One of his greatest strengths was that he was willing to eliminate mistakes. If he played and missed, the next ball was just another delivery and if it was loose he'd quite likely hit it for four." Lawry was the personification of the batsman who plays each ball on its merit. Despite Brown's compliments, he has not forgotten the other, annoying side of Lawry's attitude. As, in the first match of that 1965-66 series at Brisbane, Brown was sure he had him caught at the wicket with only his seventh ball of the innings. When Lawry never walked and after the umpire gave him 'not out', the batsman went on to score 166 in 419 minutes. The Englishmen promptly aired their opinions to Bill in quite vociferous fashion, but Lawry, unruffled, just absorbed the comments and got on with his game. "We weren't over the moon about it," Brown said, "and we never disguised the fact, but we didn't keep moaning because he gave us exactly what we expected him to give us - nothing. It was good, competitive cricket and Bill typified the spirit of the Australian side." England wicketkeeper, Alan Knott, saw a lot of Lawry behind the stumps and he too felt the Victorian could be a mightily tough opponent. "Lawry was one of the nicest people you could wish to meet but on the field he was fiercely competitive. I have seen him going up to appeal for a leg-before decision when fielding at square leg, and when he was batting he would do anything to avoid been given out, rubbing himself anywhere if there was an appeal for a catch at the wicket."*

Another England fast bowler that later did battle with Lawry, was John Snow, who played against him in England in 1968 and in Bill's final Test series in 1970-71 when bowling at his quickest. Their contests were rarely dull: Snow, full of hostility and aggression; against Lawry, the most hardened campaigner around at blunting the pace threat of any fast bowler. At Birmingham in the third Test of 1968, the Sussex quick hospitalised Lawry early in the first innings,

* Alan Knott, It's Knott Cricket, Macmillan Ltd. (London), 1985

breaking his right-hand little finger. Although, revenge was sweet for the Australian when he struck 135 at The Oval in the fifth Test. Snow, with 31 wickets, continued his good form in the 1970-71 series, which England won 2-0. Lawry, though, remained a barnacle that even Snow struggled to remove; typified at Sydney when Lawry carried his bat for 60 when his team were dismissed for 116 in the second innings, after Snow had given his Test best performance of 7 for 40. "He was that sort of batsman," admits Snow. "He hung around, like Boycs and John Edrich I suppose, though John was probably more aggressive. Bill always used to fight it out. He didn't exactly throw the bat at the ball. Bill was always a very solid player and was an accumulator rather than a hitter. He didn't give much away - he had lots of patience. From my point of view, it was tough bowling to him because he was very good technically and he gave you nothing; he used to make very few mistakes."

Lawry's most painful time as a Test cricketer came in 1969-70 when, under his captaincy, Australia were comprehensively defeated at the hands of a fiercely strong South Africa team just prior to their ban. Not only did Australia lose every Test match in the series, for Bill personally, runs were hard to come by. Apart from his 83 at Cape Town in the first Test, he struggled to find consistency in his batting, though he was not on his own at this difficult time. By now, Bobby Simpson had long since retired and Lawry had installed his Victorian colleague, Keith Stackpole at the top of the batting order along side him. It seemed to be the perfect balance with Lawry the steadying influence to Stackpole's often-offensive style. However, Stackpole believes this partnership was one of the reasons why Lawry struggled towards the end of his career, which resulted in him failing to score a century in his last 14 Tests. "Bill was a tremendous performer for Australia," says Keith, "and he'd enjoyed a wonderfully successful partnership with Bobby Simpson, and I feel that when I opened with him, it adversely affected his game. Quite often, I would get to 30 and Bill would still be on five. Instead of sticking to his own game, I think he tried to keep up (with me) and this meant he then began to play the kind of shots that he wouldn't usually attempt. Also, I was not a great runner between wickets; I preferred to hit boundaries. Bill had been used to running quick singles with Simmo and accumulating his runs, but when I opened with him, I think his game suffered because of these things." Australians will always be grateful to the service that Bill Lawry gave his country, in such a patriotic and determined manner. David Brown acknowledges Bill's shortcomings as a batsman, but knows how important his sort is to a team. "He could be dour and selfish on a good pitch, content to fill his boots rather than get on with it for the team. However, he would rate highly for someone who I would want in my side. If I had him and Boycott to go out at the start of a Test match, I know I could enjoy a day off and watch them place the team in a good position."

BILL LAWRY - TEST MATCH STATISTICS

TESTS: 67   INN: 123   RUNS: 5234
AVERAGE: 47.15   HS: 210   50: 27   100: 13

OVERALL RECORD   NB - W.M. Lawry opened in every Test match innings

V ENGLAND
TESTS: 29   INN: 51   RUNS: 2233
AVERAGE: 47.51   HS: 166   50: 13   100: 7

V INDIA
TESTS: 12   INN: 23   RUNS: 892
AVERAGE: 46.95   HS: 100   50: 7   100: 1

V PAKISTAN
TESTS: 2   INN: 4   RUNS: 89
AVERAGE: 22.75   HS: 41   50: 0   100: 0

V SOUTH AFRICA
TESTS: 14   INN: 28   RUNS: 985
AVERAGE: 36.48   HS: 157   50: 4   100: 1

V WEST INDIES
TESTS: 10   INN: 17   RUNS: 1035
AVERAGE: 69.00   HS: 210   50: 3   100: 4

COLIN McDONALD - PERSONAL FILE

FULL NAME: Colin Campbell McDonald

DATE OF BIRTH: 17th November, 1928

BIRTHPLACE: Glen Iris, Melbourne

EDUCATION: Scotch College, Melbourne; Melbourne University

PLAYING ROLE: Right Hand Bat

TEAMS: Australia; Victoria 1947/48 - 1962/63

TEST DEBUT: 1951-52 v West Indies, Sydney

TESTS: 47

MOST PRODUCTIVE GROUND - H: Melbourne, 523 runs (47.54) in 6 Tests
                                                  A: Kingston, 184 runs (92.00) in 2 Tests
FIRST-CLASS DEBUT: 1947-48

FIRST-CLASS RUNS: 11,375

FIRST-CLASS WICKETS: 3

HIGHEST SCORE: 229 Victoria v South Australia, Adelaide, 1953-54

NICKNAME: CC

PERCENTAGE OF TEST INNINGS AS OPENER: 97.59%

FOR THE RECORD: Brother of I.H. McDonald (Victoria); At Adelaide in 1952-53 against South Africa, Colin and A.L. Hassett put on 275 for the second wicket, which became the highest partnership for Australia for any wicket against that country; With R.N. Harvey, he set an Australian record for the highest third-wicket partnership in Tests - 295 against West Indies at Kingston in 1954-55; Toured Rhodesia and Pakistan with an International XI in 1961-62; Played 60 times for Victoria; On his retirement from cricket, he became one of the leading figures in Australian tennis and had considerable input into the construction of Flinders Stadium in Melbourne, that hosts the Australian Open.

COLIN McDONALD (Australia)

Test cricket is the zenith for all cricketers from all nations. It provides players with the greatest stage possible to display their skill. Their ability can not be judged effectively until they have played at this level in, at least, a handful of matches. So often, Test match baptisms expose cricketers that are simply not up to the task. However, given enough time, some will eventually perform to the required standards when they have adapted to the immense climb from domestic cricket. In the case of Colin McDonald though, he adjusted to the rigours of Test match cricket with admirable aplomb. In his first ten Tests he scored 884 runs at an impressive average of 52; figures which include five fifties and two centuries. Colin had soon masterminded the required formula to conquer Test cricket. "I had a good start and I guess I did adapt well," he said. "Certainly my early Test matches were played in Australia and the West Indies on pitches with which I was familiar. The most demanding feature of rising up through Test cricket is the absolute necessity of intense concentration on every ball. There are many players who have natural ability but there are no successful Test cricketers who are not possessed of great concentration."

He made his debut against the West Indies at Sydney. Australia had already won the series and were 3-1 up with one to play when Colin was introduced with fellow debutantes Richie Benaud and George Thoms. McDonald had opened the batting with Thoms for Melbourne University, so a good understanding was instantly born between them. Colin's greatest examination came against the well-respected spin twins, Ramadhin and Valentine. This was a battle, though, the young Australian always felt confident of winning. "Ramadhin and Valentine were very fine bowlers and had great success, but I seemed to get by against them - excuse my unintended arrogance!" He had been an opener all his life, and, unlike many opening batsmen, it wasn't for the love of facing the quicks; more to do with a desire that had remained with him from childhood, solely to bat "and the best way to be assured of that was to grab the bat first," he admits. "It had nothing whatsoever to do with a liking to bat against fast bowlers. I believe that I learned to handle fast bowling through hard experience - I was probably a more natural player of spin. My innings against Jim Laker at Manchester and various innings' against Tayfield, Ramadhin, Valentine and Gibbs bear witness to this belief." Indeed McDonald did seem to have a preference for the slow bowlers. His stubborn 89 at Manchester in 'Laker's Match' in 1956 took him 337 minutes, on a spiteful pitch that offered great purchase to the spinner, emphasised by Jim Laker's 19 wickets in the game. Another favourable aspect to coincide with Colin's Test debut was his knowledge of the wicket at Sydney. "Batting on familiar pitches is a great help when learning to cope with the ferocity of Test cricket," he said.

Despite scores of 62, 82 and 67 in his first four Tests, the major breakthrough came in his fifth Test against South Africa at Adelaide in 1952-53. He registered 154 and put on 275 for the second wicket with Lindsay Hassett, setting an Australian record for the highest partnership for any wicket against South Africa. He recalled: "Every Test match batsman, to be worth his salt must make a century, and therefore, there was a sense of satisfaction. Much of it was made in partnership with that very great batsman, Lindsay Hassett; a wonderful learning experience. I also remember Don Bradman, then a selector, suggesting that I should be more forceful with my cover drive. Oh to have his ability!"

His name was now generating interest around the cricketing sphere, but it wasn't until the West Indies tour in 1954-55 that McDonald really established himself in the Australian team. The Windies bowling attack may not have appeared the kind of heart-bumping prospect it became in later years, but still, there were players included who were often a competitive match for most opposition: Frank King, Denis Atkinson, a young Gary Sobers and the spin twins Sonny Ramadhin and Alf Valentine all featured. Colin has fond memories of that series. He said: "The Caribbean tour was a watershed for me. It was there that I established myself in the Australian team; never to be dropped thereafter. Our win was remarkable in that we were opposed by Weekes, Worrell, Walcott, Smith, Sobers, Atkinson, Ramadhin, Valentine and others. Mind you, we had some pretty good players in Morris, Harvey, Miller, Lindwall, Archer and Benaud. It is probably true to say that the West Indies team at the time lacked a great fast bowler, despite the rather erratic and wasteful ferocity of King. It was different with the great Wesley Hall in 1961. The batting of the West Indies was, nevertheless, wonderful to behold." Colin amassed 449 runs in the five-match series at an average of 64.14. He scored 110 in the second Test at Trinidad and 127 in the fifth Test at Jamaica. That contribution in Kingston was combined in a 295-run partnership with Neil Harvey for the third wicket, which became another Australian record that McDonald featured in. The left-handed Harvey, a gifted stroke-player who notched over 6,000 runs in his Test career, was a good foil to the right-handed Colin. "It was always wonderful to bat with Neil Harvey. Everything seemed easy with him at the other end. He demolished bowlers when batting well, resulting in a certain amount of rubbish been delivered to the other batsmen."

As Colin acknowledged, he was fortunate to play the first 13 Tests of his career on wickets he was used to. The pitches in the West Indies, where he had fared so well, were not too dissimilar to those in Australia. However, his first conditional transition in Tests was to come on the 1956 tour of England - a country where he had toured previously in 1953 without featuring in the Test series. Despite 78 at Lord's and that fighting 89 at Manchester when Laker dominated, Colin struggled to come to terms with the English wickets, averaging only 24.30 in the series. After touring in 1961 also, his average in all Tests in England amounted to a mere 22.53. He said: "It can be a great leveller when encountering totally different conditions as I first experienced in England in 1953. It was a humbling experience which necessitated some important adjustments in technique and which were to serve me well later on. The most important lesson was that cricket is essentially a side on game - chest towards point rather than towards the bowler."

His record on the sub-continent against Pakistan and India is another subject to debate critically. Both countries are often the 'bogey' team for opening batsmen, given their lack of genuine quick bowlers over the generations, which usually serves against the preferences of most openers. McDonald, though, was a good player of all types of bowling. He believes performances cannot always be judged fairly from the evidence of what is noted in the scorebook. "Playing cricket in India and Pakistan was a negative experience for me. Let me make it quite clear that I enjoyed the countries and the peoples but we played under very difficult conditions, vastly different from today, constantly dealing with indifferent health and poor accommodation. It is churlish to blame the conditions as the excuse because there were certainly some very good cricketers playing in those countries at the time. It does not alter the fact that we played on some very ordinary pitches, including three on the mat; conditions which did not suit me. I have no doubt that, had I the opportunity to play against those countries in Australia, I would have improved my batting average!"

After that triumphant Caribbean tour in 1954-55, he became a regular fixture in the side, though he had to wait four years before his next Test century, following the 127 in Jamaica. His performances were still of a consistent level throughout, which included a 99 in Cape Town, but the three-figure totals were eluding him. That was, until the 1958-59 Ashes series, when his form returned in emphatic style, with 519 runs in the series at 64.87. He made a Test best 170 in the fourth Test at Adelaide and followed that with 133 in the next match on his home ground at the MCG. Not only was it a series for personal celebration, Australia as a team enjoyed a comfortable 4-0 victory in the rubber. Recalls Colin: "An Australian always wishes to do well against England, therefore it was specially pleasing to do well in that series. The difference between the players of today and then was the level of fitness. For the first time in my cricketing career, I made a conscious decision to get fit. I spent three months attending a gymnasium and I have no doubt that that effort was rewarded. For practical purposes we were amateurs, but with the advent of professionalism came an incentive to get fit. I, like many others, would have been a much better player in today's climate."

121

On the 170, an innings which made him the 50th Australian to score a hundred against England, he said: "That was, technically, my best Test match innings even though Brian Statham put the first ball of the match over the top of my middle stump. The following innings in Melbourne gave me a great deal of satisfaction in that it was played in front of my home crowd on that greatest of stadiums, the Melbourne Cricket Ground. The Prime Minister at the time, Sir Robert Menzies sent me a congratulatory telegram." He added, with a great deal of pride: "I must admit to a feeling of satisfaction in opening the innings in Test matches on famous arenas before large crowds." He has much justification to be proud of such occasions. The career of a Test cricketer holds memories to cherish, dearly, whether they are pleasant or unpleasant. Especially the times encountered with the great bowlers. Colin reflects: "The greatest fast bowler that I ever faced was Keith Miller, because he had little difficulty in getting me out in the few times that I played against him. In terms of speed alone, it's hard to pick from Miller, Lindwall, Adcock, Tyson and Statham. The best slow bowler I faced was Hugh Tayfield because he never left you alone, every ball was good and different; a master of flight, spin, speed and accuracy." Richie Benaud captained McDonald in 20 Test matches and he appreciated the qualities that Colin brought to that Australian side. Says Richie, "Colin was a tough opener, not a player of the hook shot, and he often took many blows from the pacemen. He was very courageous throughout his career and a splendid team-man. From the batting point of view he was an excellent cutter and a good driver. His strengths though, were his courage and his ability to read a situation when batting."

COLIN McDONALD - TEST MATCH STATISTICS   ( ) = As Opener

TESTS: 47   INN: 83 (81)   RUNS: 3107 (3073)
AVERAGE: 39.32 (39.39)   HS: 170 (170)   50: 17 (17) 100: 5 (5)

OVERALL RECORD   + = Opened in every innings against that country

V ENGLAND

TESTS: 15   INN: 28+   RUNS: 1043
AVERAGE: 38.62   HS: 170   50: 5 100: 2

V INDIA

TESTS: 7   INN: 10 (9)   RUNS: 224 (197)
AVERAGE: 22.40 (21.88)   HS: 53 (53)   50: 1 (1) 100: 0

V PAKISTAN

TESTS: 4   INN: 7+   RUNS: 174
AVERAGE: 29.00   HS: 44*   50: 0 100: 0

V SOUTH AFRICA

TESTS: 10   INN: 18+   RUNS: 786
AVERAGE: 46.23   HS: 154   50: 5 100: 1

V WEST INDIES

TESTS: 11   INN: 20 (19)   RUNS: 880 (873)
AVERAGE: 46.31 (45.94)   HS: 127 (127)   50: 6 (6) 100: 2 (2)

BRUCE MITCHELL - PERSONAL FILE

FULL NAME: Bruce Mitchell

DATE OF BIRTH: 8th January, 1909 Died 2nd June, 1995

BIRTHPLACE: Johannesburg

EDUCATION: St. John's College, Johannesburg

PLAYING ROLE: Right Hand Bat, Off Break Bowler

TEAMS: South Africa; Transvaal 1925/26 - 1949/50

TEST DEBUT: 1929 v England, Birmingham

TESTS: 42

MOST PRODUCTIVE GROUND H: Johannesburg 655 runs (50.38) in 8 Tests
A: The Oval 448 runs (112.00) in 3 Tests
FIRST-CLASS DEBUT: 1925-26

FIRST-CLASS RUNS: 11,395

FIRST-CLASS WICKETS: 249

HIGHEST SCORE: 195 South Africans v Surrey, The Oval, 1935

BEST BOWLING: 6-33 Transvaal v Border, East London, 1937-38

NICKNAME: Mitch

PERCENTAGE OF TEST INNINGS AS OPENER: 60%

FOR THE RECORD: Put on 260 with I.J. Siedle for the first wicket against England at Cape Town in 1930-31, setting a South African Test record that remains the highest versus England; Added 299 for the seventh wicket with A. Melville for Transvaal against Griqualand West at Kimberley in 1946-47, for another South African record in first-class cricket; Wisden 1936; Holds the record for the most runs in Test cricket for South Africa.

BRUCE MITCHELL (South Africa)

Bruce Mitchell was a combative, uncompromising customer, who made bowlers graft for his wicket. It wasn't the kind of entertainment that crowds love to see that he provided, but if you appreciate tenacity, application and an unwavering will to win, then you would never fail to have been impressed by the way in which this South African went about his cricket. From long back to modern times, the one thing that has always been said of South Africa is their competitiveness and pugnacious approach. Whether it was Ali Bacher's all-conquering unit in the sixties, Kepler Wessels' Test newcomers in the early nineties or Hansie Cronje's talented battlers in the mid-nineties, there's a spirit about the team that was emphasised by Bruce Mitchell all those years ago. "He was a pretty dogged sort of opening bat and difficult to get out," recalls former England bowler, Sir Alec Bedser. "He was certainly up there in the ratings as an opening bat. Although he wasn't an excitable batsman, as he just pushed along at his own pace, he was an effective opening bat. I would call him a good all-round solid player," said Bedser, who dismissed Mitchell in his final Test for 99 at Port Elizabeth in 1948-49. The likes of Mitchell, those with such a non-enterprising but dependable style, never receive the kind of acclaim through history as the more flamboyant batsmen, that are more likely to excite and enthral spectators. This opinion is probably strengthened more in the modern day due to the emphasis on the entertainment factor, summed up by limited overs cricket. Everything is geared around putting 'bums on seats'. Nothing wrong with that, but the more pressing issue is who wins the game. Every side needs a Viv Richards, a Sachin Tendulkar or a David Gower, but there is as much a need to have players in your side who are willing to roll their sleeves up when the going gets tough, or not, and work hard at bettering whatever the situation. Bruce Mitchell was in this category, comparable to the likes of David Boon of Australia and John Edrich of England. Where there's flair in a good side, there should always be a steadying influence too. Bedser continued: "Bruce was a good competitor. He got on with his job with the minimal amount of fuss as we never used to keep shouting like they do today. We played Test cricket in the days when it meant something, as there weren't too many played in those days. Now, there's one all the time."

Strangely, Mitchell began in first-class cricket for Transvaal as more of a bowler, with his slow off-breaks. In his first Currie Cup match at the age of 17 against Border in 1926, Mitchell had figures of 5-23 and 6-72. Such impressive figures might point to the question of why wasn't he a middle-order player given these all-round skills, but the answer is simply that his batting ability was just so much greater than his bowling. This soon became obvious. He toured England in 1929 while still only 20, but he proved himself a shrewd selection and an extremely precocious talent. Although he began the tour as a man unlikely to play in the series, his early-tour performances changed all that. Beginning down the order, captain 'Nummy' Deane gradually moved him up with every promising innings, until he reached the openers position by the time the first Test match rolled around. His scores of 88 and 61 not out on debut at Birmingham showed a young cricketer who was not at all overawed by the big occasion; in fact, he was quite at home, so much so that he more or less became a Test regular for the next 20 years. Although, after a good start at Edgbaston in his first series, in the next four Tests he failed to score above 30, though this was more a minor blip in his career than a serious downward trend.

In his first series on home soil in 1930-31, again against England, Mitchell posted his first Test century at Cape Town after making 72 in the first Test at Johannesburg. At scenic Newlands, Bruce made 123 in an opening partnership of 260 with Jack Siedle (141), which became the highest first-wicket stand in all Tests for South Africa. Witnessed by the towering mountains smiling over him, Mitchell made an impression on spectators that was furthered throughout that series. He registered consistent contributions thereafter of 68 and 74 at Johannesburg once more and 73 in the fifth Test at Durban. The following season he got his first sight of the Australians in Test cricket, and it wasn't a picture he would have remembered fondly, as the Springboks lost the rubber 5-0. Mitchell averaged just 32.20 in the Tests, modest to his standards, though it was enough to place him on top of the South African averages for the series. Although he scored three fifties in the rubber including 75 and 95 at Adelaide, it wasn't a pleasurable time for him.

Drawing on his experience of English conditions from his tour there as a 20-year-old, he enjoyed a very successful 1935 tour that saw him make two centuries in the series. His 164 not out at Lord's in the second Test remains the highest score by a South African in Tests on the ground, and was made in a team score of just 278 for 7 declared. The hundred also helped his country seal its first win in England. After 58 at Leeds and 48 not out at Manchester, Bruce ended the series with 128 at The Oval. He scored 488 runs in the rubber that contributed to an average of 69.71. The Oval proved to be a successful ground for Mitchell again on the 1947 tour, where he scored hundreds in both innings'. His 120 and 189 not out, meant that he emulated his countryman Alan Melville, who had achieved this feat in the first Test of that series. In making these two centuries, he was on the field of play for all but eight minutes of the whole Test match (12 balls); a true reflection of how durable he was. Sir Alec Bedser said: "It was a good challenge bowling to Mitchell as he was tough to get out. I used to get him out caught at the wicket because he never used to move his feet much; he just stood there with a short bat-lift and played the ball from the crease." For a man like Bedser to admit Bruce Mitchell was hard to remove, this comes as a great tribute from a cricketer

126

that played tough, and who is as economical with his praise of former opponents as he was with the ball all those years ago. Alec's kind words extend further for Mitchell than merely his cricketing prowess. He concludes: "I didn't know him too well, but he was a nice man, real nice fellow - a gentleman he was."

<u>BRUCE MITCHELL</u> - TEST MATCH STATISTICS   ( ) = As Opener

TESTS: 42   INN: 80 (48)   RUNS: 3471 (2390)
AVERAGE: 48.88 (56.90)   HS: 189* (189*)   50: 21 (12) 100: 8 (7)

<u>OVERALL RECORD</u>   + = Opened in every innings against that country

<u>V AUSTRALIA</u>
TESTS: 10   INN: 20 (10)   RUNS: 573 (306)
AVERAGE: 31.83 (30.60)   HS: 95 (95)   50: 4 (2) 100: 0

<u>V ENGLAND</u>
TESTS: 30   INN: 57 (35)   RUNS: 2732 (1918)
AVERAGE: 54.64 (66.13)   HS: 189* (189*)   50: 16 (9) 100: 7 (6)

<u>V NEW ZEALAND</u>
TESTS: 2   INN: 3+   RUNS: 166
AVERAGE: 55.33   HS: 113   50: 1 100: 1

MOHSIN KHAN - PERSONAL FILE

FULL NAME: Mohsin Hasan Khan

DATE OF BIRTH: 15th March, 1955

BIRTHPLACE: Karachi

PLAYING ROLE: Right Hand Bat, Occasional Right Arm Medium Bowler

TEAMS: Pakistan; Railways; Karachi; Universities; Habib Bank

TEST DEBUT: 1977-78 v England, Karachi

TESTS: 48

MOST PRODUCTIVE GROUND - H: Lahore, 686 runs (57.16) in 8 Tests
                                  A: Lord's, 316 runs (105.33) in 2 Tests

FIRST-CLASS DEBUT: 1970 -71

FIRST-CLASS RUNS: 11,254

FIRST-CLASS WICKETS: 14

HIGHEST SCORE: 246 Habib Bank v Pakistan International Airlines,
                     Karachi, 1976-77

BEST BOWLING: 2-13 Habib Bank v Railways, Lahore, 1982-83

NICKNAME: Mo

PERCENTAGE OF TEST INNINGS AS OPENER: 89.87%

FOR THE RECORD: Put on 426 for the 2nd wicket with Arshad Pervez for Habib Bank against Income Tax Department at Lahore in 1977-78 in a semi-final, setting a Pakistan first-class record; In 1982, he became the first Pakistani to score a 1,000 runs in a calendar year; In 1982-83 he became the 3rd man to be given out 'handled the ball'; Represented English league clubs - Accrington, Walsden and Tormorden.

128

MOHSIN KHAN (Pakistan)

There can be nothing more inexcusable in sport than a player with boundless, natural talent who fails to recognise his full potential, without the want of trying. In the case of Mohsin Khan, we see a perfect example of such a crime. Blessed with all the strokes in the coaching manual and the deft timing with which to execute them so elegantly, Mohsin's ability as a batsman cannot be fairly reflected by his Test match figures. Good they might be, but could have been so much better with the benefit of a strong mental game to match his undoubted skilful batsmanship. Test cricket is not just about playing shots; the mind plays a greater part in cricket than anything and, sadly, Mohsin was often found wanting in that department. Such deficiencies led to a lack of continuity in his Test career, as he suffered the Test axe on several occasions. His long-time opening partner Mudassar Nazar, who was a player of opposite sorts with a greater desire for cricket, said: "He was never as dedicated as me, that was the trouble with him. He had a lot of talent but not as much dedication. If he had that dedication then he could have been one of the best players in the world. You find that with a lot of talented players; they never give the sport enough time (to get even better). I would tell him that many times and how much harder he should work at his game, but he'd never say anything, he was very stubborn and sure of his own game." This opinion is endorsed too, by former Pakistan captain Mushtaq Mohammed. "He played his cricket in cavalier style and probably played too many shots. At times that style would be effective but it was never consistent enough. He has a very good Test average but I think he was good enough to have averaged even higher." It is no coincidence that Mohsin's greater successes came against the stronger nations of Australia and England. The ultimate test of his ability would have been against the mighty West Indians, but he only opposed them in his three remaining Tests, faring poorly. "At the end of his Test career, he lost his reflexes and got found out by the quick international bowlers," says Mushtaq Mohammed.

His Test match career began with a series of solid, consistent totals of 44, 35, 38, 31, 46 and 41. All innings' were as a middle-order player, due to the opening partnership of Mudassar and Sadiq Mohammed. He never had to wait long though before he assumed the opener's position, where he was able to attack opposition from the outset - forming a more than useful combination with Mudassar, whose steadying influence complimented Mohsin's flamboyance. Despite leaving a useful record behind him in statistical folklore, Mushtaq Mohammed feels the Karachi-born player was never utilised correctly. "I always felt Mohsin was a middle-order batsman; I never felt he had the right technique to be an opener. I thought he was the right player to bat in the middle-order and replace the likes of myself and Asif Iqbal; had he have done that I feel he would have survived a lot more." However, Mohsin recorded some breathtaking scores as Pakistan's opening batsman and none more so than his 200 at Lord's in 1982, which enthralled appreciative spectators from both sides. Taking advantage of a depleted English attack which had lost Bob Willis before the game with injury, Mohsin carved a delightful innings that was pure geometry. His run chart ran riot, with England's most dangerous bowler, Ian Botham, conceding 148 runs from his 44 overs. It was the first double century in a Lord's Test since 1949. Mudassar, his opening partner in that match, enthused: "He was aggressive most of the time but he could knuckle down as well." His runs were made from 386 balls and included 23 fours. That innings contributed heavily towards his clocking up of a 1,000 Test runs in the calendar year - becoming the first Pakistani to do so. The greatest feat from that game at Lord's, though, was Pakistan notching only their second ever Test victory over England - their first coming in 1954. That England tour was an extremely fruitful one for Mohsin, scoring 1,248 runs at 73.41, including 203 not out against Leicestershire, plus 165 retired hurt against Worcestershire and 151 at Sussex.

Australia were a side that Mohsin faced with relish. From his 11 matches against them, he registered three centuries. The first, 135, was made in Lahore against a strong bowling attack of Thomson, Lawson and Alderman, who all struggled to come to terms with the lack of pace in the pitch. At Karachi in the first Test of that series, Mohsin became only the third batsman in Test cricket to be given out 'handled the ball'. Playing defensively to Jeff Thomson, Khan then instinctively deflected the ball away from his stumps with his hand. The two remaining hundreds came a year later in back-to-back Tests in 1983-84. This time, on the quicker surfaces in Australia, Mohsin proved he was more than a flat-track bully by attacking Lillee, Hogg, Maguire and Lawson with merciless venom. He scored 149 at Adelaide and 152 at Melbourne, while tormenting the Australians with his cocky, forceful hitting. Mudassar Nazar believes that attitude was all part and parcel of his game, which helped to create the batsman he was. "The confidence he had in his own ability was unbelievable. I will always remember how we'd pad up together before opening the innings when I would usually be slightly tense, but when I looked at him he was so full of confidence; maybe he was under tension too but he never showed it, as if it never mattered to him. Some people are like that - he was brilliant that way."

MOHSIN KHAN - TEST MATCH STATISTICS   ( ) = As Opener

TESTS: 48	INN: 79 (71)	RUNS: 2709 (2455)
AVERAGE: 37.10 (37.76)	HS: 200 (200)	50: 9 (9) 100: 7 (7)

OVERALL RECORD   + = Opened in every innings against that country

V AUSTRALIA
TESTS: 11	INN: 19+	RUNS: 786
AVERAGE: 43.66	HS: 152	50: 2 100: 3

V ENGLAND
TESTS: 10	INN: 18 (12)	RUNS: 736 (501)
AVERAGE: 43.29 (45.54)	HS: 200 (200)	50: 1 (1) 100: 2 (2)

V INDIA
TESTS: 11	INN: 14+	RUNS: 472
AVERAGE: 42.90	HS: 101*	50: 3 100: 1

V NEW ZEALAND
TESTS: 6	INN: 11 (9)	RUNS: 259 (240)
AVERAGE: 23.54 (26.66)	HS: 58 (58)	50: 1 (1) 100: 0

V SRI LANKA
TESTS: 7	INN: 11+	RUNS: 408
AVERAGE: 37.09	HS: 129	50: 2 100: 1

V WEST INDIES
TESTS: 3	INN: 6+	RUNS: 48
AVERAGE: 8.00	HS: 40	50: 0 100: 0

ARTHUR MORRIS - PERSONAL FILE

FULL NAME: Arthur Robert Morris

DATE OF BIRTH: 19th January, 1922

BIRTHPLACE: Dungog, New South Wales

EDUCATION: Newcastle High School; Canterbury High School, Sydney

PLAYING ROLE: Left Hand Bat, Left Arm Chinaman Bowler

TEAMS: Australia; New South Wales 1940/41 - 1954/55

TEST DEBUT: 1946-47 v England, Brisbane

TESTS: 46

MOST PRODUCTIVE GROUND - H: Adelaide, 640 runs (64.00) in 6 Tests
                                              A: Lord's, 286 runs (71.50) in 2 Tests

FIRST-CLASS DEBUT: 1940-41

FIRST-CLASS RUNS: 12,489

FIRST-CLASS WICKETS: 12

HIGHEST SCORE: 290 Australians v Gloucestershire, Bristol, 1948

BEST BOWLING: 3-36 Australia XI v Tasmania, Hobart, 1952-53

NICKNAME: Art

PERCENTAGE OF TEST INNINGS AS OPENER: 96.20%

FOR THE RECORD: Became the first batsman to score a century in each innings on first-class debut (148 & 111) against Queensland at Sydney in 1940-41; Served in World War II in New Guinea; MBE for services to sport - mostly cricket; MCC Honorary Member; Wisden 1949; A member of the Sydney Cricket Ground Trust; Became a successful businessman (Public Relations) after his cricket career; Became a Vice-president of New South Wales Cricket Association.

ARTHUR MORRIS (Australia)

Few spectators around the St. George club in Sydney, watching a young Arthur Morris in the mid 1930s, would have seen enough potential in the fourteen-year-old to consider him a future Australian batting great - and an opener at that. He was certainly a precocious talent, evident in his playing first-grade cricket at such a young age, but it wasn't his batting skills that originally launched his reputation. Folk would more likely have predicted another Grimmett or O'Reilly in the making, rather than a Woodfull or Ponsford, as it was his ability as a spinner that first impressed the club's superiors. Arthur recalled: "I started off as a left-hand off-spin bowler and I batted last. As I got older and stronger, I gradually moved up the scale. It was Bill O'Reilly who gave me my chance at the top of the order; he thought I had the right technique to become a good opening batsman." Indeed, whatever the great Bill O'Reilly saw in Morris soon proved a shrewd observation, as Arthur's skill rapidly progressed following his gradual promotion up the order and it became more and more obvious that he would open the batting for his country one day. If any former onlookers from St. George needed any convincing, then it came on his first-class debut for New South Wales at the Sydney Cricket Ground against Queensland. The 18-year-old left-hander placed himself in the record books by scoring 148 and 111 in the match, becoming the first player in any country to score a century in each innings of his initial first-class match. (This has since been repeated by Nari Contractor of India and Aamer Malik of Pakistan).

Morris had a strong all-round game and would surely have enjoyed as much success down the order as he did as opener. However, his great strength was playing on the back-foot and the craving he had for short-pitched bowling was often fed by opening attacks - usually to their detriment. Says Arthur, "I liked to hook and cut as I was essentially a back-foot player which, I think, is important if you're an opening batsman." His Australia and New South Wales team-mate, Richie Benaud, rates Morris with the greats. "Arthur was one of the best openers I have ever seen and was the best left-hander. Footwork was the key. He always seemed to be in the best possible position to play his attacking strokes and, if occasionally they were needed, his defensive ones as well." Such a tribute says much for his talent in general, but particularly his offensive streak. Arthur could graft with the best on difficult pitches, though it was his attacking game that most people will remember him for. He was never too keen on just 'hanging in there'. If he was at the crease, he had to be scoring - and more often than not, at a brisk pace. He didn't belong to the old subservient school of opening batsmen who were there to merely take the shine off the ball, so his colleagues down the order could prosper when he has perished. "If you can get past the openers, you know those lovely, juicy spinners are likely to come on, so then you can really enjoy yourself," revealed Arthur, with an unyielding relish. "I loved batting against spinners, especially off-spinners; I liked to get after them. If I could, I'd go down the wicket and get them on the full. Whether you're playing forward or back to spinners, you've got to get on top of them, otherwise they'll bowl a length to you all the time and tie you down." The only time he felt inadequate against a spinner was in 1951-52 when playing West Indies. He said: "I had a bit of a problem with Ramadhin - I wasn't picking him. He wasn't at all slow, in fact he came on to the bat very quickly. I had to go to the West Indies before I picked him," where he eventually made a hundred (111) against him at Port-of-Spain in 1954-55. Benaud agrees that Arthur was totally untroubled by the slow bowlers - who can often prove a thorn in the side of opening bats, that generally prefer the ball coming on to them. "He had no problems with spin. I rated him along side Neil Harvey and Lindsay Hassett as superb players of spin bowling," says Richie.

The Dungog-born Morris, always displayed a positive outlook - a characteristic indigenous to Australians, but it was also a result of an unrelenting self-belief and this confidence was reflected by many exhilarating exhibitions of batting. Opening can be a precarious position, but despite the tension that goes with the territory, Arthur forever maintained a coolness at the crease which allowed him to play his shots, unaffected by nerves. He said: "It is a very nerve-racking business going out to open - it's nerve-racking just going out to bat in general; it's not like tennis or football, you only get one chance, and it's a long walk back if you don't take it." Statistics testify that he made the most of his opportunities at the wicket, in the fact that he scored the same number of centuries as he did fifties (12). It is normal for established Test cricketers to score more fifties than three-figure totals. Whether this is down to the law of averages or whether most players lose concentration or are riddled by nerves when approaching hundred, we don't know. However, it is fact that Morris seemed totally at ease while accumulating *his* runs. "I didn't get the nervous nineties, though I was run out for 99 against South Africa at Melbourne. I didn't get all that worried about it, just took my time. You've got to have the right mental approach and think it's no different than going from nought to ten or ten to twenty. I usually felt pretty relaxed at the wicket; nothing fazed me," he admits. Such honest sentiments could well be misinterpreted as arrogance; on the contrary, Arthur was quietly sure of himself and Richie Benaud describes him as a "modest, loyal, intelligent and extremely helpful and generous man." The one time Arthur does admit to being "a little apprehensive" in a game, devoid of his usual confidence, was on his Test debut in 1946-47 against England at Brisbane. He scored just two and followed that with another low score (five) in the next Test at Sydney. At a time when some players may then have doubted their ability to play at that level, Arthur responded in typically positive fashion by scoring 155 in the second innings of the third Test at Melbourne. From here, his career turned significantly for the better. Adelaide was the venue for the fourth Test, where he hit 122 in the first innings and 124 not out in the second, becoming only the third man to score three consecutive centuries between the sides.

Arthur admits the intensity of an Ashes battle stirred his adrenaline, forcing on him a level of application and resilience that could not be emulated against the other nations. "In my time, England was the main adversary and one tended to concentrate on that more, than playing against other teams," he concedes. From 24 Tests against the auld enemy, Morris boasts an average of 50.73, including eight hundreds. The triumphant 1948 tour of England was Arthur's finest period in his career, scoring 696 runs in the five-match series at a superb average of 87. Even the legendary Don Bradman, the captain, could only muster a *mere* 72 average in the rubber! Given this, it is no surprise the Aussies took the series 4-0. Of the tour, Arthur remembers: "I was playing the best cricket of my career at that time, it was a good tour for me. I liked batting on English wickets and I liked batting in dull conditions; I always preferred that to batting in bright sunlight." Before he greedily amassed all those runs, like a sweet-toothed child alone in a candy store, Arthur had to come to terms with English wickets. He relates: "I had a few problems early on adjusting to the conditions, but I soon got used to them. When I got that hundred (105) at Lord's in the second Test, followed by the 290 against Gloucestershire, I was okay then." That double century was a phenomenal innings - and quite a way to find your feet in a different environment. Sir Alec Bedser, a former adversary who shared many a new-ball confrontation with Arthur, recalls: "He got that 290 at Bristol on a turning wicket, facing Tom Goddard, who was a bloody good off-spinner. The amazing thing about that knock was that he was out by 5.15! He got a hundred before lunch and another hundred between lunch and tea. Arthur played the spinners very well, he used to down the wicket to them."

On that 1948 tour, Arthur is better remembered for his run-scoring achievements in the Test series, which contributed a great deal to Australia's Ashes victory. He followed his century at Lord's with two fifties at Manchester, but his greatest hour came in the fourth Test at Leeds. Requiring 404 to win on the fifth day, it appeared to everybody that all Australia should realistically hope for was a draw, though Morris (182) and Don Bradman (173 not out) eventually proved there really was a third possible outcome - an Australian victory. They shared a second-wicket partnership of 301 in only 217 minutes, creating the highest fourth innings total to win a Test match (which remained until 1975-76 when India scored 406-4 to beat West Indies). "I never thought we'd win that one," recalls Arthur. "We didn't know that we were in a position to win it until after lunch. We knew we had to really get cracking, and when we did that, we could see that we *could* win the game. Up to that time, our main thought was probably saving it more than anything. Everybody else thought we were going to get beaten so it was a great thrill to win in the end, because the press were writing that it was the first win for England against Australia since the war. On a turning wicket, it was a great satisfaction to change their opinions. I saw on the Internet recently that I was bowled a lot of full tosses in that innings - well I made them bloody full tosses! If you've got a wicket that's turning and you can hit them on the full toss, then why not go down the pitch and hit them on the full? The ball doesn't do anything that way. I was absolutely amazed when I read that." Sir Alec Bedser, who was on the receiving of that barrage of runs, remembers the occasion with considerably less satisfaction, still sounding like the fierce competitor he was in his playing career. "It was very disappointing. We dropped a few catches and Norman Yardley made some captaincy errors; he put Len Hutton on to bowl just before lunch and they got about 35 from three overs off him. We handed it to them on a plate really."

Arthur built on his Headingley success by scoring 196 in the fifth Test at The Oval, helping his side to an innings victory. "In terms of being the most responsible and in the context of the game, that innings would be the best of my career. It was a real turner and I had to concentrate very hard." On another day, he would probably have received more adulation for such a finely crafted innings, but this Test match happened to be Donald Bradman's last, which inevitably overshadowed other matters in the Test. Morris was the non-striker when the Don entered the arena, requiring four runs for a Test average of 100. Following an emotional ovation, Bradman was bowled for nought. It was a sorrowful moment. Arthur shared his grief, as a player who had been greatly influenced by the batting genius. Morris reflects: "It was a sad occasion and quite an anti-climax really. Don just put his bat under his arm, like he always did whether he'd scored a hundred or a duck, and simply walked off. I think if that had occurred in today's game, Eric Hollies would have done three cart-wheels and his team-mates would have chased him round the ground, trying to kiss him! As it was, somebody just went 'I say Eric, well bowled old chap.' A little bit different from when the colour televisions came along." Of Bradman, Arthur says, "I believe he's the greatest batsman that cricket has ever seen. Obviously he was at his greatest pre-war, but he was still a great player after the war. He and Bill O'Reilly - my captain at St. George and the best bowler I ever saw, were probably the two biggest influences on my career."

One of the most pleasurable aspects to come out of a career in Test cricket, is the friendship with former adversaries. I once heard Shane Warne say in a press conference in Melbourne that having a beer and a yarn with his old opponents in years to come, means as much to him as taking wickets. These moments are important to professional cricketers and Arthur is no exception. He has maintained a close friendship with the man he considers the best bowler he ever faced - Sir Alec Bedser, and his twin brother Eric. Once a year, they visit Arthur in Sydney, when tales of 50 years ago are exchanged. "No batsman could have batted more against one bowler than I did against Alec," Morris declares. "He used to come on with the new ball and then he'd return later with the old ball - the time I found him to be at his most dangerous when he bowled his cutters. I relished the battle more against Alec than with any other bowler. I respected him and I think he respected me as a batsman. We ended up about even over the years, so we'll call it a draw!" Their battles were riveting, pure theatre. Alec dismissed Arthur eighteen times in Test matches. Says Alec, "I bowled first with the new ball, he came in first, so it stands to reason that you're going to get one of the openers out a fair percentage of the time; well, you ought to otherwise you shouldn't be playing. If the ball was swinging, I used to make it go away from Arthur, which was dangerous, but unlike a lot of bowlers today, I liked to pitch it up just short of a length - get them driving. The stumps are only 28 inches high, so if you bowl too short you're not going to bowl him or get an lbw. That was probably one of the reasons why I got Arthur out so often."

ARTHUR MORRIS - TEST MATCH STATISTICS   ( ) = As Opener

TESTS: 46   INN: 79 (76)   RUNS: 3533 (3381)
AVERAGE: 46.48 (45.68)   HS: 206 (206)   50: 12 (12) 100: 12 (11)

OVERALL RECORD   + = Opened in every innings against that country

V ENGLAND
TESTS: 24   INN: 43+   RUNS: 2080
AVERAGE: 50.73   HS: 206   50: 8   100: 8

V INDIA
TESTS: 4   INN: 5 (4)   RUNS: 209 (109)
AVERAGE: 52.25 (27.25)   HS: 100* (47)   50: 0   100: 1 (0)

V SOUTH AFRICA
TESTS: 10   INN: 17+   RUNS: 792
AVERAGE: 46.58   HS: 157   50: 3   100: 2

V WEST INDIES
TESTS: 8   INN: 14 (12)   RUNS: 452 (400)
AVERAGE: 32.28 (33.33)   HS: 111 (111)   50: 1 (1) 100: 1 (1)

MUDASSAR NAZAR - PERSONAL FILE

FULL NAME: Mudassar Nazar

DATE OF BIRTH: 6th April, 1956

BIRTHPLACE: Lahore

EDUCATION: Government College, Lahore; Lahore University

PLAYING ROLE: Right Hand Bat, Right Arm Medium Pace

TEAMS: Pakistan; Lahore; Punjab; Pakistan Universities; Habib Bank; Pakistan International Airlines; United Bank

TEST DEBUT: 1976-77 v Australia, Adelaide

TESTS: 76

MOST PRODUCTIVE GROUND H: Lahore, 810 runs (54.00) in 11 Tests
                                                 A: Birmingham, 178 runs (29.66) in 3 Tests
FIRST-CLASS DEBUT: 1971-72

HIGHEST SCORE: 241 United Bank v Rawalpindi, Lahore, 1981-82

BEST BOWLING: 6-32 Pakistan v England, Lord's, 1982

NICKNAME: Mud

PERCENTAGE OF TEST INNINGS AS OPENER: 93.96%

FOR THE RECORD: Son of Nazar Mohammed (Pakistan 1952-53); His maiden Test century of 114 against England at Lahore became the slowest ever hundred in first-class cricket (557 minutes); Once held the record for the highest partnership in Test cricket with Javed Miandad (451 v India at Hyderabad in 1982-83). This feat equalled that of W.H. Ponsford and D.G. Bradman in 1934, but still remained the highest third-wicket aggregate until 1990-91; Played minor counties cricket for Cheshire and Lancashire League cricket for Burnley; Recently owned two frozen food shops in the north of England.

MUDASSAR NAZAR (Pakistan)

"There were two ambitions I had as far back as I can remember: One was to play for Pakistan and the other was to be an opening batsman. There was never anything else I wanted to do," Mudassar admits proudly, after playing 76 Test matches for his country. Given such an insight into his earliest aspirations in life, Mudassar can reflect happily on a cricket career where he achieved more than he ever dreamed of. He was born the son of Nazar Mohammed, an opening batsman in the first ever Pakistan Test team, so cricket was always likely to dictate his soul in a country where the sport is almost religion. Having a father of such high cricketing pedigree had a significant impact on his career. He recalls: "My father was a national cricket coach and he would go to colleges and clubs and I would trot along and watch him. From the sidelines I used to pick things up." His father spoke time and again of how a sound defence is the most vital component in the batsman's game, particularly that of an opener. Mudassar absorbed this advice and still preaches that same tune today. "The game-plan is defence, whether you are an opening batsman, middle-order batsman or a tail-ender. If you haven't got the defence you will always struggle. It was drummed into me by my father that your defence must be brilliant if you are an opening batsman and that your wicket must have a cost."

Something Mudassar could rarely be accused of was throwing his wicket away, as he became one of the most reliable players of his era. To his detriment though, his great strength at building an innings was not always appreciated and he received criticism for batting too slowly - a reputation that upset him: "The criticism hurt a bit but I just took it on the chin." The innings that sparked the critics into motion was his 114 in Lahore against England when aged just 21, playing only his second Test. He batted for 591 minutes in total, but the 557 minutes he took to score his century made him a record breaker for scoring the slowest century in all first-class cricket. Inevitably he became a target of criticism for his over-long effort, but the sad aspect of the whole experience was that he was merely batting to captain's orders, yet in carrying them out to the letter he was barracked for it. He said: "This was at a time when some of the leading Pakistan players had joined Kerry Packer and the authorities in Pakistan wanted these guys driven out so they would never play for Pakistan again. They elected a new captain, Wasim Bari, who was one of the best players we ever produced but as a captain he was an amateur. His instructions to me was *not* to get out." This was partly because the attitude of the Pakistan hierarchy was, 'we are not to lose', in trying to prove the team was good enough without their stars who had defected to Packer. The net result, reflected in Mudassar's innings, was that chances of victory were neglected in favour of survival. Mudassar continued: "I distinctly remember just before tea-time, I came down the track and hit a loose shot. Straight away I had these gloves sent to me with the message, 'What are you trying to do? Your job is to stay there.' That is how the slow century came into it." Despite the negative murmurs following that innings, Mudassar extracted only positive things from it. Prior to the game he was a late replacement for Sadiq Mohammed, and to replace such a distinguished player caused him to doubt his own ability. Although the marathon effort at the crease changed all that. "To think that I was stepping into his shoes, made me wonder whether I was good enough for Test cricket. But what that hundred made me realise was that I was good enough and that by sticking around for ten hours I could be part of the team and play Test cricket. Many senior players told me after, that they thought I would be part of Pakistan cricket for a long time to come which meant a lot to me; it gave me self-belief." The century whetted his appetite for further success as he developed a ravenous hunger for runs, when many 21-year-olds might have been content to sit on a sole hundred and congratulate themselves on reaching Test status. Nazar revealed: "Many cricketers only play one or two Tests, but as soon as I played Test cricket I realised it wasn't enough and that to be remembered I would need to score a lot of runs over a number of years."

The sentiments of Mudassar may appear selfish to some, but most opening batsmen who have achieved highly will all admit to a degree of selfishness. Phrased differently it is only mental toughness, meant to inspire the individual to personal glory and usually his team also. Few cricketers have looked as well suited to Test cricket as Mudassar, who was always prepared from an early age to play the longer form. He feels modern-day players are spoiled by the emphasis on one-day cricket, but he does acknowledge that the shorter version improved his game. "One-day cricket made me a better player because I became more inclined to play my shots in Test matches. It made me a more complete player. Nowadays players are geared more for limited overs cricket and when they get their baptism in Test matches I feel there are flaws that wouldn't be there if the emphasis wasn't on one-day cricket so much. When I came into first-class cricket, my game was based purely for Test matches or three or four day cricket, which is what I'd always played at college." Former Pakistan captain Mushtaq Mohammed, believes Mudassar was a great servant to his country and a most reliable and consistent performer. "He proved to be a very productive player for Pakistan. He came into the side as an opening bat and did very well. He was solid and played within his limitations."

The series where Mudassar proved his true ability, that may not have always appeared so apparent before, was in 1982-83 against India in a six-match rubber. He scored 761 runs at an incredible average of 126.83, including four centuries and his Test best 231 in Hyderabad. He remembered: "It all started on tour in

England. I didn't get many runs in the Test matches but I scored heavily against the counties. Then I batted consistently against Australia, before the Indian series. It was a brilliant time for me and probably the peak of my career." His runs inspired Pakistan to a crushing 3-0 series win over the Indians. The rivalry between the teams is always very strong and this was no exception. "The atmosphere is very intense, but the spirit amongst the players has always been very good. It's unfortunate that the crowd get involved, but I feel the more cricket the sides have played against one another the better the spirit has become." Mudassar felt particularly proud to be opposing his cricket hero Sunil Gavaskar, the man he considers to be the best opening batsman ever. Another whom Mudassar enjoyed the battle with was India's most lethal weapon, Kapil Dev, who was by now well on the way to his record number of Test dismissals. "He was a great bowler and he got me out a few times. Kapil's greatest delivery was the out-swinger that went very late; he swung it an awful lot."

The innings that he rates as his best is an intriguing choice, as he chooses not to nominate any of his ten centuries but his score of 50 at Lahore in the 1982-83 series against India. "The pitch was damp and really grassy, unlike most of them in that series. Imran lost the toss and we were put into bat. I distinctly remember him coming back into the dressing room and he was due to bat at seven, but he put his pads and helmet on and took his place in the front row of the pavilion. Mohsin and myself were padding up and wondered what was going on. That what was the best innings I played out of them all, in what was very trying conditions." Trying conditions of another sort were the ones he endured off the field against his enemies within the Pakistan Cricket Board (formerly BCCP). For one reason or another, certain individuals were not Mudassar Nazar supporters and, he feels, this was the main reason why he was constantly moved down the order away from his preferred opening role. For a long time there was a campaign to employ Mansoor Akhtar as opener along side Mohsin Khan, but Mudassar refused to go quietly from the team and his consistent runs ensured he stayed in the side. He remembers: "There were a lot of politics in Pakistan cricket. They couldn't throw me out of the team so I was dropped down the order. I didn't like it but I was just happy to play for Pakistan in any capacity, like Alec Stewart has in the past with England. It was a joke to start batting at six when you're used to batting at one; it's a totally different game altogether. But I found that in my era, batting at six was a doddle. It might have been different 20 years earlier, though, when a lot of good spinners were around and the odd fast bowler coming back into the attack." This is typical defiance from one of Pakistan's great fighters. His additional skill of bowling medium pace, sometimes with alarming success, created further reason to admire a man who achieved all he ever wanted in life...and more.

MUDASSAR NAZAR - TEST MATCH STATISTICS   ( ) = As Opener

TESTS: 76   INN: 116 (109)   RUNS: 4114 (3787)
AVERAGE: 38.09 (37.12) HS: 231 (231)   50: 17 (15) 100: 10 (9)

OVERALL RECORD   + = Opened in every innings against that country

V AUSTRALIA
TESTS: 20   INN: 31 (29)   RUNS: 930 (849)
AVERAGE: 31.00 (30.32) HS: 95 (95)   50: 5 (4) 100: 0

V ENGLAND
TESTS: 18   INN: 26 (25)   RUNS: 858 (858)
AVERAGE: 34.32 (34.32) HS: 124 (124)   50: 4 (4) 100: 3 (3)

V INDIA
TESTS: 18   INN: 26 (23)   RUNS: 1431 (1210)
AVERAGE: 59.62 (57.61) HS: 231 (231)   50: 3 (2) 100: 6 (5)

V NEW ZEALAND
TESTS: 9   INN: 15+   RUNS: 364
AVERAGE: 26.00   HS: 106   50: 1 100: 1

V SRI LANKA
TESTS: 6   INN: 9+   RUNS: 346
AVERAGE: 49.42   HS: 81   50: 4 100: 0

V WEST INDIES
TESTS: 5   INN: 10 (9)   RUNS: 184 (159)
AVERAGE: 18.40 (17.66) HS: 41 (41)   50: 0 100: 0

SAEED ANWAR - PERSONAL FILE

FULL NAME: Saeed Anwar

DATE OF BIRTH: 6th September, 1968

BIRTHPLACE: Karachi

PLAYING ROLE: Left Hand Bat, Slow Left Arm

TEAMS: Pakistan; Karachi; Agricultural Development Bank of Pakistan (ADBP); United Bank

TEST DEBUT: 1990-91 v West Indies, Faisalabad

TESTS: 34

MOST PRODUCTIVE GROUND H: Rawalpindi, 439 runs (54.87) in 5 Tests
A: Colombo (PSS), 230 runs (115.00) in 1 Test
FIRST-CLASS DEBUT: 1986-87

HIGHEST SCORE: 221

BEST BOWLING: 3-83

PERCENTAGE OF TEST INNINGS AS OPENER: 96.49%

FOR THE RECORD: Began his Test match career with a pair against the West Indies at Faisalabad in 1990-91; Played in the 1996 World Cup in India, Pakistan & Sri Lanka; Captained Pakistan in the 1997-98 three-Test home series against South Africa. He managed just 40 runs from five innings, while the team lost the series 1-0; Scored hundreds (145 & 126) against Australia in consecutive Test matches in 1998-99, though Pakistan lost the series; Signed to play county cricket for Derbyshire in 1998, but had to withdraw due to international commitments. He was replaced by Michael Slater.

SUNIL GAVASKAR (India)

GRAHAM GOOCH (England)

GORDON GREENIDGE (West Indies)

GARY KIRSTEN (South Africa)

NAVJOT SIDHU (India)

BOBBY SIMPSON (Australia)

MARK TAYLOR (Australia)

JOHN WRIGHT (New Zealand)

SAEED ANWAR (Pakistan)

Generally, opening batsmen fall into one of two categories: Those who view their role as a mechanism to providing a sound start for the side, with the least amount of flamboyance and the greatest amount of caution (Boycott, Edrich, Turner, Mudassar, Lawry, Atherton). And then there are those who *also* believe their job is to provide a good start, but with little worry of dismissal and more concern for boundaries. The names of Greenidge, Fredericks, Stackpole, Slater, Washbrook, Jayasuriya all come under the latter description, and so too does Saeed Anwar. The scoreboard has so often rattled furiously when Anwar is batting. He is not a player who likes to settle in or adjust to the conditions first. He is more a player that gains in confidence and composure once he sees his total soar early on. The start of an innings really is the battle of superiority between quick bowler and opening batsman, and Anwar feels reversing the pressure on to the bowler is imperative, though his actions appear to be more reflex than premeditated. As one would expect, his methods are never dull. "A Test match shouldn't be boring," he said. "You have to be aggressive and positive and attract the crowd. That is how I always try to play. If you look at the world's best batsmen - Lara, Tendulkar, Mark Waugh and Jayasuriya - you'll notice that they're all open stroke-makers who are never boring."

Saeed is one of the most electrifying batsmen in world cricket, though not at the expense of grace. He plays wonderfully straight and, particularly, his cover drives are as agreeable to the coaching manuals as Koalas are to Eucalyptus. His technique, though used in unorthodox and frenetic fashion, will never upset the purists and it is a style he intends to market around the world to good affect. Anwar's well-defined game derives from his early days before his conversion to an opener. He admits: "I suppose my background with batting in the middle-order has made me a more attacking player; playing shots comes natural to me. As a youngster I liked Gordon Greenidge and Desmond Haynes, but it was Viv Richards that I really admired. He was always positive and good to watch." Although registering a 'pair' on his Test debut against the West Indies, Saeed later proved himself a player that Pakistan could depend on to score runs consistently. The transition to becoming an opener, though, was basically forced on him. Says Anwar, "The Pakistan middle-order has been strong for a long time with Salim Malik, Ijaz Ahmed, Inzaman and Javed Miandad previously, and I never really had much opportunity, so to make the team, I had to open." It has been an extremely successful switch for both Saeed and Pakistan. He averages in the mid-forties in Test cricket, while his form in one-day cricket has been equally triumphant: During the Pepsi Independence Cup in May 1997 contested between Pakistan, India, Sri Lanka and New Zealand, Saeed surpassed Viv Richards' world record of 189 not out for the highest score in limited overs cricket. Playing against fierce rivals India, the explosive batsman from Karachi smashed 194 from only 146 deliveries. The showpiece innings included 22 fours and 5 sixes. In one particular over he struck the hapless Anil Kumble for three consecutive sixes, in an over that cost 26. The skill he has used in which to master the short form of cricket, almost scarred his career. When he made only 23 runs from his first four Test innings', pundits questioned his temperament for five-day cricket. Fortunately, his reaction to the over-eager critics came soon after, when he scored 169 against New Zealand in 1993-94. He recalls: "That innings took a lot of pressure away from me. There were a lot of people who regarded me as just a one-day player, so it was an important innings in that respect. Since then, I feel I've become a good all-round player and I'm happy with my form. In the majority of the Test matches I have played in, I have usually contributed well towards the team. Opening is the most difficult thing in cricket. It takes a lot of concentration, while you've also got to score runs off the quicks."

Saeed has a clear passion for scoring runs, evident in the way he treats bowlers with contempt, dismissing their loose deliveries with a greedy and very thankful flashing blade. His batsmanship lends a great deal to the team's plight, though he does posses long-term targets of a more selfish nature. "By the time I retire I would like to have an average over 50 in Test cricket and an average over 50 in one-day cricket, and I feel that is possible." Who would doubt such aspirations? He has suffered a little with inconsistency at times throughout his Test career, though this is a criticism that can be aimed at any batsman who plays his strokes as freely as Anwar. Players of this kind look terribly irresponsible when they are dismissed early, though we must never forget the many occasions where the likes of Saeed Anwar score so prolifically and quickly, giving the bowlers precious time in which to take 20 wickets. Statistically, his career is a successful one with an average of 44, though slightly intriguing at the same time. He averages 69 against Sri Lanka, 60 against England, 59 against Australia, 52 against New Zealand and just under 38 against the Zimbabweans; but against West Indies and South Africa, just 19 and 23 respectively. These nations, along with his own, are famously renowned for having the greatest pace attacks in the world. Should we read anything into this statistical pattern? It is certainly a fact that when faced with the firepower of Allan Donald, Shaun Pollock, Curtly Ambrose, Courtney Walsh and even Heath Streak, Anwar has exhibited obvious fallibility's. His 176 at The Oval in 1996 was against an England side devoid of their only real genuine quick bowler in Darren Gough. Maybe such a criticism is merely coincidental but as they say, 'the scorebook doesn't lie'. On the positive side, he has shown the ability to adapt to different conditions. This test will be further examined when he tours the Caribbean and Australia, but with a current average of 40 outside of the sub-continent, he's proving a mature and versatile player. His 145 in Rawalpindi against Australia in October 1998 was an innings of great importance to his side, failing narrowly to carry his bat. Eventually, it proved a futile effort in a heavy innings defeat but nobody will forget such an innings, where he proved to one or two that his concentration and stubbornness is as strong as his will to score runs - quickly!

SAEED ANWAR - TEST MATCH STATISTICS   ( ) = As Opener

TESTS: 34   INN: 57 (55)   RUNS: 2551 (2547)
AVERAGE: 45.55 (47.16) HS: 176 (176)   50: 16 (16) 100: 8

OVERALL RECORD   + = Opened in every innings against that country

V AUSTRALIA
TESTS: 5   INN: 9+   RUNS: 604
AVERAGE: 67.11   HS: 145   50: 3 100: 2

V ENGLAND
TESTS: 3   INN: 6+   RUNS: 362
AVERAGE: 60.33   HS: 176   50: 2 100: 1

V NEW ZEALAND
TESTS: 5   INN: 8+   RUNS: 418
AVERAGE: 52.25   HS: 169   50: 1 100: 2

V SOUTH AFRICA
TESTS: 7   INN: 12 (11)   RUNS: 279 (279)
AVERAGE: 23.25   HS: 118 (118)   50: 1 (1) 100: 1 (1)

V SRI LANKA
TESTS: 4   INN: 6+   RUNS: 415
AVERAGE: 69.16   HS: 136   50: 4 100: 1

V WEST INDIES
TESTS: 4   INN: 5+   RUNS: 96
AVERAGE: 19.20   HS: 65   50: 1 100: 0

V ZIMBABWE
TESTS: 6   INN: 11 (10)   RUNS: 377
AVERAGE: 37.70 (41.88) HS: 81 (81)   50: 4 100: 0

NAVJOT SIDHU - PERSONAL FILE

FULL NAME: Navjot Singh Sidhu

DATE OF BIRTH: 20th October, 1963

BIRTHPLACE: Patiala, Punjab

EDUCATION: Punjab University (Law Graduate)

PLAYING ROLE: Right Hand Bat

TEAMS: India; Punjab 1981-82 -; North Zone -;

TEST DEBUT: 1983-84 v West Indies, Ahmedabad

TESTS: 49

MOST PRODUCTIVE GROUND - H: Bangalore, 376 runs (94.00) in 3 Tests
A: Colombo (SSC), 231 runs (57.75) in 2 Tests

FIRST-CLASS DEBUT: 1981-82

HIGHEST SCORE: 286 Indians v Jamaica, Kingston, 1988-89

NICKNAME: Sherry

PERCENTAGE OF TEST INNINGS AS OPENER: 87.83%

FOR THE RECORD: After playing his first two Test matches in 1983-84, Sidhu did not play in Test cricket again until 1988-89; In 1997 in Trinidad against West Indies, he scored 201, which became the second-slowest double century on record. It took him 671 minutes to compile. (Brendon Kuruppu of Sri Lanka holds the record with 777 minutes); From March 1997 to March 1998, Sidhu registered 1,061 Test match runs at 58.94. This equates to more than a third of his total Test runs scored in 12 months, from a current 15-year career; A devout Sikh, he is famous world-wide for playing his cricket in a turban.

NAVJOT SIDHU (India)

For someone that entered the cricket arena like a Roman slave set to confront the lions in the Coliseum, Navjot Sidhu has fared exceptionally well. So many Test cricketers speak of how their childhood dream was to play cricket professionally or to represent their country, but in the case of Sidhu, he is an exception to the rule. His introduction to cricket was more forced than voluntary. "There was a tremendous influence on my cricket career by my father, he was the one who brought me into this game," Sidhu admits. "In fact, my father coaxed me into cricket because I was never interested in the game. He was so adamant that his son would be an international sportsman - he thrust the sport on me, and gradually to prove points for my father's sake I began to like it and enjoy the challenge." Navjot's father, Bhagwant Singh Sidhu, passed away before his son really made his name in Test cricket, but by that time Sidhu junior began to show signs that he would eventually become the great Indian batsman that Bhagwant had so wanted. "All my cricket, right from childhood to where I am now, I give as a tribute to my father. It's a dream that he visualised for me that I am now fulfilling. Although I didn't like the sport initially, when he passed away, I played for his sake to keep his dream alive."

Sidhu's elevation in world cricket in recent years has been a relatively sudden one. He is an enigma in Test cricket to think that he began his India career in 1983-84, remains a regular today, and yet has only played 49 Tests. Compared with Mohammed Azharuddin who began in 1984-85 and now has 92 Tests to his name, Sidhu's regular absences through that time would seem peculiar given his undoubted talent, but it is not something that overly concerns him. "I've had my ups and downs and a lot of injuries in my career, but I've taken things in my stride and learned to come back when the chips are down, to fight it out," he says positively. As he talks, his positive outlook on life is so apparent and it becomes clear to see why he has fought back from these frequent times of adversity. "In cricket you have good times and bad times. It's the game of glorious uncertainty. You've got to persist with the game and work hard on your weaknesses and keep learning every day. Each day in cricket is a learning experience. The moment one feels he's perfect will spell his doom."

He originally came into the Test side after scoring 122 against the touring West Indians at Amritsar. This performance earned his selection to play against the West Indies in Ahmedabad. It was an extremely difficult baptism for a teenager, to be thrown in at the deep end to face the world's quickest and most fearsome bowling attack. Not surprisingly, he sank under the weight of the great expectancy thrust upon him, making just 15 and 4. Sadly, media reaction was not as understanding as those close to him. "I was very green at that point; 18-years-old and under tremendous pressure, so I didn't play my natural game. Getting tags in Indian cricket is very common and I was then labelled 'The Strokeless Wonder' by a journalist. My father was very dejected about that article. I then felt that I had to prove that Bhagwant Singh Sidhu's son had it in him to really cut it against the quickies; so I cut out that article and stuck it on my wardrobe. Every morning I would glimpse at this article. I kept it in mind because it was something that hurt me. For three years of my life thereafter, from '83 to '86, I slogged it out and worked eight to ten hours a day to get back in the India side." Eventually, his second chance did come, against New Zealand in 1989 at Bangalore. Batting at number three, he announced his return to the side in style by scoring 116 and 43 not out. "I particularly enjoyed the challenge against Richard Hadlee," Sidhu reveals.

From that breakthrough against the Kiwis came the toughest test of all for Sidhu later that season - a tour of the Caribbean against Viv Richards' world champions. By this time he had endured the lonely wilderness of Test isolation for long enough and Navjot was now determined to prove a point against the same team that triggered his downfall as an 18-year-old five years previously. He said: "The West Indies are a big challenge and it's a feather in your cap if you can score runs against what is probably the fastest bowling attack in the world. You need guts and a good temperament to stand up against a West Indian attack." These were qualities he exhibited that series. At Bourda, Guyana, he made an assured 42 not out, and for the first time in his Test career he was given an extended chance in the opener's berth. Although he scored only 29 runs in his next four innings', he ended the series on a high note in Jamaica, striking a brave 116 against Ambrose, Bishop, Walsh and Marshall. "That's probably the best innings I've ever played in my life," he said. "The wicket was very fast and had uneven bounce, but most importantly the bowling attack was exceptional. It was a fearsome bowling attack and to get a hundred against them...well, I still treasure it. More than concentration it needed guts to stay out there, take a few blows and fight on. Ian Bishop, in those days, was the fastest bowler I've ever faced." Sidhu continued his relish for taking on the West Indies in 1994-95, scoring 107 and 76 at Nagpur, and his best Test knock in 1997 of 201 at Port-of-Spain, which was the second slowest double century recorded. Only Sri Lanka's Brendan Kuruppu had taken longer to reach 200 (777 mins) than Sidhu (671 mins). "Occupancy of the crease was very important in that Test match," he said. "I needed to stay there and kill time. That was a big one and another innings I treasure, but it doesn't compare to the innings in Jamaica because it was a flat track with no bounce and a dull game."

Trying to sum up Sidhu's approach as a batsman is a complicated business. Just when you think he is a defensive player that absorbs all the hostility out of a bowling attack like a sponge, he will then play the most enterprising and entertaining innings you'll ever see. His cover driving, square cutting, on driving and pulling are all shots he executes superbly, while his lofted drives against the spinners shows a man in complete control. When asked if he has any particular game-plan, he answers in such a self-assured and organised manner that leads one to feel he has studied the art of the opening batsman and arrived at the best formula possible. "Basically I feel that an opening batsman has to bat through sessions, which is very important; important for any team that if you don't lose a wicket in the first session and the foundation is good, the batsmen coming in later can really build on it." The specifics of his role against the various bowlers are also something he is sure of. "With pace bowlers, you have to grind them initially. Give them the first hour when the ball is new, you should be cautious, then you can take the next five...see, easy."

On the slower bowlers he commented: "The spinners, though, need to be dominated. A spinner should be guessing where to bowl to you and you should be guessing where he's going to bowl. If you try to play them from the crease, they will have a line of attack and a length to keep you pegged down. But once you step out, they'll either be pitching it short or full. You've got to put the pressure on them, if you don't they'll be at you." During the recent 1997-98 series in India against Australia, Sidhu's aggression at the top of the order, particularly against the spinners, was a significant reason in his team's 2-1 series victory. The opposing captain, Mark Taylor, said of him: "He's the most attacking opening batsman that I've ever seen of spin bowling - he just goes after it. He was as big a thorn in our side as Tendulkar. He got India off to a start every time and really put us on the back foot." Former Indian wicketkeeper, Farokh Engineer, is another admirer of Sidhu's method against the slower bowlers. "He plays them very well and is still controlled when being aggressive. Indian batsmen face that many spinners in India that it becomes so easy for the top players."

The only series that Sidhu has played against rivals Pakistan, was in 1989-90, away from home soil. Competition between the sides is fierce and the cricket is played hard, though the off-the-field spirit is very healthy between the teams. Navjot enjoyed the series, scoring three very good fifties after beginning the rubber with a duck. He recalls: "It was a big challenge for Imran Khan - he really wanted to beat us, so he had the wickets prepared accordingly. Apart from Lahore (the first Test and the only match where Sidhu failed to notch a fifty) which was flat, the other three pitches were very green and very fast." The four-match series was drawn 0-0, though India were in a precarious position in the final Test in Sialkot, but Sidhu played a fighting innings to save the day. "That 97 is my other most cherished innings," he reveals. "We were 38 for four and me and Sachin had to bat for a very long time and battle it out to save the match." His 97 in Sialkot is one of four occasions where Sidhu has been dismissed in the nineties. Some batsmen have a distinct problem with the tension when approaching three figures, though this effervescent Indian refutes any such claim directed at him. "I might have a few sleepless nights when I've retired, but it's all part of the game and you've got to carry on. It's not a question of nerves or concentration, it's just bad luck; you can get a good ball at any time."

Navjot Singh Sidhu has toured England twice and both trips proved troublesome for him. The latter one in 1996 saw him return to India some two months before the rest of the squad, after a personal conflict with team officials. This is something that he has put well behind him and he harbours no ill feeling or regrets about the events. As he says, "I don't look back or forward, I take life in day-tight compartments and try to live life to the full and enjoy the moment." The 1990 tour was slightly less eventful, though it was still a difficult time in terms of run scoring. He made just 56 runs from five knocks, dismissed on each occasion by Angus Fraser. The tall Middlesex seamer exposed deficiencies in Sidhu's game, but being the professional he is, it was a weakness that was soon addressed and rectified. "Technically, I wasn't equipped (to play him). I was going forward too soon and my weight transfer was all wrong. Shortly after I was dropped and I then watched videos of myself repeatedly and discussed them with Kapil Dev, Mohinder Amarnath and Sunil Gavaskar. All of them told me that my balance was wrong, which is why Angus Fraser gave me a lot of problems with the swing he was getting."

There have been more good times, though, for Sidhu to reflect on his career, than bad: Like the consecutive series' against Sri Lanka in 1997-98. He averaged 52 in the two matches in Colombo, and then averaged 72 in the return three-match rubber in India. Whenever the low points do come, though, Navjot Sidhu will forever be prepared, as his attitude is tailored that way. He said: "I've always been a learner and even today I feel that I don't know the ABC of cricket. My retirement is not far away, but when it comes I'll still be a learner. I've always been a man of limitations, but within those limitations, I work hard - that's my motto in life: To enjoy tomorrow, you have to work hard today," which is as much as this man will disclose as to his plans for the future. Whatever he does, he will leave behind an eventful career that was responsible for making many spectators very happy, which is not bad for a guy that didn't like cricket!

TESTS: 49   INN: 74 (65)   RUNS: 3154 (2863)
AVERAGE: 43.80 (44.73)   HS: 201 (201)   50: 15 (15) 100: 9 (8)

OVERALL RECORD   + = Opened in every innings against that country

V AUSTRALIA
TESTS: 6   INN: 10+   RUNS: 443
AVERAGE: 44.30   HS: 97   50: 4 100: 0

V ENGLAND
TESTS: 6   INN: 9+   RUNS: 291
AVERAGE: 32.33   HS: 106   50: 1 100: 1

V NEW ZEALAND
TESTS: 7   INN: 10 (3)   RUNS: 431 (159)
AVERAGE: 47.88 (53.00)   HS: 116 (98)   50: 2 (2) 100: 1 (0)

V PAKISTAN
TESTS: 4   INN: 7+   RUNS: 269
AVERAGE: 38.42   HS: 97   50: 3 100: 0

V SRI LANKA
TESTS: 11   INN: 13+   RUNS: 935
AVERAGE: 71.92   HS: 131   50: 3 100: 4

V WEST INDIES
TESTS: 13   INN: 22 (20)   RUNS: 718 (699)
AVERAGE: 34.19 (36.78)   HS: 201 (201)   50: 1 (1) 100: 3 (3)

V ZIMBABWE
TESTS: 2   INN: 3+   RUNS: 67
AVERAGE: 22.33   HS: 61   50: 1 100: 0

BOBBY SIMPSON - PERSONAL FILE

FULL NAME: Robert Baddeley Simpson

DATE OF BIRTH: 3rd February, 1936

BIRTHPLACE: Marrickville, Sydney

EDUCATION: Tempe Intermediate High School, Sydney

PLAYING ROLE: Right Hand Bat, Leg Break Googly Bowler, Slip fielder

TEAMS: Australia; New South Wales 1952/53 - 1977/78; Western Australia
        1956/57 - 1960/61

TEST DEBUT: 1957-58 v South Africa, Johannesburg

TESTS: 62

MOST PRODUCTIVE GROUND H: Adelaide, 805 runs (73.18) in 6 Tests
                         A: Manchester, 370 runs (123.33) in 2 Tests
FIRST-CLASS DEBUT: 1952-53

FIRST-CLASS RUNS: 21,029

FIRST-CLASS WICKETS: 349

HIGHEST SCORE: 359 New South Wales v Queensland, Brisbane, 1963-64

BEST BOWLING: 5-33 Australians v Glamorgan, Swansea, 1964

NICKNAME: Simmo

PERCENTAGE OF TEST INNINGS AS OPENER: 63.06%

FOR THE RECORD: His 311 in 1964 is the highest score in an Old Trafford Test,
and was the highest by a Test captain. It remains the third highest score in a Test
match by an Australian behind M.A. Taylor and D.G. Bradman; Wisden 1965;
Retired in 1968-69, but returned in 1977-78 to captain NSW and Australia;
Captained Australia in 39 Tests; Was a prolific slip fielder. His 110 catches in 62
Tests compares favourably to W.R. Hammond's 110 in 85; Former Australian
coach; Technical advisor for India from 1997-98.

BOBBY SIMPSON (Australia)

This pugnacious, talented Australian was born to open the batting. Added to his qualities as a superior slip fielder and a more than useful leg spinner, Bobby Simpson possessed the most determined temperament that a Test cricketer could hope to have. Although he could exploit the weakest of attacks with merciless venom and excel on the most docile of pitches with a punishing attacking game, he was never more in his element than when there was a plight to battle for. His overall Test batting average was an impressive 46.81, though his 55.56 average as opener proves he was far more effective when given the responsibility of opening the innings. In fact, Simpson began his Test career in 1957-58 at Johannesburg in the middle-order, but after making 60 and 23 not out on debut, he struggled to get going initially. In his next five Tests he managed just 53 runs, and this barren spell resulted in him being dropped for the next two years. His breakthrough came in the home series against the West Indies in 1960-61, when he scored 445 runs in the five-match series and averaged a fraction under 50. This was at a time when Wes Hall was a terrifying proposition, as he usually was, though Simpson relished the challenge. He said: "The first time I came across Wes was for an Australian XI against the West Indians at Perth. Colin McDonald was playing and he opened with me and he took strike. The first ball from Wes not only bounced over Colin's head but also the wicketkeeper's head and it half-volleyed the boundary fence. Colin looked up and said, 'Oh shit!' That was the first time that I appreciated just how quick he was. When I faced Charlie (Griffith) a few years later, I found that he could bowl a quicker spell, but Wes was consistently quicker. Even at the end of a day's play, Wes would still come steaming in at you. He didn't say a lot but he certainly let you know he was there. We are still great mates, and even recently when I was coaching Bermuda, we got together and chatted. Out of the blue, Wes said to me, 'Bobby, I could never hit you could I?' I said, 'Have you waited 30 years to tell me that?' He said, 'I used to get everybody else but I couldn't hit you!' And don't forget in those days we never had the front foot rule or the leg side fielding restrictions, so they could go as close as they liked to a 'Bodyline' fielding plan. And with the front foot rule, they were really bowling a metre closer to you than they do today."

Bobby was famous for his personalised way of coping with quick bowling and he profited significantly from his ability to keep his eye on the ball, whether hooking or letting the bouncers go by unchallenged. "I always believed that if you didn't hook you shouldn't get hurt," said Bobby. "I always swayed inside or outside of the ball if I wasn't going to hook and I found that if you got out of the way easily, it frustrated bowlers. Basically, if you watch the ball, you can't get hit on the head. The people that get hit today are the ones who are ducking out of the way and taking their eyes off the ball. When we played we never wore helmets and I reckon there are more injuries nowadays because of that; people take their eye off the ball. We became accustomed to handling it and knew we *had* to watch the ball." Often, when opening batsmen take on the most sharpest of bowlers around, the kind that are a genuine health hazard, in their obduracy, tenacity and courage, it is easy to assume that these batsmen enjoy the battle, though as far as Simpson goes, this would be a distorted interpretation. "I'm not a mad-man," he announced coolly. "Only crazy people say they enjoy facing fast bowlers. Anybody that says they enjoy facing fast bowlers, I think you've got to doubt their sanity. The great pleasure is succeeding against them. When you've had a good day, you know you've really achieved something. Roy Marshall summed it up pretty well when he said one day, 'There are two mad-men that play this game. The fast bowler, because who wants to run that fast on a hot day and use up all that energy, and the opening batsman, who's got to be mad to face a mad-man'!"

After a promising comeback in the Test arena against the West Indies when he exhibited his mettle as an opener, Simpson was adversely affected once more on his first Ashes tour in 1961, when he was asked to bat down the order. "That was unfortunate because I was probably the best opener in Australia at that time," says Bobby, "but I was also a pretty good leg spin bowler. We had a lot of injuries, and when Richie (Benaud) got injured, I had to drop down the order to do a lot more bowling. In the first three Tests I batted in several different positions from one to seven. It wasn't until I started opening again that I got runs. When you're up and down all the time it does upset your game. What made it all the more annoying was the fact that I'd had a wonderful season before as opener against the West Indies, but then all of a sudden, I became the pinch hitter; but that was the role I had to play for Australia." From then on, in the main, Simpson opened the batting and this coincided with the most successful period of his career.

Despite consistent run scoring, including nine totals over 70 and three innings' in the nineties, the New South Welshman had to endure 30 agonising Test matches before he posted a century. It was a situation that caused him frustration more than worry due to his consistency. "That was stupid really because I'd been getting stacks and stacks of runs in first-class cricket, but somewhere along the line the hundreds were eluding me. But once I got a hundred I got one regularly after that." In hindsight, Simpson has found reason to explain his century drought. "Sometimes, situations dictate and at other times it's poor concentration at the wrong time; looking too far ahead instead of the ball you're about to receive." When that first Test century did arrive, though, there were no problems with concentration; as, at Manchester on the

1964 Ashes tour when he was skipper, Bobby compiled a mammoth 311. After electing to bat first on a batsman-friendly wicket, he extended his relish of the Englishmen's offerings for an hour into the third day. Within his duties as captain, Simpson was then more concerned with the plight of the side and winning the match than with beating Gary Sobers' Test record or Don Bradman's Australian record of 334. After gaining a 1-0 lead in the series in the third Test, the match prior, Bob was determined to maintain Australia's dominance in the series. However, in reply to Australia's 656 for 8 declared, England ensured a drawn game when they scored 611. On the triple century, he commented: "I always felt that when I did get to three figures it was going to be a biggy, and that was an ideal time to do it. The first day the wicket was very lively and the ball was darting around, but after that it flattened out into a batsman's paradise and it was just up to me to take advantage of it. The very fact that I'd broken through was a huge relief, and once you make that breakthrough, it takes the monkey off your back. I never really thought about going for the record. As captain I had a declaration total in mind and on the third morning I just went out and threw the bat to try and accelerate (the score). I was never good enough to beat a Bradman record anyway; he'd taken half the time to get his score."

To emphasise his good form, and fitness, which is an aspect frequently attacked by pundits looking back at the game of yesteryear, on the tour of India and Pakistan shortly after that Ashes series, Simpson helped himself to a century in both innings' at Karachi. This was at a time when the wickets posed little threat of turn as they do today. "In those days, Karachi was a really easy batting wicket," Bobby concedes. "I'd been there before for a representative team and scored a lot of runs. It was interesting that after that series we had played four back-to-back Test matches after the Indian tour. I have a quiet chuckle when I hear players today complaining at having to play just (two) back-to-back Tests. We played four in four weeks, and that was after a long tour of England."

Only months later, Bobby's Australians were touring again, this time in the Caribbean. Approaching the peak of his career, Simpson failed to score more than 30 in the first three Tests, but when confronted with a 2-0 series deficit in favour of the West Indies, he extracted all his fighting qualities to post a battling 201 at Barbados in the fourth Test, though the game ended in a draw. This score combined in an Australian record first-wicket partnership of 382 with his regular opening colleague, Bill Lawry. "That was badly needed," Simpson recalls. "We just *had* to win that match to have a chance in the series." In this rubber, Charlie Griffith was given his first sighting of the Aussies and he teamed up in a ferocious new-ball attack with Wes Hall. It was

157

a potentially damaging combination that Lawry and Simpson eventually tamed. "By that time, Bill and I had got used to the pace of the wickets and knew how to play Charlie (Griffith)," revealed Bobby. "I was batting a foot outside of my crease and taking an off-stump guard. He bowled from so far wide of the crease that to hit the stumps he had to pitch it well wide of off-stump, and I found that if he let one fly, invariably, it would fly over my left shoulder. Occasionally, he gave you one to square cut. The left-handers found Charlie easier to handle because he bowled it going away from them. For me, taking the off-stump guard was the reason why I was able to handle him from then on." However, the initial duel was considerably more tense and one which Bobby will never forget. "The first ball I faced from him, as he was running in to bowl I thought good, he's just going to have a warm-up. Then all of a sudden my off-stump just exploded, but fortunately the umpire had called no-ball, so I certainly got into line quicker after that! Bill Lawry at the other end couldn't stop laughing as we'd heard about this bloke but we hadn't seen him."

In the home series of 1965-66 against England, Bobby scored what he considers to be one of the very best innings' he ever played in Test cricket. It was at Adelaide in the fourth Test, where he compiled 225 and helped his country achieve victory by an innings. "The interesting thing about that was the fact I didn't play in the first and third Tests. First I had a broken wrist, and then I played at Melbourne in the second Test and then had to miss the third Test through chicken pox, which is a terrible thing for an adult to have. I found that innings the most demanding physically because I probably still wasn't 100% fit. In terms of technical ability, that was as good an innings as I ever played in Test cricket. Bill and I played very well there and very sensibly, just pushing the singles and not doing anything stupid. We frustrated the Englishmen and it got to the stage where the bowlers were screaming at the fielders and the fielders were screaming at the bowlers, as we were happily picking up ones and twos all the time." The following season in 1966-67, Bobby enjoyed a successful tour of South Africa from a personal viewpoint scoring 483 runs at 48.30, though Australia lost the five-match series 3-1. After losing the first Test quite convincingly, in the second Test at Cape Town Simpson displayed his fighting qualities once more in making 153, on the same wicket that Graeme Pollock made a double century. This is one of the striking observations of 'Simmo' - he always seemed to perform when his team really needed something special from him. Times of adversity extracted a little extra from his reserves. "At that time we didn't have a great team," Bobby admits, which meant there was more pressure on him to score runs. "We had lost all the players from the Benaud era just about: Alan Davidson had gone, Neil Harvey had gone, Richie had gone himself, 'Slasher' Mackay had gone, so we were scratching around trying to rebuild. You've got to make the most of what you can do. At that time I had reached my peak as a batsman. Although you may play more responsible and careful, to a certain extent it restricts your shot making when you might have played a bit freer at another time." Such a scenario has plagued other great batsmen, and it is a shame that this kind of talent should be weighed down with worry of team failure if he himself does not score runs. Without the extra concern and forced caution, Simpson might well have been remembered as a more enterprising batsman because he certainly had the ability to be a more flamboyant player.

Bobby played in what was supposed to be his final Test series in 1967-68 against India. He averaged 58 in the three Tests that he played in. He later returned a decade later from the backwaters of grade cricket to lead his country when the stars had defected to the Kerry Packer circus. Prior to his initial retirement, it seemed unthinkable that a 31-year-old player at the peak of his game should retire, but he felt future security for his family was too important an issue to ignore. However, before reaching this decision, he proved what a terrific player he still was, and against a very adept Indian spin attack. "I got a hundred in each of the first two Test matches, and for the first time in my career I threw my wicket away to give someone else a chance; because I knew I wasn't going to England in '68. Before the third Test I said to the selectors that I wouldn't mind standing down as captain but I'd still like to play, so they dropped me and brought me back for the fourth Test, which I thought was pretty rough treatment. I shouldn't have opened my mouth should I! I thought I was doing the right thing but it cost me a Test match." On the details behind his return to the Test arena ten years later, again against India, he commented. "I always fancied my chances against the spinners, and part of the reason I made the comeback was because we were playing against a lot of spinners. I had every confidence in my ability to handle an Indian spin attack even when I was forty-odd. After I retired, I was still making more runs than anybody in club cricket, and it became a standard joke that the chairman of selectors would ring me up and say, 'Do you want to be captain of New South Wales?' (The state wasn't doing very well at the time) Bradman played a big part in my decision. He told me how he played till he was 40 because he had lost six years to the War. His confidence in me convinced me that I still had a responsibility to the game. He had been a great counsel to me throughout my whole career, from a young boy up until I was captain. I also had the advantage of playing Test cricket before and so I knew what it was all about. I was probably a more mature cricketer at 40 than I was at 30. In fact I found that I was outlasting the youngsters at the end of a days play because I was mentally tougher than they were. Quite often, for the last hour of the day, I would take myself out of slip and field at cover just to rouse the guys up a bit!"

It is a tribute in itself to think that Bobby returned from being in the Test wilderness for ten years to come back and captain his country at the highest level possible in a further ten Test matches. Although he batted down the order and though his run-making was not as prolific as it had been when he first retired he still managed another two centuries at home against India. His biggest test came against the West Indies in the Caribbean in 1977-78. This time it wasn't Griffith and Hall providing the bullets, but a four-pronged battery of quick bowlers that helped West Indies to dominate world cricket for a long time thereafter. With the drama of television coverage well established by that time, many assumed these bowlers were quicker than their fast-bowling contemporaries through previous generations, but Simpson refutes this claim. "They were certainly no quicker than Wes and Charlie, or the likes of Gordon Rorke and Frank Tyson for that matter. Once they get to a certain category, they're too bloody quick anyway. The talk that they bowl faster nowadays is just so much rubbish." That tour was a tough one for Simpson given the amount of star players that had been lost to Packer's riches. "It was very difficult going over there with a considerably weakened team and they were at full strength until the World Series took some of their stars like Desmond Haynes and Gordon Greenidge. When we played their second XI we ended up beating them quite easily. It was a very tough assignment with the whole Packer business going on. They were trying to recruit players from my side. On the other side, they were losing their stars; there were just so many shenanigans going on."

After his taste for the big time had again been well and truly whetted, Bobby was happy to continue for at least one more season after the West Indies tour, and given the inexperienced squad forced on Australia, his all-round qualities were badly needed. However, the selectors did not see things this way. "Yes, I would like to have carried on for another series but the Australian board wouldn't back me. Considering they brought me back to help out when the side needed me and my experience, I thought it was strange that they dropped me when the side was still well short on experienced players. As it happened, they went and got beat by India and Pakistan. I know I would have bludged some runs from somewhere."

TESTS: 62   INN: 111 (70)   RUNS: 4869 (3664)
AVERAGE: 46.81 (55.56) HS: 311 (311)   50: 27 (19) 100: 10 (8)

OVERALL RECORD   + = Opened in every innings against that country

V ENGLAND
TESTS: 19   INN: 31 (22)   RUNS: 1405 (1244)
AVERAGE: 50.17 (62.20) HS: 311 (311)   50: 9 (7) 100: 2 (2)

V INDIA
TESTS: 11   INN: 21 (9)   RUNS: 1125 (559)
AVERAGE: 53.57 (62.11) HS: 176 (109)   50: 6 (4) 100: 4 (2)

V PAKISTAN
TESTS: 2   INN: 4+   RUNS: 316
AVERAGE: 79.00   HS: 153   50: 0 100: 2

V SOUTH AFRICA
TESTS: 15   INN: 27 (18)   RUNS: 980 (789)
AVERAGE: 39.20 (43.83) HS: 153 (153)   50: 6 (4) 100: 1 (1)

V WEST INDIES
TESTS: 15   INN: 28 (17)   RUNS: 1043 (756)
AVERAGE: 40.11 (50.40) HS: 201 (201)   50: 6 (4) 100: 1 (1)

MICHAEL SLATER - PERSONAL FILE

FULL NAME: Michael Jonathan Slater

DATE OF BIRTH: 21st February, 1970

BIRTHPLACE: Wagga Wagga, New South Wales

EDUCATION: Wagga Wagga High School

PLAYING ROLE: Right Hand Bat, Cover fielder

TEAMS: Australia; New South Wales 1991/92 -; Derbyshire 1998

TEST DEBUT: 1993 v England, Manchester

TESTS: 40

MOST PRODUCTIVE GROUND - H: Perth, 497 runs (99.40) in 3 Tests
A: Rawalpindi, 219 runs (73.00) in 2 Tests
FIRST-CLASS DEBUT: 1991-92

FIRST-CLASS RUNS: 8,645 (as at 28-3-98)

FIRST-CLASS WICKETS: 1 (Waqar Younis lbw)

HIGHEST SCORE: 221 Australians v Karachi, Karachi, 1998-99

BEST BOWLING: 1-2 Australia v Pakistan, Rawalpindi, 1994-95

NICKNAME: Slats

PERCENTAGE OF TEST INNINGS AS OPENER: 100%

FOR THE RECORD: Had to choose between cricket and hockey as a teenager, after representing New South Wales in both sports; Scored 152 at Lord's in only his second Test match at the age of 23; Was a member of the 1996 World Cup squad in India, Pakistan & Sri Lanka, but he never played a game; Signed to play for Yorkshire in 1997, but had to withdraw when he was selected for the Ashes tour to England; If he failed to make it at cricket, Michael believes he would have studied at university and become a PE teacher while playing amateur hockey as well.

MICHAEL SLATER (Australia)

Michael Slater is an exhilarating stroke-player who enthrals spectators irrespective of allegiance and he sees no reason to consolidate at the start of his innings to merely comply with conventions of the opening batsman. He views a cricket bat as a weapon to score many runs in as little time as possible, as opposed to an implement to defend the stumps for long periods. Having described his impetuous approach to batting, it would be easy to assume that Michael is a loose, irresponsible player better suited down the order. Contrary to such opinion, Slater's Test match average of 45.59 from 40 games testifies that he is as solid in defence as he is fluent in attack. It is no surprise to learn that the exciting and explosive player from Wagga Wagga, New South Wales, developed an intense childhood affinity with the riveting displays of certain batsmen from the Caribbean. He revealed: "My first real hero as a child was Viv Richards because of the way he played. But when I became an opener at 15, I thought the partnerships of Greenidge and Haynes were superb. They were an inspiration to me as a kid and I suppose the way I play now - playing my shots, being aggressive when I can - is in a similar vane to them. I back my technique and if the ball's there I go after it. I don't want to change my game too much, but I am looking to become a player that can always be relied on to go out and get runs often."

Although his attacking game helped provide a good footing to his Test career, this aspect of his cricket was also his undoing in 1996, though somewhat harshly, when he was dropped from the Test team for 16 months. Given that his average was 47 after 34 Tests, few would agree that he was in bad enough form to deserve such treatment. In the four Tests prior to his omission, his scores were 219 (Test best), 62, 13 not out, 0, 15, 44 and 0. Hardly the horror run that merits the chop. However, it is fact and now in the past. Slater responded sufficiently in India in 1997-98 to re-claim his once-regular position at the top of the batting order with Mark Taylor. On the experience, he said: "It was confusing at the time because it wasn't as though I'd had a real bad run of outs, so from that point of view it was hard to work out why it happened and why they wanted to make a change. Matthew Elliott came in after scoring a lot of runs in Shield cricket, but I had the understanding that you didn't get dropped until you had a big run of outs. In every career, a player has his highs and lows, but I didn't feel as though I'd had that low, so it was hard to accept. What made it harder were the people close to me like family and friends saying, 'Why, what have you done (wrong)?' That next season I tried to accept it and I was fighting with myself trying to convince myself that I had come to terms with it, but I really hadn't. It took me the whole season to come to terms with the situation."

The reason for his omission was poor shot selection; which exhibited a two-faced attitude shown by the Australian selectors. His offensive, unorthodox technique was accepted when the runs were constantly flowing, but as soon as he played a couple of poor shots and suffered the embarrassment of a long sit in the pavilion, all of a sudden, Slater became this irresponsible, undisciplined opening batsman. His style of play never changed and yet his average was still over 47! Slater believes there was also a hidden agenda for his dismissal from the team. He feels the selectors were worried about picking a man for the forthcoming series against the West Indies, who was not on top of his game. "Shot selection was mentioned. They got nervous, I think, running into the West Indies series. The Test match before in India I played an ordinary shot and got a duck, after top scoring in the first innings. That shot got a bit of air-play and made the selectors nervous before such a big series." His comeback in India began nervously. In his first two matches back, in Madras and Calcutta, he made a collective total of 29 in four innings'. In Bangalore, though, in the final Test after Australia had already lost the series, Slater bounced back. Under tremendous pressure, where he needed to prove the selectors correct in recalling him, he scored 91 in typical Slater fashion. His 50 came up in just 52 balls with 11 fours; hardly the form of a player riddled with worry. "I knew I had to go out and play my natural game," he said, "and if it never came off, I wouldn't have lost anything because I was trying to do it my way. I'm proud of myself for turning it around. It would have been so easy to lie down and die and go out there nervous and scratch around." On his technique, he added: "The more shots you play the more risks there are, and that's why I get criticised. Because I play a lot of shots, I'm going to get out playing shots and sometimes that can look bad. But I've played that way right through my career and I've scored a lot of runs playing that way." Australian coach, Geoff Marsh, feels the time that Slater spent in the Test match wilderness, served him well. "Michael matured as a person and as a player during the time he spent out of Test cricket. Although he was dropped because of poor shot selection, you would never want Michael to change the way he plays and lose that aggression because he wins Test matches for you with that approach. He still has an extremely bright future ahead of him."

Passion is a word you would associate with the way in which Slater goes about his cricket, whether scoring runs or plying his supreme athleticism and agility in the field. He is a proud cricketer who wears his baggy green cap with pride. Such characteristics show through his transparent demeanour. He said: "I always want to field in the baggy green, I'll never wear a white floppy in the field. The baggy green symbolises Australian cricket, which means a lot to me. I do play with great passion and occasionally I'll sit back and think of what it took to get there and what it all means to me." Representing Australia at cricket was the only thing that Michael ever really aspired to during his adolescence, though at seventeen, he had to choose between cricket and hockey. He played for New South Wales at both sports and it was a tough choice but one that he always knew the answer to, as he explains. "It became harder to combine the two. My first love was always cricket and I realised that if I continued the way I was going, then I could make a decent living out of cricket. Everybody has dreams and playing for Australia was something that I always wanted to do. After playing state under 19s, followed by the Cricket Academy, I then knew it was possible to turn the dream into reality. Now, I never sit back and say 'I've done it' because I'm very much one for looking ahead. I love what I'm doing so much that I just want to concentrate on scoring more runs for Australia and winning more Test series'."

Michael first announced his potential on the biggest stage of all at Lord's in 1993, when, in only his second Test match, he scored 152. Initially, he was surprised to have even been selected to tour. His only target that season was to establish himself in the New South Wales side, though, he eventually established himself in the Test side months later. On debut at Manchester he registered 58 and 27, which was an experience that he did not expect so soon. "It was pretty mind-boggling that it was all happening, I just couldn't believe that I was out there playing." His first taste of Test cricket at Lord's was a different proposition and his 152 proved that nerves failed to unsettle him. "To play at Lord's has to be the ambition of any cricketer and for me to play my second Test there was a thrill in itself, but to go out and get 150…well, I still can't believe that it happened. It just capped off an amazing series of events that season." That breakthrough tour for him served more good than just runs on paper and helping to secure the Ashes in the cupboard. It also removed the pressure of Test cricket from him early on and allowed him to savour it instead of worrying about proving himself. "Sure, to get runs early in my Test career took the pressure off and made me relax and enjoy the cricket," he admits. "When I envisaged Test cricket years before, it was all about going out in the MCG or the SCG with the Aussie crowds cheering you on. After my start, I was able to enjoy that experience."

From that England tour Slater continued to plunder international attacks. One of his most cherished innings' was his 110 in Rawalpindi while touring Pakistan in 1994. He averaged 48.80 in the three Test matches, against one of the strongest bowling attacks in world cricket. Not only did this tour prove his ability to handle the best bowlers, but it also said much for his all-round game at being able to prosper in different conditions. First England, then South Africa (95 in Durban) and Pakistan. He commented: "It's always nice to perform in testing conditions. To be a consistent performer you have to be able to adjust to different conditions, so that hundred in Rawalpindi was a big moment in my career. You hear a lot about how difficult it is facing the spinners in the sub-continent, so against Mushtaq (Ahmed) I had to concentrate hard and be fully switched on." There was also the 'small' matter of Waqar Younis and Wasim Akram to contend with, which is no minor feat. "Akram is a real quality quick," Slater praised. "He's left-arm and you don't face too many of those, he swings it both ways, he's very quick, he has everything. I was really pumped up for it because, at that stage, they were regarded as the best opening pair in the world and I wanted to do well."

If England thought they had seen the best of Slater in 1993, they soon discovered that there was still more to come from the player. In the 1994-95 Ashes series, the young New South Welshman scored 623 runs including 176 at Brisbane, 103 at Sydney and 124 at Perth, culminating in a series average of 62.30. It would appear the bowling of an Englishman is the perfect cure for hangover as far as Slater is concerned. He averages 51 against them in his Test career and he does admit, "traditionally England and Australia is a series that every Aussie likes to play in." The only person to cause him any discomfort consistently for England is Devon Malcolm. Their contests have rarely been dull. "In Perth that series, Dev bowled me the quickest spell that I've ever faced," said Slater. Maybe it was no coincidence that when Michael scored 176 at Brisbane, which he regards as his favourite Test innings because of the way it set a rhythm for the series, Malcolm was injured and didn't play.

An experience that particularly disappointed him was the 1995 tour of the West Indies, in which Australia won the series 2-1 and subsequently became the unofficial world champions. He said: "It was a good tour in terms of the team's success, but I underachieved and I was batting better than my performances showed. It was disappointing because I really wanted to get over there and do it against the West Indies, especially against Ambrose, Walsh and the Benjamins; if you get runs against them, you know you can get runs against anyone." One feels that he will get his chance to triumph in the Caribbean at another time, against an equally potent attack. I would not like to bet against him doing much, much better next time. Michael Slater is a refreshing asset to cricket. He entertains, puts 'bums on seats' and furthermore, he scores a lot of runs. Slater does think about his future in cricket, though he is now more wary of getting too carried away with his success, after receiving the Test axe for 16 months. "While I do set myself goals and look at the big picture occasionally, I am very mindful now of not getting too far ahead of myself. I just want to be a very consistent opening bat for Australia for as long as I possibly can. The time period I've got in my mind to play until is around 34-35, so if I can be consistent then I'll be playing for all the time I want to be playing in."

MICHAEL SLATER - TEST MATCH STATISTICS

TESTS: 40	INN: 70	RUNS: 3055
AVERAGE: 45.59	HS: 219	50: 12 100: 8

OVERALL RECORD NB - M.J. Slater has opened in every Test match innings

V ENGLAND
TESTS: 11	INN: 20	RUNS: 1039
AVERAGE: 51.95	HS: 176	50: 3 100: 4

V INDIA
TESTS: 4	INN: 8	RUNS: 206
AVERAGE: 25.75	HS: 91	50: 1 100: 0

V NEW ZEALAND
TESTS: 3	INN: 4	RUNS: 305
AVERAGE: 76.25	HS: 168	50: 1 100: 1

V PAKISTAN
TESTS: 9	INN: 15	RUNS: 621
AVERAGE: 41.40	HS: 110	50: 3 100: 2

V SOUTH AFRICA
TESTS: 6	INN: 11	RUNS: 436
AVERAGE: 43.60	HS: 95	50: 3 100: 0

V SRI LANKA
TESTS: 3	INN: 5	RUNS: 309
AVERAGE: 77.25	HS: 219	50: 1 100: 1

V WEST INDIES
TESTS: 4	INN: 7	RUNS: 139
AVERAGE: 23.16	HS: 41	50: 0 100: 0

KEITH STACKPOLE - PERSONAL FILE

FULL NAME: Keith Raymond Stackpole

DATE OF BIRTH: 10th July, 1940

BIRTHPLACE: Collingwood, Melbourne

EDUCATION: Christian Brothers' College, Clifton Hill, Melbourne

PLAYING ROLE: Right Hand Bat, Leg Break Bowler

TEAMS: Australia; Victoria 1959/60 - 1973/74

TEST DEBUT: 1965-66 v England, Adelaide

TESTS: 43

MOST PRODUCTIVE GROUND - H: Adelaide, 393 runs (65.50) in 4 Tests
A: Kingston, 186 runs (93.00) in 1 Test

FIRST-CLASS DEBUT: 1959-60

FIRST-CLASS RUNS: 10,100

FIRST-CLASS WICKETS: 148

HIGHEST SCORE: 207 Australia v England, Brisbane, 1970-71

BEST BOWLING: 5-38 Victoria v Queensland, Melbourne, 1965-66

NICKNAME: Stacky

PERCENTAGE OF TEST INNINGS AS OPENER: 80%

FOR THE RECORD: His father, K.W. Stackpole, also played for Victoria; Following his 207 in 1970-71, he became the first to score a double century in an Australia v England Test at Brisbane; Made 47 catches in his 43 Tests; Wisden 1973; MBE for services to cricket; Represented Ramsbottom in England's Lancashire League and Collingwood in Melbourne; After his cricket career, he became involved with the Australian sporting media, notably TV and radio commentary and newspaper columnist.

KEITH STACKPOLE (Australia)

A glance at Keith Stackpole's Test match average will reveal to you a score of good to mediocre standard, and though averages are the fairest method of assessing a player's true ability over a period of time, in the case of Stackpole, such a marking system does not do justice to the player. Yes he averaged 37.42 by the close of his Test career, which is not a particularly great average, but there is so much more to learn about this cricketer that statistics will never reveal. He was an aggressive player who was more concerned about the plight of his team than his own cause. Maybe this approach led to his downfall on too many occasions, but he was forever at his best when taking the attack to the bowlers. There is no better example of this than his first Test century in only his fourth Test, when he scored 134 batting at number eight. This was at a time when he was selected as an all-rounder, for his leg-breaks as well as his batting ability. "I don't like to talk about my own cricket much, but that 134 was quite unique. I was 34 at lunch and got out from the last ball before tea at 134, getting a hundred in a session. My defence was offence; I had to play shots. I found that against bowlers like Underwood and Prasanna, I couldn't play with my bat-pad all the time, I would just have got out, so I took up the challenge and soon found that most bowlers don't like being hit." Stackpole registered just 75 runs in his last five Test matches, and this significantly bruised his final average, but as he admits, averages were rarely a concern to him. "If I took out six of my worst Test matches I would be averaging in the mid-forties, but averages never worried me. The only time that I've been concerned about my average is now, because that is how people judge you. I think a fair reflection of my Test career would be an average of around 40, but they don't lie and that's how you're judged. One of my all-time heroes was Peter Burge. He was a tremendous batsman, but he was like me and only averaged in the late thirties. Burgey was one of the best Australian players that I ever saw. I used to love watching attacking players. Even as an opponent I'd much prefer to be out there when Ted Dexter was tearing you apart or when Colin Milburn was after you, as opposed to a Kenny Barrington, though I admired his technique and attitude to the game."

That 134 at Cape Town, which contributed towards an Australia victory, would have been enough to assure most players of their place in the side for a while, though Keith suffered at the hands of a selection panel who were keen to change a losing sequence. "It was nice to get that hundred but people soon forgot about it and I wasn't picked the next season; because we were beaten 3-1 they felt changes had to be made. Therefore, I didn't play against India and I missed out on a trip to England in 1968. That made me into a better player though, I became much tougher." His next series was at home to the West Indies in 1968-69. Although his return to Test cricket was not prolific, there was a major adjustment in his game from the third Test that positively affected the remainder of his career: His elevation in the batting order to open the innings with Bill Lawry. Even for his state side, Victoria, he never opened, going in at three. However, the selectors felt it would be a good idea to swap him and Ian Redpath, which became a move that suited both players. Immediately he showed himself to be at home in his new role, scoring 58 and 21 not out, while Australia also won the game. "I never looked back once I started opening," Stackpole admits. "It was kind of strange how it all happened. We'd just finished off the West Indies first innings about 25 minutes before lunch on the second day. As we were walking off, we got to about 20 yards from the gate at the SCG and Bill Lawry says, 'Stacky put the pads on.' I thought he wanted a lunch watchman!"

His solid performances at the end of that West Indies series at the top of the order earned him a tour of India in 1969-70. Given his preferred offensive style that was always helped by the hard, bouncy wickets that he played on in Australia, it was to be an interesting test for Keith to see whether he could also handle the slower-paced wickets on the sub-continent. It was an examination he passed with distinction. In the first Test at Bombay he scored 103, going on to average 46 in the five-match series that his side won 3-1. "This might sound funny but India was the making of me as a Test cricketer. It taught me more about technique and to put more value on my wicket. It taught me to be tighter against bowlers like Prasanna and Bedi. I reckon if you can make runs in India, you can make runs anywhere. I was also lucky in the fact that opening gave me the chance to get a feel of the wicket and get my eye in before the spinners came on; where as at number five the spinners are in their rhythm and the ball is scuffed up." The 103 in Bombay was scored under particularly difficult conditions. Australia batted second and after day two, on the eve of the rest day, Keith had reached fifty and was still not out. Shortly after play, though, he suffered great hydration and cramp. The team was staying on the ground and after everyone had gone up to their room, Keith became marooned on the toilet, suffering from a severe bout of cramp. Fortunately for Stackpole, Doug Walters came back for something, heard him shouting and instantly got help. He had to be carried up to his room, where he remained entirely throughout the rest day. On the hundred, he commented: "It was a great thrill to make a hundred, particularly against Prasanna and Bedi, as they were great bowlers. Prasanna, without doubt, was the best off-spinner I ever faced. He was better than Lance Gibbs; he had more heart and turned the ball more. When you were up at the non-strikers end and Prasanna was bowling, you could literally hear the rip and the balling buzzing through the air. He used to impart so much spin on the ball. I used to play a waiting game against him and just keep them out until he bowled one full when I would hit him over the top. Then he might drop one shorter, and I'd be waiting to punch it. I really enjoyed that tour and I never thought it would be the last time an Australian side would win a series there for over thirty years!"

Following a demoralising tour of South Africa in 1969-70 for both Stackpole and Australia, where they went down 4-0 in what became the Springbok's last Test for 22 years, Keith enjoyed a highly successful Ashes series in 1970-71. He had made his bow in Test cricket five years previously against England with little success, but this time he scored heavily, though Australia lost the rubber 2-0. The battle for the Ashes has witnessed many enthralling personal duels through generations, and few more exciting than Stackpole's contest with England quick bowler, John Snow. The Victorian was never more in his element than against an aggressive fast bowler, and he faced many probing quickies during his career, though he rates Snow as the greatest. "I liked playing bouncers, I liked playing short bowling. It was a challenge to play against fast bowlers," Stackpole reveals. "The most fearsome of all bowlers was Wes Hall. He was a great character; he used to run in as fast as he used to bowl. Wes used to glare, he used to laugh, he would try and intimidate you and quite often he would follow through after delivery and end up right next to you. The best fast bowler I ever played against, though, was John Snow. I opened up against John more than I did against anyone in my career. Snowy was the best, yet he bowled stupidly against me. He never kept the ball up much or bowled many yorkers or try to get me caught in the slips on the drive. I was one of few guys in the Australian side who his bowling suited. Although, if you asked me to name the best five deliveries I ever got in my career, Snowy would have bowled three of them. He had a real good leg-cutter. He was a top bowler. I never had the greatest technique but I think Snowy and myself had a lot of admiration for one another."

In the first Test of that 1970-71 series, Stackpole set his stall out from the very beginning. At Brisbane he made 207 - his highest Test score. In a drawn game, 'Stacky' provided great entertainment for the Queensland crowd, though he was nearly run out in his teens when Boycott threw the wickets down. The decision was mulled over for the remainder of the series. "I genuinely believe I was in. If you asked me whether I was out in the last over on the last day's play in Sydney, caught Knott bowled Underwood, I'd tell you yes, I snicked it even though I was given not out. And on the first morning in Melbourne also against England, Snowy bowled me a bouncer and I tried to duck out of the way and it flicked my glove and went through to Knotty. Again I was given not out but I hit it. In this instance, though, in Brisbane, I'm sure I was not out." His 136 at Adelaide in the fifth Test was less controversial and also an innings which Keith considers better than the double century in Brisbane. Here in South Australia, his reaching three figures had an extremely meaningful cause, in helping to save the match and preventing an irretrievable 2-0 lead to the opposition. It also led to a special moment for him after play with one of the game's greatest sons. "That was the time I had my longest ever conversation with Sir Donald Bradman," Stackpole recalls. "He came into the dressing room and said, 'Well played. I didn't think you had it in you to concentrate for so long.' That got my back up at the time. I thought you cheeky bleeder. If you didn't think I could concentrate why didn't you come to me earlier. But now I realise it was my fault. I should have had the guts to go to him and say, 'Donald, can you give me a couple of hints?' He was approachable, but most people feared him. I have this one regret that I didn't have enough guts to have more meaningful conversations with him to find out more. In those days, we were renegades, we never got paid a lot, we felt we had an axe to grind, and with Donald being a selector and Chairman of the Board you felt you were fighting him in more ways than one."

In 1972, the Ashes battle continued in England, where Keith prospered once more. It was another situation where pundits doubted his technique in different conditions, but he served huge helpings of humble pie to many an 'expert'. Five fifties and one hundred in the five-Test rubber culminated in a series average in the fifties; on a tour that he was desperate to be on after missing out in 1968. "It was very satisfying. The ambition of any Australian cricketer is to go on a tour of England," he said. "One of the greatest moments of my cricket life was that first morning at Lord's, as you go up through the dressing room you can see the stud marks on the floor that have been left by the great players that have played there. Then you go to nets and in those days about 500 people used to turn up to watch you practise. They used to scrutinise you and assess you. At the time, it was still quite moist and if you ever got bowled you could hear a gasp behind you and whispers of, 'This guy hasn't got a very good technique'." Whoever those doubting English supporters were soon choked on their words when he hit the winning runs for his 57. The series finished 2-2, but not without incident. "The funniest moment of my career occurred at Trent Bridge when I got a hundred (114) but was dropped twice in the forties. When Tony Greig eventually got me out off a little outswinger, he was on his haunches thumping his fist into the ground. As I passed him when I was walking off, I said, without looking at him, 'You're nothing but a fucking teddy bear.' His head nearly swung off his shoulders and he started chasing me muttering obscenities, but I just carried on walking. The next day the press had a real go at him for trying to intimidate the batsman; little did they know I'd started it! We were bitter enemies in those days but now we're very close friends."

Stackpole's run of form continued on tour in the Caribbean in 1972-73. Australia won the series 2-0. "It was a good tour for me but it could have been better," admits 'Stacky'. "I underestimated a couple of bowlers. My problem was, if I didn't think a bowler was any good I just used to go after him too early, like Keith Boyce. I never rated Boycey." Stackpole began positively from the outset that series and the raw West Indies fast bowler Uton Dowe, who had been talked up by many islanders, suffered more than anybody. After Stackpole's 44 in the first innings and his 142 in the second, a banner in the crowd was raised that read: 'Haven't you heard about the Ten Commandments? Dowe shall not bowl.' "In those days, they used to line you up and play the national anthem on the first morning of a Test. Opposite me in the line-up was Dowe. We were like two heavyweight boxers going head to head in a world title fight. I can remember just staring at him and every time his eyes made contact with mine they'd look away. I knew then I had him." Keith feels he played a more important innings, though, in the fourth and final Test, when he made 76 not out "In Guyana, we got 135 to win the game with no wickets down. They had a couple of spinners playing as it was a turning wicket and conditions weren't that easy to bat on. We won easily in the end because we still played aggressively. Right from the start we tonked it, but we'd have lost it if we had just tried to sneak up on the total."

It was unfortunate that in his final Test match against New Zealand, Stackpole made a pair. He admits that playing the Kiwis failed to inspire him like an Ashes match or a battle versus the West Indies. He said: "There have only ever been two Australian players to be out from the first ball of a Test match: One is Warren Bardsley, and he had to wait 46 years for someone to join him - that was me - back in 1974, and already I've been waiting 24 years for some other bastard to join me!" After scoring 122 on his home ground in 1973-74, his remaining five Tests all against New Zealand brought him just 75 runs. He attributes his writing in the newspapers as a distraction, coupled with a wavering interest for cricket at the time. "The penultimate day of my last Test was the only day in my cricket career, including league and Shield cricket, where I didn't watch the game, which I always used to do. I just sat in the dressing room playing cards with Doug Walters, because I was disappointed and had lost the urge a bit." Still, Keith Stackpole had by this time entertained so many cricket supporters and will be remembered as such. His former Australian team-mate Greg Chappell said: "He was ideally suited to opening, as he was a pretty nervy character and he got a bit edgy when he was waiting around. Stacky preferred to get after them straight away. He loved facing fast bowlers, and I think his aggressive style worked well for him." Another team-mate who has a lot of respect for Keith is fast bowler Dennis Lillee. "Stacky was in a similar vane to Greenidge and Haynes," Lillee praised. "He thought of defence as a last resort. Stacky was a hitter of the ball, not a carresser of the ball, and he was certainly a guy that could get you off to a good start and help demoralise an attack early, which is always important for a team." Given such honest tributes from two of Australia's greatest ever players, who needs averages?

KEITH STACKPOLE - TEST MATCH STATISTICS   ( ) = As Opener

TESTS: 43	INN: 80 (64)	RUNS: 2807 (2390)
AVERAGE: 37.42 (40.51)	HS: 207 (207)	50: 14 (14) 100: 7 (6)

OVERALL RECORD   + = Opened in every innings against that country

V ENGLAND

TESTS: 13	INN: 24 (20)	RUNS: 1164 (1049)
AVERAGE: 50.60 (55.21)	HS: 207 (207)	50: 7 (7) 100: 3 (3)

V INDIA

TESTS: 5	INN: 10+	RUNS: 368
AVERAGE: 46.00	HS: 103	50: 1 100: 1

V NEW ZEALAND

TESTS: 6	INN: 10+	RUNS: 197
AVERAGE: 19.70	HS: 122	50: 0 100: 1

V PAKISTAN

TESTS: 1	INN: 2+	RUNS: 37
AVERAGE: 18.50	HS: 28	50: 0 100: 0

V SOUTH AFRICA

TESTS: 9	INN: 17 (8)	RUNS: 441 (187)
AVERAGE: 25.94 (23.38)	HS: 134 (71)	50: 1 (1) 100: 1 (0)

V WEST INDIES

TESTS: 9	INN: 17 (14)	RUNS: 600 (552)
AVERAGE: 40.00 (46.00)	HS: 142 (142)	50: 5 (5) 100: 1 (1)

HERBERT SUTCLIFFE - PERSONAL FILE

FULL NAME: Herbert Sutcliffe

DATE OF BIRTH: 24th November, 1894

BIRTHPLACE: Harrogate, Yorkshire

EDUCATION: Pudsey School

PLAYING ROLE: Right Hand Bat

TEAMS: England; Yorkshire 1919 - 1945

TEST DEBUT: 1924 v South Africa, Birmingham

TESTS: 54

MOST PRODUCTIVE GROUND H: The Oval, 916 runs (91.60) in 7 Tests
A: Melbourne, 724 runs (103.42) in 4 Tests
FIRST-CLASS DEBUT: 1919

FIRST-CLASS RUNS: 50,138

FIRST-CLASS WICKETS: 2

HIGHEST SCORE: 313 Yorkshire v Essex, Leyton, 1932

BEST BOWLING: 2-16 Yorkshire v Surrey, The Oval, 1937

PERCENTAGE OF TEST INNINGS AS OPENER: 98.80%

FOR THE RECORD: During World War II, Sutcliffe was an Army Major; His Test average of 60.73 from 54 matches remains the highest by any England player; Sutcliffe registered 151 first-class centuries in his career and lies sixth in the all-time list of most centuries scored; For Yorkshire in 1932, while scoring 313, he shared a record opening stand with P. Holmes of 555 against Essex at Leyton. It remains the fifth highest ever partnership in first-class cricket, and the second highest first-wicket stand; On retirement from cricket, he served as an England Test selector from 1959 to 1961; He later became a successful businessman.

HERBERT SUTCLIFFE (England)

You only have to look at the statistical record of Herbert Sutcliffe to appreciate just what a truly magnificent batsman he was. There are cricketers who are very good, but there's also those who can only ever be described as 'great', to properly pay them the relevant tribute - Herbert Sutcliffe falls into this category, and near the peak of it too; along with his famous opening partner for England, Jack Hobbs, who Herbert always acknowledged was a far more stylish player than he. Sutcliffe had his limitations and rarely defied those boundaries. His rich and disciplined talent was instantly obvious to many onlookers when he scored 1,839 runs in his first season with Yorkshire in 1919. That initial glimpse of his skill so impressed Wisden, that they chose the youthful Sutcliffe as one of their 'Five Cricketers of the Year.' After this beginning, he had set himself an unusually high standard to consistently emulate throughout his career; but given his genius, more than emulate that beginning, he went on to better it on a consistent basis to become one of England's greatest ever batsmen. In fact, his final Test average of 60.73 is the highest by any England Test cricketer. To maintain such an average from his 54 Tests is further testimony to his greatness. Furthermore, Sutcliffe was the only player to register 1,000 runs in all of the 21 inter-war years; scoring more than 2,000 runs on twelve occasions and 3,000 runs on three occasions.

Yorkshire has unearthed some fine talents down the generations, particularly opening batsmen. Indeed, Leonard Hutton and Geoffrey Boycott are two of England's finest in Test history, though, despite the many records that duo monopolised between them, Sutcliffe has the most column inches of the record books devoted to his name. Sutcliffe's baptism in Test cricket appeared to be a comfortable one for him, given his impressive performances right from the word go, but it was more to do with his craft as a batsman than any weaknesses of the opposition. After his first ten Test matches, Herbert was averaging an incredible 79.76, with 1,000 runs to his credit, including five centuries. His first series was in 1924 against South Africa. Following on from his promising debut at Birmingham where he scored 64, he recorded his first Test century (122) in only his second match. In making that 122, he shared a record first-wicket stand of 268 with his long-time opening partner, Jack Hobbs, which became England's highest first-wicket total at Leeds. The pairing of Hobbs and Sutcliffe was so formidable and so consistently prolific that opposition bowlers often felt beaten before a ball was bowled. The duo were an institution in cricket.

There aren't too many Englishmen that boast an average over fifty against the old enemy, Australia, but Sutcliffe's average against them of 66.85 makes him one of the few to enjoy the offerings of the Australians through the years. His intentions were made painfully clear to the Aussies in his first match against them at Sydney in 1924-25, when he scored 59 and 115. These contributions were further improved on in the next match at Melbourne, which, incidentally, is his most successful Test venue outside of England. He recorded a century in both innings (176 & 127) and really announced himself as a man who would be a thorn in the Australian side for a long time to come. A promise he later kept. Those two centuries at Melbourne earned him several statistical honours; as he became the first player to score a hundred in each innings of a Test against Australia; the first Englishman to score three successive centuries in Tests; and in batting throughout the third day's play, it became the first such instance in the Test arena. Before that 1924-25 run-soaked series was complete, Sutcliffe plundered another century. Again at Melbourne, he scored 143, which not only meant it was his third successive three-figure total at Melbourne, but it also made him the first Test cricketer to compile four hundreds in one rubber. Despite finishing that series in somewhat of an anti-climax with a nought at Sydney, the damage he had already inflicted on the hapless Australians was massive. He scored 734 runs in the five-Test series at an average of 81.55. His departure from the country would, I'm sure, have been a huge relief for the Australian bowlers, and for the country as a whole. When Herbert Sutcliffe was at the crease in that series, his confidence was so high and his batting so assured and commanding that the statisticians on the ground were busier than the wicketkeeper!

Few Test batsmen score two hundreds in both innings' of a Test. However, Herbert Sutcliffe achieved this feat twice. Added to his superior performance at Melbourne in 1924-25, he repeated it against South Africa in 1929. At The Oval, where he averaged 91.60 in his seven Tests on the ground, Sutcliffe registered 104 and 109 not out and became the first player to achieve this feat twice in Tests. Again, like the series against Australia five years previously, he hit four centuries in the rubber, scoring 114 at Birmingham and 100 at Lord's also. His form was so electric it seemed peculiar when he made just 60 runs in four consecutive innings' during the middle section of that series, including nine at Manchester. His shortcomings at Old Trafford, though, were soon remedied when he made 74 against Australia a year later and 109 not out the following year in 1931. That hundred was an interesting one, considering the Test only began at 3.15 on the third day due to heavy rainfall. By the time the match was abandoned as a washout after just 195 minutes of play, Herbert had registered his fifteenth century in Tests.

The famous 'Bodyline' series was played in 1932-33 and Sutcliffe played a significant part in England's comprehensive 4-1 series victory. Although much of the credit went to England's fast bowlers, Harold Larwood and Bill Voce and quite rightly so, Sutcliffe more than contributed with 440 runs at a solid average of 55. This included his 194 at Sydney, which remained his highest Test score, eclipsing the 176 at Melbourne in 1924-25. It was his sixteenth and final Test century and his eighth against Australia. In getting there he overtook Jack Hobbs's record of 15 Test hundreds. Although he failed to score a century in any of his last 14 Test matches, his run scoring remained consistent if not prolific. To further emphasise his downward spiral (to his standards), he made just 3 and 38 in his final match at Lord's against South Africa, which was the game where the Springboks recorded their first win in England. It was a totally reversed scenario to how he began his Test career against the same nation 11 years prior, in such breathtaking fashion. However, Herbert Sutcliffe will forever remain in cricket folklore as one of the greatest batsmen of the twentieth century.

HERBERT SUTCLIFFE - TEST MATCH STATISTICS   ( ) = As Opener

TESTS: 54   INN: 84 (83)   RUNS: 4555 (4522)
AVERAGE: 60.73 (61.10) HS: 194 (194)   50: 23 (23) 100: 16 (16)

OVERALL RECORD   + = Opened in every innings against that country

V AUSTRALIA
TESTS: 27   INN: 46 (45)   RUNS: 2741 (2708)
AVERAGE: 66.85 (67.70) HS: 194 (194)   50: 16 (16) 100: 8 (8)

V INDIA
TESTS: 1   INN: 2+   RUNS: 22
AVERAGE: 11.00   HS: 19   50: 0 100: 0

V NEW ZEALAND
TESTS: 4   INN: 4+   RUNS: 250
AVERAGE: 83.33   HS: 117   50: 0 100: 2

V SOUTH AFRICA
TESTS: 17   INN: 27+   RUNS: 1336
AVERAGE: 55.66   HS: 122   50: 5 100: 6

V WEST INDIES
TESTS: 5   INN: 5+   RUNS: 206
AVERAGE: 41.20   HS: 63   50: 2 100: 0

MARK TAYLOR - PERSONAL FILE

FULL NAME: Mark Anthony Taylor

DATE OF BIRTH: 27th October, 1964

BIRTHPLACE: Wagga Wagga, New South Wales

EDUCATION: Mt Austin High School, Wagga Wagga; Chatswood High
School, Stoney; University of New South Wales

PLAYING ROLE: Left Hand Bat, Slip Fielder (Taylor-Warne fielder-bowler
combination is the most successful in Test cricket)

TEAMS: Australia; New South Wales 1985/86 -;

TEST DEBUT: 1988-89 v West Indies, Sydney

TESTS: 99

MOST PRODUCTIVE GROUND - H: Brisbane, 866 runs (61.85) in 9 Tests
A: Peshawar, 426 runs (426.00) in 1 Test
FIRST-CLASS DEBUT: 1985-86

FIRST-CLASS RUNS: 16,467 (as at 28-3-98)

FIRST-CLASS WICKETS: 2

HIGHEST SCORE: 334* Australia v Pakistan, Peshawar, 1998-99

BEST BOWLING: 1-11 Australia v Pakistan, Rawalpindi, 1994-95

NICKNAME: Tubby

PERCENTAGE OF TEST INNINGS AS OPENER: 100%

FOR THE RECORD: His 839 runs on the 1989 tour of England places him third
in the list of the record aggregate runs in a series; Succeeded A.R. Border as
Australia captain in 1994; He captained Australia to runners-up in the 1996 World
Cup; Has skippered Australia in 45 Tests to date; His 334* in Peshawar equalled
D.G. Bradman's record of the highest Test score by an Australian.

MARK TAYLOR (Australia)

Although Mark Taylor has become one of Australia's greatest and most successful batsmen in Test history, it's his lesser-publicised strengths that impress me as much as any statistical record he has achieved. He now shares Sir Donald Bradman's record for the highest score in Tests by an Australian with his 334 not out in Peshawar, though his more personal qualities rate equally as high: The stocky New South Wales player is one of the most honest cricketers you could wish to meet. Whether in triumph or adversity, Taylor, as captain, maintains a cool, always upbeat exterior and rarely is he reluctant to share his innermost thoughts on the state of play when asked the question. Never was this more apparent than during his run drought that spanned 21 innings without a Test 50, from 1996 to 1997. He was the first to admit that he was fortunate to keep his place in the team, acknowledging the fact that the team was winning under his captaincy, and was his saving grace. Throughout that period of mental torture, when he was constantly under the media microscope, he forever kept his cool and always stood up to his responsibilities. "They won't see me in a press conference crying and breaking down or losing my cool," Taylor promised. "I think you've got to be stronger and understand what your job is and what their job is and tell them what you think is the truth - that is all you can do. You have to keep an equilibrium between success and failure, whether winning or losing, getting a hundred or two ducks, especially as captain. If your players see you down they're going to be down."

One man who knows Mark Taylor better than most people is his former opening partner Geoff Marsh, now coach of Australia. Marsh has been able to view Taylor's mood from close quarters and has been impressed by his observations. He said: "Mark had about six *really* bad months from the West Indies series to the England tour, but the thing that I admired about him was, not once did he ever give up on a media conference. He went out and faced the media every time, and though they were doing their jobs, the pressure he was under was unbelievable, but he stood firm and never brought his problems into the dressing room. The strength of the guy is incredible; like Mark Waugh has said, you can't ruffle him. When Mark Taylor speaks in the dressing room you can hear a pin drop - he's fantastic with the guys and gets his message across. It was his inner strength that got him through those twelve months and that goes to show the power of the man."

This well chronicled, personal crisis of Taylor's, is the only real down side or hardship of any length that he has suffered in his otherwise rosy Test career. However, it wasn't your average poor run of form, as Mark admits, "It really was a shocking spell. I'm not the kind of person who likes to make excuses, but during that time it's the worst I've ever seen Test wickets. There's no doubt that I was batting poorly - mentally it was getting harder and harder - but there were only a couple of times when I felt 'this is a good wicket,' right from where my problems began against the West Indies at home. It was only Adelaide that was a good wicket and I got 11 and the team got 500. That was my chance (to come good)." From that moment on, for the next six months, the situation degenerated for Taylor. On tour in South Africa in the three-Test series, he managed just 80 runs. Technically and mentally he was struggling and there seemed to be no escape for him. Media pressure on him, who were calling for his head, was tremendous. However, the Australian selectors kept faith in him as a winning captain and a very successful slip fielder. "When I went to England it was make-or-break," he admits. "I was either going to score some runs at the start of the series or I was out."

Again, the Taylor resilience defied the media, public opinion and the bookmakers plotting the odds of the next captain, when he struck a determined 129 in the second innings of the first Test at Birmingham - after making just seven in the first innings. England won the match but Taylor won his personal battle, with an innings of immense character when everything was on the line. "Before that match I was as low as you can get. The pressure was on big time," he said. After making only seven in the first innings he went out for a meal that night with his parents, feeling extremely low. Mr. and Mrs. Taylor urged their son not to throw in the towel but he knew that not only was he struggling, so was the team, and part of the reason for that was him. "I explained to them, though, that if it all finished after that Test I'd still be happy. I'd captained my country, made 14 Test centuries as an opening batsman and knew I had done a good job. That's the attitude I took out with me in the second innings. Before I was worrying too much, thinking, 'Maybe this is the last innings, I have to get some runs, I have to break this drought, I have to prove people wrong' - you don't have to do anything, apart from enjoy the competition, because once you lose that you shouldn't be playing. It helps sometimes if you can be a little blasé about things and just relish the challenge with the bowler." As Geoff Marsh confirms, it was a sterling effort by Taylor to turn things round when the odds were stacked heavily against him. "He lost his confidence to the extent where he was feeling uncomfortable at the crease and couldn't hold his bat properly. To come through it with a century by saying, 'Bugger it, I'm just going to go out there and hit the ball,' when the pressure was on most - it was just a great display of mental toughness."

Mark's distinguished Test career began in 1988-89 against the West Indies on his home ground at Sydney. He had long been a consistent run scorer in

183

Shield cricket, although that season he hadn't scored a century before his selection. Australia were 3-0 down in the series with two to play and they adopted a 'Let's try something different attitude', which materialised into the selection of Mark Taylor. This created a right-hand left-hand opening combination with Geoff Marsh, and David Boon dropped down to number three. His initial glimpse of Test cricket was an eye-opening experience. Says Taylor, "After facing the first couple of overs I really didn't think I was good enough. I got my first run off Ambrose, which I tried to flick off my hip, but it hit me on the glove and went down to fine leg. I thought, 'Jeez I'm in trouble here. I think I'm out of my league!' Eventually I made it to lunch and got out shortly after for 25. It got easier the longer I stuck around, even against those guys, so I learnt a lot from my first dig." In the next Test match in Adelaide, again it was not overly successful, but it did tell him a lot more about his ability and helped him to kick on to greater heights. "In the second innings I got 36," he recalls. "I hit a couple of hook shots in front of square off Patrick Patterson, who was probably the quickest bowler in the world at the time. I thought that if I'm playing that shot it must mean that I can see the ball well enough to hit the fastest bowler in the world for four, so I can't be too much out of my league. I got a lot of confidence from those two Test matches and I went back to Shield cricket and made three hundreds in three matches, because I felt I had broken through to another level and my confidence went through the roof."

Statistically, Taylor's Test career reads impressively against all countries, except the West Indies. Although 28 is not an atrocious average considering the standard of the Windies' bowling attacks he has confronted over the years, it is still below average for his own standards. Habitually, Mark is at his best when the battle is on and the competition is fierce - such conditions bring out the tiger spirit in him, but in general, it has not happened for him against the West Indies. "For an opening batsman, they've always been the toughest side to play against because they are at you all the time," Taylor said. "Right from the word go the West Indies really work on you, and they work on you as captain as well. The times I've played well I've probably wanted to do too well and got out playing bad shots. The times I haven't played well they've just nailed me. If you're down early in a series against them, they will keep you down and they're the best at it. Very few batsmen come back from two or three bad Tests to finish the series well."

From the five Test series' he has been involved with the West Indies, Taylor has only performed successfully with the bat in one of them, consistently. That was in the Caribbean in 1990-91, where he scored 441 runs in the five-Test rubber at an average of 49. Again it was a losing series for Australia, but consolation for Mark came with his personal achievements. In Jamaica he made 58, 61 in Trinidad, 76 in Barbados, before completing the series on a high note with 59 and 144 in Antigua to help win the game. Mark rates that series top in terms of competitiveness. "That was the toughest cricket I've ever played," he admitted. "For on-the-field toughness, I would go as far to say it was an ugly series. Both sides really went at each other hard. We had a beer together, as teams, on the first night of the first Test and that was it for the rest of the series. In Jamaica in the first Test, Ambrose bowled me three bumpers in a row to start the series off and I thought, 'Oh, here we go.' It was always likely to be tough though, as they were the kings and we were trying to knock them off. It's always going to be tough between Australia and the West Indies but it should never get that bad."

Through his career, as most opening batsmen do, Mark experienced many riveting new-ball duels with various bowlers. One quickie who received the wrath of Taylor's bat more than most is England's Devon Malcolm. He has returned the punishment on occasions, though more often than not, the Aussie opener has won out. There is no greater example of this than on Taylor's first full Australian tour, to England in 1989, where he amassed an incredible 839 runs in the six Test matches. Prior to striking a ball, Mark was totally overawed by the prestige surrounding the whole experience, and never dreamed it would be so successful. "I thought, 'What an opportunity, my first tour is an Ashes tour. Even if I don't play a game or if I do play a game and don't perform - at least I've been on an Ashes tour. What a buzz that'll be for when I finish playing.' That's how I approached the whole tour," he admits. Initially, he struggled to come to terms with English conditions and failed to make an impact in the run-up to the series. "I felt terrible," he revealed. However, his fortune transformed dramatically at Taunton against Somerset in the final game before the first Test, where he made two fifties in the match. Thereafter, his scores in the Test series resembled the fruits of a letter to Santa Claus: 136 and 60 at Leeds; 60 and 27 at Lord's; 43 and 51 at Birmingham; 85 and 37 not out at Manchester; 219 at Nottingham and 71 and 48 at The Oval. It was consistency personified. The Nottingham Test brought Taylor and Malcolm together for the first time, but it was not to be a happy debut for Devon, as the Australian openers (Taylor and Marsh) put on 329 for the first wicket. Agonisingly for the Englishmen, Mark edged Angus Fraser through the slips while still on three, which became a costly let-off. Inevitably, there were some forgettable bowling figures around with Fraser going for 2-108, Botham 0-103, Hemmings 0-81 and Malcolm 1-166. On the battle with Malcolm, Taylor recalls: "Although he bowled sharp, he bowled short and at that stage in the series it was just where I wanted it. Every time Devon came on, I hit his first ball for four and that set the tone for the rest of the innings. Every time he came on I just went 'bang' and that got me going, but he probably thought, 'Oh here's trouble.' Throughout my career I've always looked to hook Devon, where as with other quicks, I'll just get out of the road. Some of the guys feel he's the quickest they've ever faced, and that includes the West Indies. Some guys find him very awkward, but he's always been a guy I've been able to pick up better than others." His 1993 tour of England was another successful one that included two centuries in the first two Tests. The 111 at Lord's satisfied him particularly. "It's nice to say that you've done that at the end of your career," he said proudly. That was Australia's second consecutive Ashes win in England, though the series victory over the Poms in 1994-95 gave him greater pleasure, when he was captain.

Following on from that run-crazed 1989 tour of England, Taylor continued his good form at home. The first team to suffer was Sri Lanka. He scored 164 not out at Brisbane and 108 at Hobart in consecutive Tests. He is more proud, though, of the series that followed against Pakistan. In the three Tests he registered 52, 101, 77, 59 and 101 not out, against what he nominates as the best all-round bowling attack he has ever faced of Imran Khan, Wasim Akram, Waqar Younis, Aquib Javed and Mushtaq Ahmed. He enthused: "In Melbourne I got a fifty and a hundred and that's as good a bowling as I've ever faced in Test cricket, consistently. Akram bowled the best spell of fast bowling I've ever faced. What he was doing with the ball - I've never seen anyone do again. AB (Allan Border) and I put on over a hundred and we played and missed twice an over off Akram. We just said, 'No bat lift for Akram, let's just try and pick up a few ones.' I was playing him almost like French cricket. The only chance of getting a four was a flick down to fine leg!" At the end of that Australian season, an amazing first year in Test cricket had drawn to a close. His reputation had travelled the full circle. "I had to pinch myself to believe it was all happening," he said. "I went from a guy who walked out on his Test debut in January 1989 thinking he wasn't good enough, to a player that people were rating as the world's number one. It was unreal."

Another of his highs came when he was appointed captain of Australia in 1994, to replace Allan Border. His first mission in charge was a tour to Pakistan. The first Test in Karachi was a bittersweet moment for him, as, while captaining his country for the first time, he made a pair. There could have been fewer ways to celebrate such an occasion in more tragic circumstances. "It was one of the flattest wickets I've ever played on as well," Taylor acknowledges honestly. "As I was walking back to the pavilion after getting the pair, a few thoughts went through my mind: I thought, 'Have I taken on too much here? But then I figured that if I only get the captaincy for one Test, then it will be one more than most blokes get," again focusing on the positive aspect of a situation many others would struggle to salvage any sort of consolation from. With such an attitude, it is no coincidence that Taylor has gone on to become one of the best Australian captains in Test history. His finest hour as skipper came on the 1995 tour of the West Indies when Australia defeated the reigning 'world champions' 2-1. It wasn't a successful tour for him with the bat, though this was no disgrace on that tour. He said: "We had 120 hours of Test cricket scheduled, but we only played 72. It was a real bowler-fielder orientated series. I felt I was batting all right but anytime anybody made a mistake he was out. There was only one dropped catch in the series, by Courtney Browne who missed Steve Waugh on 42 in Jamaica, and he went on to get 200 and win us the match and the series. That was typical of how the series went."

Following the months of misery that bedeviled Taylor in 1996 and 1997, he announced his return to form in Australia by hitting 112 against New Zealand at Brisbane in November 1997. It was a vintage Taylor innings, digging his side out of deep trouble and helping them to a score of relative comfort. On a track that offered much early on to the bowlers, he grafted his way to three figures, while displaying an excellent show of controlled aggression. Anything that was outside off stump that was neither full nor short, he left alone with sublime judgement; but when there was anything slightly short or full it received the relevant, dismissive treatment. Brisbane is his most successful Test venue in terms of runs scored. He commented: "It's one of my worst grounds as a Shield player because it's usually got a bit in it for the bowler on the first day. I enjoy the challenge of the wicket there because it's one of the best Test wickets in the world as it's fair for everyone. I've seen batsmen score runs on it, I've seen fast bowlers take ten wickets in a match there, and I've seen Shane Warne take ten wickets in a match there. Also, it's the first Test of the summer and I generally play my best in the first Test. Maybe I get complacent and lose the edge as a series goes on," he offered.

Mark's positive approach is cemented so much into the foundations of his cricketing outlook that it becomes difficult ever to detect vibes of discontent; he harbours so little thought in the of way doubt or worry. Although, one aspect that does anger him is needless, negative or inconsistent criticism from pundits who, he feels, should know better. He points to the 112 against New Zealand while still recovering from his loss of form as a prime example - six weeks before the series against the Springboks began. "By the time South Africa came round they said, 'This will be Taylor's big test. He's made a few runs against New Zealand but they aren't that good.' So they just discarded the 112 even though we were four for 40 on a green top," he complained. "Then at Melbourne against South Africa I got 20 in the first innings before Gary Kirsten dived full length at point to catch one I'd hammered at him; and in the second innings I got 59 when the wicket was turning and Pat Symcox bowled one in the rough that spun to first slip and I was given out when I didn't hit it. So it was funny that when I got 169 at Adelaide in the third Test after getting dropped on 40, but I went on to play really well, people said, 'Oh you were a bit lucky.' I thought that would be bloody right. Did you say I was unlucky in Melbourne when I should have gone on to get a hundred? You're either lucky when you make runs or you should have made more when you're unlucky. I get a little annoyed by the real harsh critics who don't look at the game, they look at you, and not at the things you do well but at the things you don't do well. They will always be there and it's something you have to live with, but sometimes you feel like hitting them," he joked.

One of his most recent Test innings was 102 not out to win the match in Bangalore against India. This, however, followed two consecutive Test defeats to lose the series 2-1, after Australia had won nine consecutive Test series' previously. Mark's shot selection accounted for the majority of his dismissals on that Indian tour but he was up against a class spinner in Anil Kumble. The skill of Kumble, on his home wickets, was given as a significant reason in Australia's failure to amass big totals. For Taylor, though, spin bowling has never been a problem in his career, unlike many opening batsmen. "I've always considered myself a good player of spin," he said. "Playing in Sydney has really helped me over the years as it's always been a turning track ever since I've played there. As an opening batsman you do prefer to face some quicker bowling up front because that's what you're used to. It's more the thought of facing something different than the bowling itself (that puts you off)." Taylor is a man who knows his own game better than anyone, and though he hasn't always stuck to it, he does acknowledge that he has his clear strengths and weaknesses. "I'm not really the kind of player who would smack a wide one for four if it was the first ball of an innings - like Haynes or Slater probably would. I prefer to see what the ball's doing and how the wicket's playing first. As soon as I hit that first boundary, especially a straight drive, then I really feel as though I can start attacking more." Just like in Peshawar. After assessing the docile wicket and the bowling he plundered the Pakistanis for an unbeaten 334. In typical selfless Taylor fashion, he spurned the chance to overtake Brian Lara's record score of 375 when he declared for the good of the team. In terms of milestones he was just content to equal Sir Donald Bradman's record for the highest Test score by an Australian. "To equal a Bradman record is satisfying enough," he offered. He was more happy at his team's 1-0 series victory - the first by Australia in Pakistan since Richie Benaud's side in 1959-60. Typical MarkTaylor!

MARK TAYLOR - TEST MATCH STATISTICS

TESTS: 99	INN: 177	RUNS: 7297
AVERAGE: 44.49	HS: 334*	50: 38 100: 19

OVERALL RECORD NB M.A.Taylor has opened in every Test match innings

V ENGLAND
TESTS: 28	INN: 51	RUNS: 2268
AVERAGE: 46.28	HS: 219	50: 13 100: 6

V INDIA
TESTS: 9	INN: 18	RUNS: 675
AVERAGE: 42.18	HS: 102*	50: 3 100: 2

V NEW ZEALAND
TESTS: 11	INN: 16	RUNS: 666
AVERAGE: 47.57	HS: 142*	50: 5 100: 2

V PAKISTAN
TESTS: 12	INN: 20	RUNS: 1347
AVERAGE: 79.23	HS: 334*	50: 8 100: 4

V SOUTH AFRICA
TESTS: 11	INN: 19	RUNS: 746
AVERAGE: 41.44	HS: 170	50: 3 100: 2

V SRI LANKA
TESTS: 8	INN: 15	RUNS: 611
AVERAGE: 43.64	HS: 164	50: 1 100: 2

V WEST INDIES
TESTS: 20	INN: 37	RUNS: 984
AVERAGE: 28.11	HS: 144	50: 5 100: 1

GLENN TURNER - PERSONAL FILE

FULL NAME: Glenn Maitland Turner

DATE OF BIRTH: 26th May, 1947

BIRTHPLACE: Dunedin

EDUCATION: Otago High School

PLAYING ROLE: Right Hand Bat, Occasional Off Break Bowler

TEAMS: New Zealand; Otago 1964/65 - 1979/80; Worcestershire 1967 - 1982; Northern Districts 1976/77

TEST DEBUT: 1968-69 v West Indies, Auckland

TESTS: 41

MOST PRODUCTIVE GROUND H: Christchurch, 679 runs (67.40) in 7 Tests
                         A: Guyana, 259 runs (259.00) in 1 Test
FIRST-CLASS DEBUT: 1964-65

FIRST-CLASS RUNS: 34,213

FIRST-CLASS WICKETS: 5

HIGHEST SCORE: 311* Worcestershire v Warwickshire, Worcester, 1982

BEST BOWLING: 3-18 Worcestershire v Pakistan, Worcester, 1967

NICKNAME: Budgie

PERCENTAGE OF TEST INNINGS AS OPENER: 91.78%

FOR THE RECORD: Before he joined Worcestershire, Warwickshire turned him down; He also represented Worcestershire at hockey; Wisden 1970; Benefit 1978 (£21,103); His 223* at Jamaica in 1971-72 became the highest score for any batsman to carry his bat in Tests; In 1973-74 at Christchurch, Turner scored a hundred in each innings against Australia and became the first New Zealander to achieve the feat; Coached New Zealand in the mid-nineties.

190

GLENN TURNER (New Zealand)

According to Tom Graveney, "Glenn was absolutely tremendous. I believe he was, technically, the batsman of the seventies." This is not a tribute spoken lightly. Graveney, a veteran of 79 Tests and a former county colleague of Glenn's at Worcestershire, saw the progress of the Kiwi right from the early days - four years prior to him becoming a Test player. In fact, it was Tom who was responsible for signing Turner, after receiving a glowing recommendation from his old friend, Billy Ibadulla, who was coaching in New Zealand. "We gave him a trial and I watched him in the nets and the ball never missed the middle of the bat, but the only thing was, he wouldn't play any shots. He never looked like getting out, but he never looked like getting any runs either!" Also present at that initial viewing of the future starlet, was Ron Headley, the county's long-serving opening batsman. He recalls: "As soon as I saw this lad in the nets I knew we had to take him on. I always wanted somebody with some guts at the other end; he'd got technique and that was his strength. However, he didn't look like he could hit the ball off the square. We became a good foil for each other, though, as opening partners. I was a bit flamboyant and would get to 30 or 40 while he'd still be on five, but eventually we learnt from each other. He became a beater of the ball and more flamboyant, while I started to concentrate a bit more."

Glenn improved so much that he went on to become one of the best Test batsmen of his era. Although, before he made the mark in Test cricket, these negative faults, of being over-cautious with his strokeplay, had to be ironed out before he could develop the potential that was so obviously in abundance. Tom Graveney has his own view of what made the significant difference in Turner's game. "The thing that turned his game around, I think, was the Sunday League. We were playing Essex at Chesterfield, replying to their 240 which is nothing nowadays, but then it was a bloody good score. Anyway, we were 7-0 after seven overs with Glenn still not off the mark. I was waving my fists from the pavilion saying 'Get on with it.' Then, in the next seven or eight overs he scored fifty. He began to play shots he didn't know he had. His timing and power was superb. From then on, he realised he could be an attacking batsman as well." His final season in first-class cricket featured his highest score of 311 not out against Warwickshire. If anything emphasised the distance that Glenn's batting skill had come, from those days in the mid-sixties, it was this innings. Phil Neale was his captain in that game, and was also a team-mate from 1974. He remembers: "I actually got a lot of stick from the crowd for declaring because he only needed a few more to beat the highest number of runs scored in a day, but the game came first and Glenn was quite happy because he'd got blisters all over his hands. Forty minutes after the start of play, Bob Willis was still in his opening spell and he was bowling to a slip while everyone else was on the boundary. Glenn had just gone at him from the word go. He murdered the Warwickshire bowling so bad that the pitch was reported as being unfair to bowlers!"

Glenn's Test career began in 1968-69 at Auckland against the West Indies and in somewhat disappointing fashion, registering nought in his first innings. Although, this kind of form was not repeated often against the West Indies, as Turner seemed to relish the battle enormously. He finished that home series with an average of 30.50. However, by the time of his next meeting with them in 1971-72, he was in merciless form, plundering them on their home soil for 672 runs at an incredible average of 96.00 over five Tests. (By this time he had already notched his first Test hundred (110) against Pakistan in Dacca). In the first Test at Jamaica he scored 223 not out in the first innings, which became the highest score for any batsman to carry his bat in Test cricket. It was the second time he had carried his bat in Tests. In 1969 at Lord's, Glenn made 43 not out in New Zealand's second innings and in doing so, became the first New Zealander to carry his bat through an innings in a Test match. That score, which took him 253 minutes to compile, brought him further acclaim from the record books, as he was the youngest player to achieve the feat in a Test at the age of 22 years and 63 days. Meanwhile, during the fourth Test in the Caribbean, Turner struck another double century; this time a massive 259 in 704 minutes at Guyana. This was the highest Test score for New Zealand, the highest score in a Guyana Test and also the record individual total for any player in the series. Coincidentally, in his previous innings he had scored 259 against Guyana on the same ground. Some of his former colleagues have offered reasons why Turner was so successful against the West Indies, who never had a Marshall or an Ambrose then, but were still a force to be reckoned with for opening batsmen. "He was absolutely still as a rock when the bowler was in his delivery stride, which is the hallmark of a terrific player," says Tom Graveney. "Glenn had great balance, he never committed himself which meant he could go either forward or back when the ball was bowled." Phil Neale is equally complimentary in his assessments of Turner's technique against the opening bowlers. "His style was his own and his timing, especially when hitting the ball in front of the wicket off quick bowling, was exceptional. His strength was his ability to pace an innings and he always made sure one end was tied down. It's interesting to note that a lot of his hundreds were scored in situations when his team won games; he was exceptional in run-chase situations."

In 1973-74, Turner produced what most New Zealand batsmen would call a dream performance, when he hit his rivals from across the Tasman Sea for two hundreds in a Test match, and securing a five-wicket victory in the process. The Australians are a competitive bunch, and none more so than the team they had in 1973-74. With the Chappell brothers in the middle-order and with Lillee and Thomson to provide the firepower with the ball, that Aussie team really was a tough unit. Such only makes Glenn's achievement all the more impressive. His 101 and 110 not out in Christchurch meant that he became the first Kiwi to score two centuries in a Test.

The very fact that Glenn had carried his bat twice in his Test career by the time he was 25 speaks volumes about his temperament at the crease. He always had a cool head and was the man whom his colleagues always knew they could rely on to produce the goods in times of adversity. Phil Neale, now a successful coach with Warwickshire, admits that there was a lot to learn from Glenn Turner, and not just from his cricket ability. "His preparation in the morning, his composure, his confidence in his own ability were all things you'd want to aspire to and learn from. He was very measured and calculated in what he did. If he ever got out to a bad decision or a bad ball, there was no throwing his bat around the dressing room, he'd just go back, put it down in its place and get on in the same way as if he'd scored a hundred," Neale enthused. "In terms of his batting, not only could he play the quicks comfortably, he played the spinners exceptionally well and he really did have a very good technique on turning wickets. He was quite inventive as he would chip two's over the in-field. Glenn was probably the first guy to explore the unorthodox way of scoring runs."

GLENN TURNER - TEST MATCH STATISTICS ( ) = As Opener

TESTS: 41	INN: 73 (67)	RUNS: 2991 (2828)
AVERAGE: 44.64 (45.61)	HS: 259 (259)	50: 14 (12) 100: 7 (7)

OVERALL RECORD   + = Opened in every innings against that country

V AUSTRALIA

TESTS: 7	INN: 12+	RUNS: 541
AVERAGE: 49.18	HS: 110*	50: 2 100: 2

V ENGLAND

TESTS: 9	INN: 16 (14)	RUNS: 510 (423)
AVERAGE: 36.43 (32.54)	HS: 98 (98)	50: 5 (4) 100: 0

V INDIA

TESTS: 9	INN: 16 (12)	RUNS: 583 (507)
AVERAGE: 38.87 (42.25)	HS: 117 (117)	50: 3 (1) 100: 2 (2)

V PAKISTAN

TESTS: 6	INN: 12+	RUNS: 431
AVERAGE: 39.18	HS: 110	50: 1 100: 1

V SRI LANKA

TESTS: 2	INN: 3+	RUNS: 71
AVERAGE: 23.67	HS: 32	50: 0 100: 0

V WEST INDIES

TESTS: 8	INN: 14+	RUNS: 855
AVERAGE: 65.77	HS: 259	50: 3 100: 2

CYRIL WASHBROOK - PERSONAL FILE

FULL NAME: Cyril Washbrook

DATE OF BIRTH: 6th December, 1914

BIRTHPLACE: Barrow, Lancashire

EDUCATION: Clitheroe Grammar School

PLAYING ROLE: Right Hand Bat

TEAMS: England; Lancashire 1933 - 1960

TEST DEBUT: 1937 v New Zealand, The Oval

TESTS: 38

MOST PRODUCTIVE GROUND H: Leeds, 509 runs (101.80) in 4 Tests
A: Johannesburg (Ellis Park), 323 runs (127.66) in 2 Tests

FIRST-CLASS DEBUT: 1933

FIRST-CLASS RUNS: 34,101

FIRST-CLASS WICKETS: 2

HIGHEST SCORE: 251 Lancashire v Surrey, Manchester, 1947

BEST BOWLING: 2-8 Lancashire v Victoria, Melbourne, 1950-51

PERCENTAGE OF TEST INNINGS AS OPENER: 93.93%

FOR THE RECORD: He ended his Test career at the same venue as where he began it - The Oval. Sadly, it wasn't a fairy tale swan-song for him, as he scored nought; In 1948-49 while on tour in South Africa, Cyril made his highest score in Test cricket of 195 at Johannesburg. That innings coincided with a record England opening partnership of 359 with Leonard Hutton; The Washbrook and Hutton team is the sixth most successful opening pair in Test cricket history; After playing all but three of his Tests by 1950-51, he played against Australia in 1956 whilst a selector; CBE for services to cricket.

CYRIL WASHBROOK (England)

Cyril Washbrook is best remembered as a batsman who liked to play the short ball, and often he prospered from playing the hook and cut shots. He preferred to adopt the attacking way of opening the innings as opposed to embracing the opener's cliché of consolidation. This was an approach that worked for him and it worked for his team also, as he was responsible on numerous occasions for getting his side off to a flying start, whether it be Lancashire or England; the arena did not affect his game. His style, that of the aggressor, complimented the slightly more circumspect Len Hutton, as they combined together as a tremendously successful opening pair for England. The two shared a record England opening partnership of 359 in South Africa in 1948-49. Played at Ellis Park, a new Test venue that was more famous for hosting rugby, Washbrook and Hutton exploited what was a flat, lifeless wicket to maximum effect in compiling the total in just 310 minutes. That stand became the world record for the first wicket, before it was surpassed by Mankad and Roy of India in 1955-56 who put on 413, which remains the record today. Still, the effort by Washbrook and Hutton remains an England record. Cyril eventually scored 195 - his highest Test innings and Hutton made 158, helping their team to a commanding first innings total of 608. Recalling the match, which ended in a draw, Sir Alec Bedser comments: "It was a lovely, easy-paced wicket and they both batted very well. Cyril was particularly aggressive, as he always was. He was always looking to score and was a very good attacking batsman. He was the ideal man to bat with Len." On the team within a team, Tom Graveney, who was the man that eventually replaced Washbrook in the Test side after he had dropped down the batting order, said: "They were a great partnership. Cyril wasn't in the same class as Len, but it's unfair to compare any batsman with Len."

World War II prevented Washbrook from making more of his talent, as it did with many players of that era. His Test debut was in 1937 at The Oval against New Zealand, where he made just nine and eight not out. Due to the war, he then had an agonising nine-year delay before he was given the opportunity to play Test cricket once more. On his return to the arena in 1946, he scored 27 and 24 not out against India at Lord's. His first Test century came at Melbourne in 1946-47, when he put 112 on the board after getting 62 in the first innings. That occasion was one of few highs for Washbrook versus Australia, as he averaged a relatively modest 33.20 against them in his career. However, he personally enjoyed a particularly auspicious match at Leeds in 1948 when Don Bradman was skippering the Aussies. His 143 and 65 in the Test was, sadly for him and for England, not enough to ensure victory or a draw when an England win seemed the obvious outcome for much of the game. The U-turn in events, provided by Arthur Morris (182) and Don

Bradman (173 not out), set up one of the greatest run chases ever witnessed in Test history. Australia required 404 to win on the fifth day and on reaching this score, they created the highest fourth innings total to win a Test match, which India surpassed in 1975-76 after getting 406 to beat the West Indies. It was a game England should never have lost, and following his superb efforts in the game, Washbrook had more reason than most to feel dejected. It was a bittersweet moment for him.

Incidentally, Leeds was a phenomenally successful ground for him. In his four Tests at the venue, he scored 509 runs at an average of 101.80. These figures include scores of 98, 103 not out and that 143 against Australia. Headingley has always been a ground renowned for wickets that favour the bowler more than batsmen. Given the reputation of Washbrook's, of his offensive approach, it would be unfair to surmise that he lacked the technical qualities to befit a player of Test class. It can be too easy, sometimes, to neglect from mind the other less obvious skills that batsmen of Washbrook's like have in their cupboard. The fact that Leeds is his best Test venue provides the evidence that this player had a lot more to his technique than the hook and pull shots, which he favoured more than driving for instance. Sir Alec Bedser confirms: "Cyril did like it short and he played the square cut and hook shot as good as anybody, but he was also a fine all-round batsman technically, and you had to be, because in those days we played on uncovered wickets, where the ball did a lot more. If he never had a defence he would have been found out very quickly." Undoubtedly, though, attacking the short ball was an exercise that Washbrook much preferred to be involved with than grafting on stodgy wickets. Tom Graveney said: "He was mainly a cutter and hooker; he loved it short. The only trouble with Cyril was that he used to hook up, so most teams used to send a man out to field in the deep. I remember Lindsay Hassett dropped him twice at long leg in one match. In the end, he pinched a policeman's helmet, held it upside down and stood there fielding with it, waiting for the next one!"

In his two Tests against the West Indies in 1950, Washbrook averaged 63.75, after scoring a century in the second innings of both matches; 114 at Lord's and 102 at Nottingham - his final Test hundred. In this series, Cyril put on 212 with Reg Simpson (94) for the first wicket. This remains the highest opening partnership for England against the West Indies. After averaging just 17 on the subsequent tour of Australia that winter, Cyril was soon dropped from the Test side. He was later recalled to the team in 1956 at the age of 41 to face his regular tormentors, Australia. At this point, Washbrook was an England selector and his responsibility as an administrator rubbed off on his batting, as he registered a pugnacious 98 when England needed such a score more than ever. At 17-3,

Washbrook joined Peter May (101) and they combined to post a third wicket partnership of 187 in 287 minutes. This proved to be a turning point in the series, which England won 2-1, and was also significant in England winning the match, which was their first victory over Australia at Leeds. This innings was typical of Cyril Washbrook according to Sir Alec Bedser, as the Lancastrian was forever the tough, disciplined professional. "He's a very nice man and a good friend of mine is Cyril. He was one of the stronger personalities in the dressing room, and he didn't used to stand for any nonsense. He wanted everything right and in place, especially when he was captain at Lancashire." Although he suffered the embarrassment of scoring nought in his final Test match, Cyril had achieved enough beforehand to be well remembered, as a cricketer who played hard and more to the point, positively.

CYRIL WASHBROOK - TEST MATCH STATISTICS   ( ) = As Opener

TESTS: 37   INN: 66 (62)   RUNS: 2569 (2457)
AVERAGE: 42.81 (43.10) HS: 195 (195)   50: 12 (11) 100: 6 (6)

OVERALL RECORD   + = Opened in every innings against that country

V AUSTRALIA
TESTS: 17   INN: 31 (28)   RUNS: 996 (892)
AVERAGE: 33.20 (33.03) HS: 112 (112)   50: 5 (4) 100: 2 (2)

V INDIA
TESTS: 3   INN: 5+   RUNS: 146
AVERAGE: 36.50   HS: 52   50: 1 100: 0

V NEW ZEALAND
TESTS: 5   INN: 7 (6)   RUNS: 234 (226)
AVERAGE: 46.80 (45.20) HS: 103* (103*)   50: 1 (1) 100: 1 (1)

V SOUTH AFRICA
TESTS: 10   INN: 19+   RUNS: 938
AVERAGE: 55.17   HS: 195   50: 5 100: 1

V WEST INDIES
TESTS: 2   INN: 4+   RUNS: 255
AVERAGE: 63.75   HS: 114   50: 0 100: 2

JOHN WRIGHT - PERSONAL FILE

FULL NAME: John Geoffrey Wright

DATE OF BIRTH: 5th July, 1954

BIRTHPLACE: Darfield

EDUCATION: Christs College, Christchurch; University of Otago

PLAYING ROLE: Left Hand Bat

TEAMS: New Zealand; Northern Districts 1975/76 - 1983/84; Canterbury 1985/86 - 1987/88; Auckland 1988/89 - 1993/94; Derbyshire 1977 - 1988

TEST DEBUT: 1977-78 v England, Wellington

TESTS: 82

MOST PRODUCTIVE GROUND H: Auckland, 1060 runs (39.25) in 15 Tests
A: The Oval, 301 runs (60.20) in 3 Tests

FIRST-CLASS DEBUT: 1974-75

FIRST-CLASS RUNS: 25,073

FIRST-CLASS WICKETS: 2

HIGHEST SCORE: 192 Canterbury v Central Districts, New Plymouth, 1986-87

BEST BOWLING: 1-4

NICKNAME: Shake or Wrighty

PERCENTAGE OF TEST INNINGS AS OPENER: 96.62%

FOR THE RECORD: Scored 1,830 runs for Derbyshire in 1982, including seven hundreds; Benefit at Derbyshire 1987; Captain of New Zealand 1988-90; Had trials for Kent before signing for Derbyshire, but destiny eventually led him back to Canterbury in 1997 as cricket coach. They were runners-up in three competitions in his first season; Has a degree in bio-chemistry.

JOHN WRIGHT (New Zealand)

Test match cricket wasn't the auspicious occasion it should have been initially for John Wright when he commenced his New Zealand career as a nervous 23-year-old. He had the talent required for a prolonged Test career, but he lacked significant qualities to go the distance. In his first 16 Tests, John was averaging just 22 and still devoid of a Test century. He had to confront his obvious deficiencies that prevented him from fulfilling his potential and that was exactly what he did. John revealed: "Psychologically I just didn't feel at home in Test cricket. I was very under-confident and I asked myself why I wasn't being successful. I had the ability, the technique and the desire, but I wasn't mentally tough. For the next ten years I worked very hard at becoming a stronger competitor mentally, focusing on how to think when I'm batting. I worked with a guy called Dr. Arthur Jackson in Sydney, who helped me to get rid of all the negative thoughts. I was getting too complicated and found I wanted it so much that I got tense and overawed and never allowed myself to play my shots."

Despite the relatively barren start to his Test career, John did enjoy a successful debut in 1977-78 at Wellington. It was a momentous event for his country, as the Kiwis beat England for the first time in their history, dating back as far as 1929-30. John's contribution was a dogged 55 in the first Innings. "It was a nice way to start a Test career," Wright admits, "especially getting our first ever win against England as well. It was a tough wicket, I batted all day before we went off for bad light - it was real grinder in a low scoring match. If the wicket was more sporting like they usually are in New Zealand, I would have scored a few more having batted the day out." It was earned against a bowling attack that eventually claimed 928 wickets combined. Willis, Hendrick, Botham and Old were no amateurs with the ball. "That four-pronged attack was the best English bowling line-up I faced. Particularly Botham and Willis. Bob Willis was quick and Botham was just a great bowler. He swung it both ways, at good pace too. He was a great competitor and always at you," says Wright. Given such a promising first innings in Test cricket, it is difficult to comprehend how John experienced the self-doubt that plagued him. "I regret those early Tests now, as I averaged over 40 in my last 50 Test matches and I would have loved to finish with a Test average over 40." So why did he retire when he did, we're entitled to ask; with an average of 53 in his last 18 Tests. Like a fine wine John undoubtedly improved with age. He explained: "I was 38 when I retired and my back was knackered. I had trouble with my back all through my career, but at 38 it was time to go."

There were not many better defensive techniques in the game than John's. He was an excellent leg-side player and could execute the cut tremendously well, but it was his resilience and courage that earned him most respect. These were the foundations his success was built on, although he admits his resolve may have sometimes worked against him: "I played defensively in Test matches; I was more attacking in my captaincy. I was probably too defensive in many respects but I was always trying to do a job for the side and see the new ball off. Sometimes I look back and think I could have been a bit more positive, because in first-class cricket I always looked to dominate, whereas in Test matches I didn't as much. There are a few reasons why, which go back to my school days when the coach said, 'You're an opener, you've got to get to lunch,' which wasn't the best advice I ever had. Also, I used to be very tense before I sorted things out psychologically. There's a great saying in cricket: 'Eighty-five percent is played up here (in the head)'."

The real breakthrough came in 1980-81 against India at Auckland. John made 110 - his first Test match century. It took him 17 matches but was worth the wait when he reached the milestone in the most splendiferous fashion, pulling Shastri for six. He recalled: "The wicket was slow and turning a long way. India included four spinners so I had to work hard and play a waiting game. It was obviously a relief and a wonderful feeling. I really enjoyed my hundreds, getting a ton was like winning a gold medal for me." Tough batting conditions always brought the best out in Wright. Whether the ball was flying past his nose or whether it was a spiteful track to bat on, he was in his element. His spluttering Test career now sparked into motion, as century number two soon followed. It was against Australia at Christchurch - his home ground. With Thomson, Lillee and Alderman to contend with, his score of 141 was a fine knock, but not enough to prevent defeat. "Thommo bowled very quick in that game," recalls John. "We got rolled over in the first innings and followed on, but by then the wicket had flattened out into a beautiful batting track. I looked to play my shots and it was one of those days where I seemed to hit everything really well. It was a good innings. Along with Michael Holding, Thommo would be the quickest I ever faced."

It was something special for John, to play a series against Australia. The two nations, divided only by the Tasman sea, are brought up on tenacity which makes for terrific competition between the sides. He said: "The side I enjoyed playing against most was Australia - I really loved it. There's a good rivalry between the two countries and I would have loved to play my cricket in Australia, though I did have three months of club cricket in Perth. They appreciate fighters." It's fitting that Wright should nominate an innings he played against the Aussies as his greatest Test knock. In a one-off match played at Wellington, John helped his side to a comfortable nine wicket victory with an unbeaten 117. "I loved that innings," he reflects proudly. "The ball was turning, there was a bit of pressure chasing and it was against Australia." Players are usually judged by statistics, though certain eras provide greater demands than others, which can distort figures when compared over generations. It may be fair to say John was unfortunate to play at a time when the West Indies employed a fearful four-pronged pace attack. From his ten matches against them, Wright averaged a fraction short of 30. Despite the hardship involved, it was a contest he revelled in. "Holding and Marshall were very sharp, so was Davis, Walsh, Roberts and Croft. They used to try to wear you down, but I loved all that. To me, ever since I was a kid, facing the quicks was the supreme challenge. I never minded it coming above my waist; it was a great feeling, very pure. It's sad that I wasn't successful against the West Indies, because I enjoyed playing them. They were good people, they played their cricket hard and for the right reasons. One of the biggest things against them is to win their respect as a competitor; hopefully I did that."

Close observation of Wright's Test record curiously shows a preference for batting on home soil. Of his twelve centuries, only two were scored on tour. Although he registered three totals in the nineties away from home, two hundreds from 67 innings' on tour raises the question - 'Did he enjoy touring?' Says John, "I've often thought about that, it's interesting. I always felt comfortable at home and I considered the New Zealand pitches to be good. On the other hand I did enjoy touring as well, though my figures might suggest differently. I coped better with touring as I got older, I think." Although statistics, at least, make John a reluctant traveller, in England he was a tremendous servant to Derbyshire. From 1977 to 1988, he was the model professional. A third of his Test centuries were scored against England, added to scores of 88, 93, 98 and 99. He admits his time was well spent. "It always helps when you're playing against them professionally. You know the conditions, you know their faces, you know you've scored runs against them before in county cricket so you are not overawed." County cricket is only one aspect of his career that he is immensely proud of. Wright is not the kind of man to reflect selfishly on all the runs he scored, catches he caught and money he made. He appreciates what cricket gave him. "One of the things I loved about cricket was how I learned to mentally organise myself. It stood me in good stead for everything else I've done in my life. I use a lot of it now in my coaching." John has shown great potential as a coach, though it's his playing days that will forever dominate his most satisfying memories. "I always loved the competitive part of cricket, I batted to occupy the crease. I just loved Test cricket and playing at the highest level; to get 5,000 runs was a big occasion for me. At least I've gone the distance and done a job for my side."

JOHN WRIGHT - TEST MATCH STATISTICS   ( ) = As Opener

TESTS: 82   INN: 148 (143)   RUNS: 5334 (5195)
AVERAGE: 37.82 (37.91) HS: 185 (185)   50: 23 (22) 100: 12 (12)

OVERALL RECORD   + = Opened in every innings against that country

V AUSTRALIA
TESTS: 19   INN: 37 (36)   RUNS: 1277 (1231)
AVERAGE: 37.55 (36.20) HS: 141 (141)   50: 4 (4) 100: 2 (2)

V ENGLAND
TESTS: 23   INN: 43+   RUNS: 1518
AVERAGE: 37.02   HS: 130   50: 7 100: 4

V INDIA
TESTS: 9   INN: 15+   RUNS: 804
AVERAGE: 61.84   HS: 185   50: 3 100: 3

V PAKISTAN
TESTS: 11   INN: 19 (17)   RUNS: 576 (510)
AVERAGE: 30.31 (30.00) HS: 107 (107)   50: 3 (2) 100: 1 (1)

V SRI LANKA
TESTS: 10   INN: 17 (15)   RUNS: 624 (597)
AVERAGE: 36.70 (39.80) HS: 101 (101)   50: 3 (3) 100: 1 (1)

V WEST INDIES
TESTS: 10   INN: 18+   RUNS: 535
AVERAGE: 29.72   HS: 138   50: 3 100: 1

MORE GREAT OPENERS 'NOT FORGOTTEN'

(Underlined statistic represents the reason why player is not featured in main section)

WARREN BARDSLEY (Australia)

An extremely reliable and patient batsman who became the mainstay of the Australian batting during his Test career. Wisden editor Sydney Pardon once wrote, 'How can England win when Australia has Bardsley.' This comment was exemplified on his first England tour in 1909 when he became the first player to score a century in both innings' with 136 and 130.

Tests: 41   Runs: 2,469   Average: 40.47   Opened in 74.24% of Test Innings'

SIDNEY BARNES (Australia)

A player capable of compiling large totals once he had settled at the crease. He played glorious strokes predominantly on the off-side of the wicket and could easily enthral spectators irrelevant of allegiance. Barnes was widely considered one of the greatest of his era, though his eccentric manner led him to drop out of the game for two years after a successful Ashes tour in 1948, where he had formed a strong opening partnership with New South Wales colleague, Arthur Morris. Eventually, Sid took his own life.

Tests: 13   Runs: 1,072   Average: 63.05   Opened in 73.68% of Test Innings'

BILL BROWN (Australia)

A steady accumulator of his runs, though always appeared untroubled when at the wicket. Would have appeared in more Tests had he not have played at the same time as several prolific opening batsmen in Woodfull, Ponsford, Fingleton, Barnes and Morris. He scored 105 at Lord's in 1934 when he opened for the first time in Tests.

Tests: 22   Runs: 1592   Average: 46.82   Opened in 82.85% of Test Innings'

JACKIE McGLEW (South Africa)

Always solid in performance, McGlew was one of South Africa's key players in the fifties. His highest Test score of 255 not out was made at Wellington in 1952-53 against New Zealand; this contributed towards a fine average of 64.70 against the hapless Kiwis from 12 Tests. His figures against the stronger nations of Australia and England, though, were not so high, averaging 30.66 and 35.52 respectively.

Tests: 34   Runs: 2,440   Average: 42.06   Opened in 89.06% of Test Innings'

VIJAY MERCHANT (India)

Sir Alec Bedser rates him as one of the best opening batsmen he ever bowled to, given Merchant's ability to play on uncovered wickets. Given his career first-class

average of 71.22 after 146 games, it shows without too much deliberation just what a magnificent cricketer he was. Unfortunately, he played little Test cricket, but he'd performed well enough to leave his mark of class on the arena for a long time after.
Tests: 10   Runs: <u>859</u>   Average: 47.72   Opened in 66.66% of Test Innings'

BILL PONSFORD (Australia)

The more enterprising of the great Woodfull and Ponsford opening partnership. It has been said that he was the only partner that Don Bradman did not overshadow when at the crease. Incredibly, Ponsford registered three totals over the 350 mark - 352, 429 and 437. He is the only player to have scored more than 400 twice. His 429 for Victoria against Tasmania in 1922-23, was made in just 477 minutes. Scored a century in his first and last Test match. On retirement, he had amassed a superior first-class career average of 65.18.
Tests: 29   Runs: <u>2,122</u>   Average: 48.22   Opened in 64.58% of Test Innings'

IAN REDPATH (Australia)

Best known for his powers of concentration and his dogmatic, combative style of batting. Redpath was the perfect man for a crisis, as he seemed to thrive on the pressure of Test cricket. Bowlers knew they had to earn his wicket, as occupation of the crease was his passion, though he could play handsome strokes when set, particularly off the back foot. When Bobby Simpson retired, he shared many useful opening partnerships with fellow Victorian Bill Lawry, before he was lowered to the middle order.
Tests: 66   Runs: 4,737   Average: 43.45   Opened in <u>50</u>% of Test Innings'

BARRY RICHARDS (South Africa)

Graham Gooch says of him, "Technically he had everything. It was just a shame that he couldn't put his talents on the big stage. He would have been a fantastic player in Test cricket. It's certainly fair to call him a great player despite his lack of Test match experience." Rated one of the very best by so many, but was sadly deprived a Test career due to politics. The average that stands after his four Tests against Australia, is certain testimony to his true ability and, sadly, we can only imagine what might have been.
Tests: 4   Runs: <u>508</u>   Average: 72.57   Opened in 100% of Test Innings'

SHOAIB MOHAMMED (Pakistan)

Son of the 'little master' Hanif Mohammed, Shoaib modelled himself on his father's technique and to good effect too, considering his lofty Test batting average. He was a victim of an inconsistent selection committee as he was often uprooted from the openers berth to steady the middle order.
Tests: 45   Runs: 2,705   Average: 44.24   Opened in <u>58.82</u>% of Test Innings'

207

ALEC STEWART (England)

As good, aggressive opening batsmen go, Stewart is up there with the best of them. He is the perfect player to defy a bowling attack early in an innings, who can quickly reverse the initial pressure from the batting side. His finest moment in Test cricket came in 1993-94 against the West Indies in Barbados, when he scored 118 and 143 in the match to lead England to a memorable victory. Sadly, Alec has often been the victim of a fluctuating selection policy whereby he has been asked to keep wicket and bat in the middle order when his greater successes have occurred at the top of the order, when facing the new ball. Since taking over the England captaincy, Stewart has been content with the keeping role, allowing Michael Atherton and Mark Butcher to open the innings.

Tests: 81   Runs: 5652   Average: 41.56   Opened in <u>52.73</u>% of Test Innings'

JEFF STOLLMEYER (West Indies)

A stylish batsman who made the highest score ever recorded in inter-colonial cricket in 1946-47, when he scored 324 for Trinidad against British Guiana. He was an exceptionally reliable opening batsman that shared many important 1st wicket partnerships for the West Indies with Jamaica's Allan Rae, though the brilliance of the more prolific 'Three W's' often stole the headlines above Stollmeyer's consistency.

Tests: 32   Runs: <u>2,159</u>   Average: 42.33   Opened in 98.21% of Test Innings'

BERT SUTCLIFFE (New Zealand)

One of the most attractive stroke-makers since the war, Sutcliffe has often been grouped with such greats as Sobers, Gower, Harvey and Lloyd as a great left-handed talent with a game rich in fluency and ease. Due to New Zealand's batting frailties in the middle order in the 1950s, Sutcliffe was employed down the order in his last 14 Tests to provide solidity and staying power, which resulted in his absence from his preferred opening role. In 1955-56 he scored 230 not out against India at Delhi.

Tests: 42   Runs: 2,727   Average: 40.10   Opened in <u>56.57</u>% of Test Innings'

VICTOR TRUMPER (Australia)

Word of mouth is an invaluable treasure in cricket history. We all rely on past opinions to evaluate former masters of the game and the thought that Victor Trumper was the greatest Australian player before Bradman, tells us just what a talent he was. Blessed with terrific power and timing, he was able to impress upon disciples of the game his craft and skill to dominate in any given conditions. He died during the First World War.

Tests: 48   Runs: 3,163   Average: 39.04   Opened in <u>58.42</u>% of Test Innings'

BILL WOODFULL (Australia)

Infamously known as a dour and defensive player hence his nicknames 'The Rock' and 'The Wormkiller', but one who could be depended upon to salvage the most hopeless of causes with his gritty and pugnacious style. His temperament was highly respected, especially during the Bodyline series of 1932-33 when he skippered Australia, and maintained his cool admirably at a time when many feathers were ruffled. Captained his country in 25 Tests of which they won 14, lost 7 and drew 4.

Tests: 35   Runs: 2,300   Average: 46.00   Opened in 81.48% of Test Innings'

HOW THEY RATE:	TESTS	RUNS	HS	AVERAGE	100
BARRY RICHARDS	4	508	140	72.57	2
SIDNEY BARNES	13	1072	234	63.05	3
BILL PONSFORD	29	2122	266	48.22	7
VIJAY MERCHANT	10	859	154	47.72	3
BILL BROWN	22	1592	206*	46.82	4
BILL WOODFULL	35	2300	161	46.00	7
SHOAIB MOHAMMED	45	2705	203*	44.24	7
IAN REDPATH	66	4737	171	43.45	8
JEFF STOLLMEYER	32	2159	160	42.33	4
JACKIE MCGLEW	34	2440	255*	42.06	7
ALEC STEWART	81	5652	190	41.56	11
WARREN BARDSLEY	41	2469	193*	40.47	6
BERT SUTCLIFFE	42	2727	230*	40.10	5
VICTOR TRUMPER	48	3163	214*	39.04	8

THE GREAT OPENING PARTNERSHIPS

(QUALIFICATION: 1750 RUNS)

	Ptr'ships	Runs	Best	Av.	50	100
1) C.G. Greenidge & D.L. Haynes	148	6482	298	47.31	26	16
2) W.M. Lawry & R.B. Simpson	62	3596	382	60.95	18	9
3) M.J. Slater & M.A. Taylor*	68	3594	260	54.45	14	10
4) J.B. Hobbs & H. Sutcliffe	38	3249	283	87.81	15	10
5) C.P.S Chauhan & S.M. Gavaskar	59	3010	213	53.75	10	10
6) L. Hutton & C. Washbrook	51	2880	359	60.00	13	8
7) M.A. Atherton & G.A. Gooch	44	2500	225	56.82	12	7
8) M.A. Atherton & A.J. Stewart*	42	2210	171	41.17	9	7
9) J.B. Hobbs & W. Rhodes	36	2146	323	61.31	5	8
10) Mohsin Khan & Mudassar Nazar	54	2057	157	39.56	16	3
11) G.R. Marsh & M.A. Taylor	47	1980	329	45.00	9	4
12) D.C. Boon & G.R. Marsh	41	1871	217	46.78	8	5
13) E.J. Barlow & T.L. Goddard	34	1806	134	56.44	11	6
14) G. Boycott & G.A. Gooch	41	1754	144	38.13	10	4

*Statistics correct at October 1998.

Published and distributed by:
Country Books
Courtyard Cottage, Little Longstone, Bakewell, Derbyshire DE45 1NN England

ISBN 1 898941 20 3

British Library Cataloguing in Publication Data:
a catalogue record for this book is available from the British Library.

Production and typesetting:
Dick Richardson, Country Books, Little Longstone DE45 1NN

Printed by:
MFP Design & Print, Manchester M32 0JT

ABOUT THE AUTHOR:

Richard Sydenham was born in Birmingham in 1974. He has written predominantly on cricket and football, notably Warwickshire C.C.C. and Aston Villa F.C. as a freelance journalist for the Birmingham Metronews. Furthermore, he has been a leading columnist for Cricket World magazine, AXA Sunday League programme and has also covered Test matches at home and in Australia and India, as well as one-day internationals in Sharjah. He now writes for the Gulf News in Dubai. This is his first cricket book.